Unlocking the Scriptures for You

JAMES—JUDE

William R. Baker/Paul K. Carrier

**STANDARD
BIBLE STUDIES**

STANDARD PUBLISHING
Cincinnati, Ohio   11-40115

Library of Congress Cataloging in Publication Data:

Baker, William R.
   James—Jude / by William R. Baker and Paul K. Carrier.
     p. cm. — (Standard Bible studies)
   ISBN 0-87403-175-3
   1. Bible. N.T. Catholic Epistles—Commentaries. I. Carrier,
  Paul K., 1935- . II. Title. III. Series.
BS2777.B35   1990
227'.907—dc20
                                    90-31393
                                        CIP

CONTENTS

Preface

Almost fifteen years ago, I became the associate minister at a western suburban Chicago church in Hoffman Estates. Many of my experiences in that foundational ministry still live with me. One of the most enduring of these is a young-adult Bible study that met in our home from the summer of 1978 until the fall of 1980. We grew phenomenally in our faith and in our relationships during those years. The Epistle of James was our first New Testament study. They prophesied that one day I would write a commentary on James. And so I have.

Almost ten years ago, I left that beloved church to pursue doctoral studies in Aberdeen, Scotland. I was guided in my research by Robin Barbour, Howard Marshall, and Ruth Edwards in the divinity department. My thesis topic concerned personal speech ethics in the Epistle of James. Many thoughts from my thesis undergird this study commentary. For those desiring to seek further commentary help in their study of James, I would recommend highly Doug Moo in the Tyndale New Testament Commentaries. For more scholarly studies, Peter Davids in the New International Greek Testament Commentary series and Sophie Laws in the Harper New Testament Commentary series provide stimulating dialogue. In my study of the Epistles of John, I have found John Stott in the Tyndale New Testament Commentaries and I. Howard Marshall in the New International Commentary on the New Testament helpful in both their discussions and their practical insight. The best purely academic study of the Epistles of John is Raymond Brown in the Anchor Bible series, but Stephen Smalley in the Word Biblical Commentary includes similar views in fewer words.

I owe a debt of gratitude both to Mid-South Christian College and St. Louis Christian College, who encouraged me to work at this project on their time. Also, I must salute those students at Mid-South who took my first course on the Epistles of John for providing stimulating debate that helped shape my views.

Finally, I must acknowledge the vital role played by my family in the completion of this project. The good behavior of my twin preschool sons, Gavin and Kyle, for two long, hot summers made it all possible. The professional copy editing and stylistic pointers of my wife, Joni, has made it better reading.

—William R. Baker

Part One

James

Commentary by William R. Baker

INTRODUCTION

Getting Acquainted With James

When you first meet someone who you know will be important in your life, you take some time to get acquainted. Those first few moments together are a vital beginning to a deeper, long-lasting relationship. These first few pages are just like that. They introduce you to the Epistle of James. They will help you significantly to develop the meaningful relationship with the Epistle of James nurtured in the rest of this study.

One of the first things you will notice as you read through James is its choppy style. The author appears to skip thoughtlessly from one topic to another. There seems to be little care for logical progression. In this way, it may remind you of Proverbs. There is good reason for this. James and Proverbs are both placed in a category of literature called wisdom literature. One of the characteristics of this kind of literature is the choppiness you have already noticed, which is created by extensive use of proverbs, parables, and other memorable forms that can stand independently.

One of the ways these independent units in wisdom literature are connected is by grouping them thematically. Another way is to use what are called linkwords or catchwords. These words link together consecutive units of thought whose logical relationship is distant. Linkwords are prominent in James, especially in the first chapter. The word *perseverance* links the third and fourth verses. The word *lack* links verses 4 and 5. The verb *give birth* links verse 15 with verses 16 through 18. The word *religion* links verses 26 and 27. Some of these are easier to see in Greek. The noun *trial* in James 1:12 and the verb *tempt* in the next verse are linkwords in the Greek (translating *peirasmon* and *peirazomai)*.

Understanding the concept of linkwords can help us perceive relationships between consecutive units in James that have no linkwords and seem logically unconnected. First, sometimes the obvious linkword is left out, but the author assumes we can make the association of ideas ourselves. A good example is the idea of being "slow to become angry" in James 1:19. It makes good sense that the idea is associated with the person who blames God for his temptations in James 1:13. Yet there is no linkword. Second, sometimes (based on an association of ideas) the author expects us to be able to link units of thought that are not consecutive. We might call this leapfrog linking. A good example is found in James 2:5, where the author expresses the idea that God chooses the poor and not the rich. This links to the earlier assertion of this same concept in James 1:9-11. Third, sometimes leapfrog linking may occur with more than one other unit. We can see that James 5:1-7 assumes both James 2:5-7 and James 1:9-11.

Another characteristic of wisdom literature is concern for how to live. The author, usually a teacher, imparts wisdom from his own experience to help his students succeed in life. Such teaching often becomes ethical in nature. We can see a number of ways in which James is like this. First, James 3:1 reveals that the author considers himself a teacher. Second, he is concerned about imparting wisdom. James 1:5 and 3:13-18 declare this specifically, but it is also easy to read the entire epistle in this light. Third, James has a proportionately high number of ethical imperatives for its size. There are thirty-two contained within the 108 verses. The vast majority of the thirty-two are concerned with what a person says, which is also a dominant concern in wisdom literature. Paul strings numerous ethical imperatives together in his writings, but these are always grouped at the end and are not contained throughout as with James. Fourth, the unifying theme of James is maturity. This is indicated by James 1:4, James 2:22, and James 3:2. The author is concerned that Christians advance in the way they live.

Understanding that James is wisdom literature is important in your getting acquainted with it. However, there is more you need to know before you study it.

First, James is Jewish. Numerous Old Testament quotations and allusions make this evident. James 2:8 quotes Leviticus 19:18. James 2:11 quotes Exodus 20:13, 14 and Deuteronomy 5:17, 18. James 2:23 quotes Genesis 15:6. James 4:6 quotes Proverbs 3:34. James alludes to the Old Testament background surrounding Abraham (2:21-23), Rahab (2:25), Job (5:11), and Elijah (5:17, 18). Also, James 1:1 alludes to the twelve tribes of Israel "scattered among the nations," and James 5:4 alludes to God as "the Lord

Almighty" ("the Lord of Hosts"), strictly a Hebrew term characterizing God's power, used most frequently by the Old Testament prophets like Isaiah and Jeremiah. In fact, in that whole passage of James 5:1-6, the author sounds very much like an Old Testament prophet as he condemns the rich who take advantage of the poor. Finally, two other indications of the Jewish nature of James are the use of the word *synagogue* in James 2:2 to refer to an assembly of Christians and the reference in James 2:19 to the hallmark of Jewish theology, "God is one."

Second, James is Greek. It is written in Greek. Old Testament references are cited in Greek and are drawn from the Greek Old Testament (the Septuagint). The author knows Greek well. He uses a large number of words (sixty-three) not used elsewhere in the New Testament, many words found otherwise only in Greek literature that came after James (thirteen), and even a few words he appears to have coined himself. He employs alliteration (purposely using words together that begin with the same letter). He plays off of words and even uses rhyme occasionally. Some of his metaphors in chapter 3, like those involving horses and ships, are common in Greek literature. The device of a hypothetical speaker, used in James 2:18 and 3:13, is also Greek.

Third, James was written by an accomplished speaker. Many of the Greek features of the writing just mentioned would make James enjoyable listening. It would keep the attention of an audience. The frequent reference to his readers as "brothers," "my brothers," or "my dear brothers" (James 1:2, 16, 19; 2:1, 5, 14; 3:1; 4:11; 5:7, 12) would also work well to keep an audience involved in a speech or, for that matter, a congregation to a sermon. Because of these features in James, it is possible that James was originally a sermon or that it brings together main points of some sermons previously delivered by the author. This is one of the reasons we enjoy James so much. We feel as if he is speaking to us.

Fourth, James is related to other New Testament books. The most obvious relationship is with the Gospels, especially Matthew and Luke. With regard to Matthew, the parallels easiest to see are with the Sermon on the Mount (Matthew 5-7). Among many that could be mentioned, James 1:12 reminds us of Matthew 5:10-12, James 5:12 of Matthew 5:33-37, James 5:2 and 3 of Matthew 6:19 and 20, and James 1:25 of Matthew 7:21 and 26. Outside of the Sermon on the Mount, the concern in James about a person's speech, most evident in James 1:19, 26; 3:1-12; 5:12, reminds us of Jesus' teaching

13

in Matthew 12:36 that at judgment people will have to account for "every careless word they have spoken."

Less obvious is James's relationship to 1 Peter. Much of the relationship involves using the same Old Testament texts. Both 1 Peter 1:24 and James 1:10 and 11 depend upon Isaiah 40:6-8. Both 1 Peter 4:8 and James 5:20 depend upon Proverbs 10:12. First Peter 5:5 and James 4:6 cite Proverbs 3:24. Surprisingly, they do not draw the same point from the common passages, which makes it unlikely that either 1 Peter or James depends on the other. There are other parallel passages that are not based on common Old Testament texts, like 1 Peter 1:6 and 7 and James 1:2-4; 1 Peter 1:23 and James 1:18; and 1 Peter 2:11 and James 4:1, but these are not precise enough to challenge the conclusion that 1 Peter and James share some common ideas and sources but are not dependent.

James's most debated relationship with other New Testament books involves Paul's writings, especially Romans and Galatians. The connection becomes apparent in James 2:14-26. This section discusses in detail the relationship between faith and works just as Paul does in Romans 3 and 4 and Galatians 3. James presents quite a different perspective from Paul's. This is especially obvious in their contrasting interpretations of Genesis 15:6 in Romans 4:3 and James 2:23. There is little reason for James to deal with the topic in the way he does unless he and his audience are aware of Paul's views on this subject. This does not mean that James must literally be dependent upon Romans or Galatians, nor that James is denouncing Paul's view. No doubt, Paul presented his novel approach to faith and works in synagogues and in churches before he wrote it down. It is quite likely that James opposes those who have taken Paul's basic idea of justification by faith and wrongly divorced it from maintaining behavior consistent with faith.

Fifth, the author of James almost certainly is James, the brother of Jesus. The New Testament refers to two others named James as followers of Jesus, but neither seems a likely author for this book. James the son of Zebedee and brother of John was martyred in Acts 12:1 and 2. James the son of Alphaeus is mentioned in lists of the Twelve (Matthew 10:3; Acts 1:13), but that is all the New Testament tells us about him. On the other hand, James the brother of Jesus is prominent in the New Testament and lived until at least A.D. 61, when he was martyred. Although he was Jesus' brother (Matthew 13:55), he was not a believer until Jesus appeared to him following the resurrection (Mark 3:21; 1 Corinthians 15:7). He was with the apostles at Pentecost (Acts 1:14) and became a leader of the Jerusalem church (Galatians 1:19; 2:9; Acts 12:17; 15:12-21). Tradition tells us he was also having such an influence among the non-Christian Jews in the city that, during a brief period between Roman procurators, the high priest Ananus quickly seized the opportunity to have James illegally executed.

Sixth, James may be chronologically the first of the New Testament books. One of the main reasons for thinking this is its distinctively Jewish nature combined with its ignoring of the Gentiles as a factor in the church. It is difficult to believe that James or anyone else could write such a book to the church after A.D. 49. James, in fact, presided over the conference held that year in Jerusalem to decide the place of Gentile converts in the church (Acts 15). Another reason for thinking James was written early are the many allusions to what Jesus taught that do not seem to depend on the Gospels as we now have them written. Thus, James was likely written around A.D. 46 or 47. The only New Testament books with suggested dates near this are Galatians, at A.D. 49, and perhaps Matthew, dated by a few scholars at 45. The factor that may call this early date for James into question is the relationship of James's discussion of faith and works to Galatians and Romans. However, James's personal contact with Paul and leadership knowledge of the church is enough to account for this discussion in the epistle.

Having become acquainted with James in this brief introduction, you should now be ready to move beyond hand-shaking to a more intimate relationship with it. I guarantee it will challenge you powerfully, as it has me, to be a mature disciple of Jesus.

If you haven't already, please take some time now, before you get into detailed discussions, to read the Epistle of James through entirely in one sitting.

CHAPTER ONE

Opening Concerns: Trials

James 1:1-18

The Author Addresses the Recipients (1:1)

The letter opens as we would expect by naming the sender and the receivers of the letter. Not enough information is given, though, for a modern postal service to deliver it. There is not even enough information for it to be returned to the sender.

The writer identifies himself not as James the brother of Jesus, nor as James the leader of the Jerusalem church, even though he is both of these. He simply says he is "James, a servant of God and of the Lord Jesus Christ," a designation that could refer to any Christian named James. This in itself tells us something about our author. He was one of the most prominent Christian leaders of his time, yet he describes himself as a generic Christian. Despite his pedigree, he does not use this as a badge of authority over his readers. He is a servant—his reader's servant, our servant. His words will have to earn their own way with us. His confidence in his message to us springs from the fact that he serves God first and foremost. His servant status, then, means his message is from God.

Other New Testament authors call themselves servants of Christ (Romans 1:1; Galatians 1:10; Philippians 1:1; 2 Peter 1:1; Jude 1). Only James refers to himself as a servant of God and Christ. A church full of converted Jews would be jolted by this pairing, and it is another indication that the letter was written in the 40s. The point would not be missed that serving God and serving Christ are interchangeable and inseparable. We serve God when we serve Christ; we serve Christ when we truly serve God. We cannot be a servant of one without being a servant of the other.

James incorporates Jesus' messiahship with His name much as we do today, as if Christ were His last name. Although this is a common practice of New Testament writers, it must have seemed strange for James to refer to his older brother as Jesus Christ. Since James grew up with Jesus, his testimony in this regard is daunting. Further, he calls Jesus "Lord," a term used by Jews to refer to Jahweh. Its purpose here is to accent Jesus' divinity but also to complement the servant status of James.

The letter is addressed "to the twelve tribes scattered among the nations." Ordinarily, this would indicate that the letter is to Jews who live outside of Israel among Gentiles (John 7:35). However, here we should understand that Christians, most of whom are Jewish at this time, living outside of Israel are in mind. As in 1 Peter 1:1, this need not be restricted to Jewish Christians since the church, composed of Jews and Gentiles, considered itself heir apparent to Israel (Romans 4:1-25; 9:24-26; Galatians 4:21-31; 5:16; Philippians 3:3; Hebrews 3:6). Very likely, James addresses former members of the church in Jerusalem who fled during the persecution mentioned in Acts 11:19 that commenced with Stephen. In that sense, James should be viewed as a letter born out of more personal, pastoral concern than we usually associate with it. Perhaps it should prod us to "keep up" with people who at one time were in our church.

Trials Lead to Maturity (1:2-4)

The road to Christian maturity winds through many difficulties. Each leg of the journey requires lessons learned from the prior stages. Problems we encounter in our lives are not to be viewed simply as roadblocks and detours to be impatiently endured but rather as integral to our end goal. We cannot get to where God wants us to be without passing through them. They are part of how God develops us to our full potential. Problems are to be viewed with joy not because we actually enjoy them, but because they are part of God's plan for us. Being Christians does not mean we lose our natural emotional reactions to stressful situations in our lives. We go to the dentist even though it is temporarily painful because we know it is for the long-range good. We can view problems with joy because God has prescribed them for us. Further, a new and more difficult problem in our life means that we have completed the previous stage of our development successfully. A problem can be viewed as a positive report card that indicates we are promoted to the next grade.

In his analysis of the Christian life in these verses, James sees three stages: trials, perseverance, and complete maturity. The first two are continually repeated until the final one is reached. The final stage provides the motivation needed to participate in the first two. The trials are many, varied, and to be expected as a matter of course.

They may be tied to our Christian stance and come in the form of persecution—physical, mental, or social. There may also be situations that arise because we are people and share the same experiences as all other people, such as distraught personal relations, economic setbacks, physical illnesses or accidents, or deaths of loved ones.

James advises that these trials that come our way are not to be viewed as arbitrary and haphazard. Rather, each is a spiritual matter. Each trial is a "testing of your faith," he says. It is a test to show our spiritual mettle. The test is not designed to cause us to fail but to prepare us to succeed. The intended result of the test is to get us to the second stage: perseverance.

This is not a passive submission to the situation, but rather an active, tenacious battling through the situation. An excellent illustration is boot camp. The point of the drills and the obstacle courses is not to produce failed weaklings but to produce strong, aggressive, confident soldiers who are prepared for much more difficult tests, real battles. James asserts that the key to arriving at the perseverance stage each time is to deal with each and every test as a spiritual matter. Approaching the situation with spiritual confidence, or joy, will also help.

The third stage is the final result of repeatedly completing the first two. In one sense, it is an ideal. No one becomes perfect in this life. Yet there is still the very attainable goal of reaching our full potential for God in this life. This is also complete maturity, the words *mature* and *complete* being taken as expressing one idea. It is not only a reward, but also a motivation to help us get through the trials. It is the reason we should be able to stand back and look at the troubles we go through as positive experiences. To alter the familiar bumper sticker, "The more lemons and the bigger lemons life gives you, the better lemonade you will make for God."

Further reflection on these verses tells us that the Christian walk, which is not easy to begin with, never gets easier. As in John Bunyan's classic spiritual allegory, *Pilgrim's Progress,* the path gets more and more difficult, the problems harder to work through. This observation provides us a way to check our own spiritual pulse. If our Christian life is easy (slow pulse), maybe this means we have stopped along the path or are walking around in circles instead of following the path that slopes up or narrows. It will be natural to stop once in a while to rest, but we dare not rest too long, or we will lose sight of our goal of spiritual maturity. On the other hand, if our

Christian life is hard (fast pulse), this probably means we are follow-ing the path properly and are in the middle of the spiritual develop-ment God desires for us.

Wisdom Comes from Prayer (1:5-8)

If we are not convinced that the Christian life consists of trials, perseverance, and complete maturity as explained in James 1:2-4, then we need help. In contrast to "not lacking anything," we lack something vital: wisdom. Wisdom, James informs us, is not some-thing we can pick up at the quick shop. It is not available in stores. Rather, wisdom is distributed freely by God to those who ask. God wants us to understand the Christian life. Wisdom contributes to the goal of complete maturity.

The introduction of wisdom as a key ingredient for living is con-sistent with this book's status as wisdom literature. The fact that James introduces this subject by means of the linkword *lack* is all the more confirming. (See "Getting Acquainted With James.") James's advice that anyone lacking wisdom "should ask God" is founded in the Old Testament idea that God is the source of wisdom (1 Kings 3:28; 4:29; Proverbs 2:6). Another foundational Old Testament idea is that proper respect for God is the first lesson in wisdom (Job 28:28; Psalm 111:10; Proverbs 1:7; Micah 6:9). This may be why James chastises the doubter in James 1:6-8. Finally, James understands wisdom to be a matter of skill rather than of in-telligence. This is consistent with the tendency for the Greek transla-tion of the Old Testament (the Septuagint) to use the Greek word for *wisdom* to translate the Hebrew word for *skill,* as in Exodus 31:3. Wisdom is knowing how to live the way God desires us to (Deuteronomy 4:5, 6). As James will say in 2:13, wisdom is shown in our behavior. Older people are generally wiser than younger peo-ple because of their greater experience in living through tough times.

James's confidence that God will grant wisdom to the person who asks "in faith" corresponds to Jesus' teaching in Matthew 21:21 and Mark 11:22-24. Although James asserts the positive, he concentrates on the negative. The one who doubts when he prays for wisdom "should not think he will receive anything from the Lord." The pri-mary problem is not the amount of confidence the petitioner has when he utters his prayer. Rather, the problem is that he does not have confidence in the nature of God generally. He does not truly believe that God "gives generously to all without finding fault." The petitioner's lack of confidence in approaching God for wisdom reveals a sea of confusion within. He is drawn to one view of God one moment but to another the next. His life corresponds to God's will one day, but he rebels the next. He is "double minded," or more literally, "double souled." He is "blown and tossed by the wind." The person is fickle and unreliable through and through. He is "unstable in all he does." His faith, such as it is, is superficial generally. The person is far—very far—from being a person who trusts God implicitly. How could God grant this person of spiritual wanderlust any prayer requests, much less his petition for something as precious as God's wisdom?

In James 1:5-8, then, James tells us not only that the key to understanding how God wants us to live is wisdom, but also how to obtain it. He tells us that successful prayer for wisdom, or for anything else, is based upon a sturdy faith in God. Wishy-washy faith gets us nowhere with God.

Poverty Is a Blessing, Wealth a Curse (1:9-11)

We normally think of prosperity as a blessing and poverty as a curse. Socially this may be true, but spiritually it is just the reverse. In spiritual potential, the poor person has the advantage and the prosperous person the disadvantage. Yet each person's situation, whether poor or prosperous, is a trial through which he must persevere and thereby progress toward the spiritual maturity God desires for him. The challenge for rich and poor alike is to dig beneath the external circumstances of life to the inner spiritual realities. We need to see ourselves as God sees us.

For the most part, James intends these verses to illustrate the assumption in James 1:2-8 that all Christians encounter trials in life. Employing opposite ends of the economic spectrum accomplishes this superbly. However, these verses also introduce further comments he will make about rich and poor in James 2:2-7 and 5:1-6, and perhaps even 4:3, 4, 13-17. As in the current passage, his general point of view is harsh toward the rich but encouraging to the poor. This reflects both Jesus' attitude as portrayed in the Gospels (Matthew 6:19; 19:23, 24; Mark 4:19) and the attitude of the Old Testament (Deuteronomy 6:10-12; Psalm 37:16; Proverbs 10:2).

The major question of interpretation for James 1:9-11 is whether or not James considers the prosperous person a Christian. He says that the rich person "will pass away like a wild flower" and "fade away even while he goes about his business." That makes us think he cannot mean a Christian, for it sounds like the condemnation of judgment. Also, in James 2:2-7 and 5:1-6, there is a general consensus that James does not consider the rich to be Christians. Because of a widespread famine in Palestine (Acts 11:28, 29) and the ostracism of new Christians by the Jewish community, it is further suggested that James considered all Christians to be poor and the rich to be their persecutors.

The line of reasoning above has its merits, but the phrasing, logic, and immediate context suggest that James has in view a prosperous Christian. First, in terms of the phrasing, the word *brother* describes both the one "in humble circumstances" and the one "who is rich." In the New Testament, *brother* commonly designates a fellow Christian. Second, in terms of logic, the irony of suggesting that a person should take pride in what amounts to his own eternal condemnation is too twisted to be taken seriously. Third, in terms of context, what is said before and after these verses suggests that the passage is to be taken as an illustration that Christians are to view their circumstances in life as tests of their faith in the sense of opportunities to persevere and mature. Of course, James 1:5-8 and 12-18 entertain the possibility that those who profess to be Christians may fail their tests both immediately and ultimately. This is true for those who are prosperous as well as for those who are poor. However, James's negative language about the rich shows he is less hopeful for the rich. In this perspective, he simply takes seriously Jesus' teaching in Matthew 19:24 that it is easier for a camel to pass through the eye of a needle than for a rich person to enter the kingdom of God.

The paramount test of faith for the prosperous person, then, is how he views his wealth. If he recognizes God's point of view, he knows it is a hindrance to his maturing relationship with God. Daily he must remind himself that it does not increase his value before God even though it does increase his value with regard to the society in which he lives. He must take James's words, based upon Isaiah 40:6 and 7, as a stern warning that both his goods and his very life are transitory. They can be taken at any moment, just as in the case of Job or in Jesus' parable of the arrogant rich man who added barns (Luke 12:13-21).

On the other hand, the paramount test of faith for the poor person is how he views his poverty. If he recognizes God's point of view rather than society's, he knows that it is a blessing rather than a curse. Unlike the rich person, his very circumstances in life force him to depend upon God. They are a great asset to his spiritual development. Rather than being down-in-the-mouth because of his poverty, he should take seriously James's encouragement to revel in his position of favor before God.

None of us likes to think of himself as either poor or rich. Because of this, it is easy for us to dismiss this passage as irrelevant to us. However, we are naive if we think that our American, middle-class mentality lets us off the hook. As has been stressed consistently, the intent of James 1:9-11 is to illustrate the point that, for all of us, the situations in which we find ourselves, whether economic, social, or something else, are tests of our Christian faith. We must all examine our lives to identify the biggest roadblock keeping our faith from growing. Most likely, this will be different for each one of us. We must admit, though, if we are truly middle class, that materialism and self-reliance come very high on our lists. These obstructions relate most closely to the problems of the rich.

God Provides Blessings, Not Temptations (1:12-18)

When we sin, the responsibility lies squarely on our shoulders. We find it difficult to admit this, so we look to scapegoats. We pass the buck and say it was our friend's fault, the devil's fault, or even God's fault. But the sin is ours, and the quicker we admit it, the sooner we will move past it better prepared to resist the next temptation. We are wrong to pass the buck, especially when we blame God for our failure. If we do so, we grossly misunderstand His character. He is not in the business of tempting any more than He is able to be tempted. Rather, He is in the business of blessing. He is good, not evil; so He gives us good things. In fact, all good things we receive are from Him. (Those Christmas presents are not from Santa, after all!) The greatest of these gifts, of course, is the gospel embodied in His Son.

James continues to develop his theme that the inevitable trials we encounter in life are opportunities to strengthen our spiritual character. He re-anchors this theme in James 1:12, using three key words he has not used since James 1:2-4: *persevere, trial,* and *test.* In the introduction, we called this "leapfrog linking." However, by no means does James abandon the message of James 1:9-11. There is no linkword, but success for the prosperous person and the poor person in their respective trials is in mind when he says, "Blessed is the man who perseveres under trial" (James 1:12). He simply moves from the illustration of James 1:9-11 to the principle that applies to all. Having returned more directly to his main theme in James 1:12, he goes on in James 1:13-18 to address another problem (like lack of wisdom in James 1:5-8) that prevents many people from persevering through their trials in life. In this case, it is the tendency to blame God when we cannot persevere. James attempts to correct this problem by explaining the true character of God.

When James says that the persevering man is "blessed," he means that he "will receive" a blessing from God that is "the crown of life." This blessing is an objective reality based upon the person's successful encounters with the trials life offered him. The translation of *blessed* as "happy" in the Today's English Version, the Jerusalem Bible, the New English Bible, and the Living Bible is inappropriate and misleading. The person may be happy because he is blessed, but that is an emotional state based upon subjective feelings. Being blessed by God, here as well as in the Beatitudes (Matthew 5:3-12), is a spiritual state based upon objective reality. God chooses to bless the persevering person, not only because he has remained faithful, but because his faith has deepened. He has continually moved toward the complete maturity God desires for him.

As a result of this perseverance, God gives him the "crown of life" that has been reserved for him. If a royal crown is in mind—as in Revelation 4:4; 6:2; 12:1—then the crown is more an inheritance than a reward. On the other hand, if the bay or olive wreath for the victor in an athletic contest is in mind—as in 1 Corinthians 9:25 and 2 Timothy 2:5—the sense is that God is observing the competition as judge and the crowns await those who are ahead. In either case, James hopes that knowledge of this awaiting crown will provide motivation for the person to persevere and to be successful. The additional description of those who receive the crowns from God as "those who love him" indicates that their motivation for achievement should spring from their love of God. As in Revelation 2:10, the crown of life itself is eternal life.

Beginning with James 1:13, the word translated "trial" in James 1:2 and 1:12 is translated "tempt." This difference is not a result of any grammatical change (even though the word changes from a noun to a verb) but comes because of a changed perspective. In the earlier uses, external circumstances of life are in view. From that perspective, they are morally neutral. From God's perspective, as James has stressed, they are opportunities to prove one's faith and to grow in spiritual maturity. Now James shifts to consider the internal ramifications of life's trials. From that perspective, these are temptations. As a person finds it increasingly difficult to persevere and begins to contemplate abandoning the struggle to do God's will, he may very well start blaming God for the entire situation. In effect, he shifts from trusting God to distrusting him. The next step is giving up. In order to prevent this failure, as with his approach to dealing with the doubting prayer in James 1:5-8, James tries to help by clarifying the true nature of God's character. To say, "God is tempting me," is entirely unwarranted because God wants good to result from life's trials. His intentions are positive. He is in the stands cheering us on. He is doing all He can to help, short of making our decisions for us. If He did that, of course, our spiritual successes would be counterfeit—nothing more than cheap imitations of the real thing. What good would that do us? So James asserts that "God cannot be tempted by evil, nor does he tempt anyone" (James 1:13). God has nothing to do with evil. It has absolutely no effect on Him. He is totally separate from it. To blame Him for any evil that results from our trials is wrong.

The true character of God is developed in James 1:16-18, but before he goes on to that, James vividly pinpoints in verses 14 and 15 where the blame truly lies. Quite simply, the blame is ours. God has given us free moral choice. As a result, responsibility for sin lies with each individual. We cannot blame our parents, our environment, our friends, our enemies, God, or even Satan. It is especially notable that Satan is never mentioned in this section. On the contrary, as James says, "Each one is tempted when, by his own evil desire, he is dragged away and enticed" (James 1:14). It is our own evil impulse that converts a trial in our life, which is morally neutral, into a temptation.

Now James does not think all our desires are bad. We have both good and bad desires. The struggle for control of our character is much like the old cartoons that picture an angel and a demon competing to influence the cartoon character. But just as those cartoons try to teach, a person must learn that he is accountable for choosing the voice to which he will listen and that he will have to pay a price for responding to the evil influence. Rather than understanding the evil influence to be external, though, James understands it to be internal. The logical result is that we tempt ourselves. Thus, when James uses the fishing metaphor "dragged away," which would be better understood by us as "reeled in," he paints the ludicrous picture of our reeling in ourselves, and when he uses the hunting metaphor "enticed," he sketches a scene in which we are enticed by the bait in our own trap.

The word translated "desire" in the New International Version is translated "lust" in the King James and New American Standard Bible. Although the more generic translation is usually preferable, the sexual nuance conveyed by "lust" is particularly appropriate when James attempts to describe the stages of sin in verse 15. It appears he has in mind a man's encounter with a prostitute as the backdrop for his points. (One could make a worthwhile comparison with Proverbs 5 and 7.) Clearly, it is his own lust, or desire, that brings him to her door. And, although the conception may be private, the resulting child makes the sin public. If what he has done is rape, under certain conditions, Old Testament law provides for his execution (Deuteronomy 22:13-30). However, the death to which James refers is more likely the natural death of the child once his life has been lived out. Thus, James speaks of sin as "full-grown."

The overall point is to demonstrate the difference between viewing life situations as trials or as tests resulting in the positive sequence of faith, perseverance, complete maturity/crown of life or viewing life situations as temptations with the resulting negative sequence of evil desire, sin, and death. The end result of sin is death, and the blame is the individual's own evil desire. The end result of perseverance is eternal life, and the credit goes to the person's faith.

James clearly distinguishes sin from evil desire and temptation. Evil desire "gives birth to sin," but it is not sin. Temptation may lead to sin, but it is not sin. We must not get down on ourselves because we are tempted to sin, nor because we hear the voice of evil in our heart. These occur because of our human condition. We cannot help that. Sin occurs when we heed that evil voice and yield to that temptation. To overcome these and to listen rather to the voice of God is the perseverance of faith.

In James 1:16-18, James determines to provide an accurate description of God's character in contrast to the false one represented in verse 13. Thus, when he says, "Don't be deceived, my dear brothers," he refers primarily to the idea of blaming God for temptation and the sin that may result. Not only is God not connected to the evil temptations that may befall us, He is responsible for "every good and perfect gift" that comes to us. All the good things that happen to us are from Him. We can be sure of this, James suggests, because God is the "Father of the heavenly lights." He is the source of all light, having created the sun and the stars. Light in Jewish theology symbolizes purity, goodness, and truth as opposed to darkness, which represents impurity, evil, and falsehood. So not only does the observable blessing of sunshine and the other blessings of life on earth that result from it come from God, but His association with light (as opposed to darkness) demonstrates the purity of His character. We see this is James's point when he emphasizes that, unlike the sun's light, which does produce shadows, God "does not change like shifting shadows." He is consistently good and pure in character with no connection to evil. As Larry Bryant has put it so well in song, He is "Father of lights, scattering even the darkest of nights," and "Father of love, showering all perfect gifts from above."

Having asserted that God is responsible for all the good that occurs in the world, and having supplied evidence to support this principle in James 1:17, James goes on to point out how God has demonstrated it to be indisputable. In fact, we ourselves provide that indisputable demonstration. As "firstfruits," we are a good gift. The major question in interpreting this verse (James 1:18), though, is to determine exactly who James has in mind when he says that God "chose to give us birth through the word of truth, that we might be a kind of firstfruits of all he created."

Three options are present. The first is Israel as a nation, which is described as firstfruits in Jeremiah 2:3. The Old Testament also refers to Israel as begotten by God (Deuteronomy 32:18), God's son (Hosea 11:1), and chosen by God (Deuteronomy 7:6; 26:19). Despite the substantial Old Testament support, this is the least likely option since there is nothing in the overall context to suggest that James is addressing strictly Jews.

The second option is people in general. The appeal, then, would be to the creation of man as the highlight of God's creative work. He was given dominion over the rest of creation (Genesis 1:28). There was a decision by God to make man (Genesis 1:26), as well as the involvement of His spoken word. Luke 3:38 speaks of Adam as God's son, and Paul speaks of all mankind as God's offspring (Acts 17:28). Although the reference to God as "the Father of the heavenly lights" in verse 17 does support a creation context for the remarks in James 1:18, James's remarks in this epistle have not been directed to people in general. Rather, they have been directed to Christians to help them persevere under trial.

For this reason and others, the third option, that James refers to Christians, is the best. In this sense, the word of truth refers to the gospel as it is described in Colossians 1:5; Ephesians 1:13; and 2 Timothy 2:15. Becoming a Christian is commonly referred to as rebirth in the New Testament (John 3:3; 1 Peter 1:3), and Christians are said to be chosen by God (John 17:6; 2 Thessalonians 2:13; Ephesians 1:4). Paul speaks of Christians as firstfruits in Romans 16:5 and in 1 Corinthians 16:15. In terms of context, this option also correlates well with the uses of "the word" in James 1:19-27.

Actually, a fourth option is possible if one is uncomfortable with choosing between the second and third options. It is possible that James wants God's creation of man and God's re-creation of Christians to stand together as a dual demonstration of the idea that He gives us good gifts. He crowns creation with man; He crowns His creation of man with the re-creating of some into Christians. He gives life, and He has given eternal life. In this sense, James purposely uses language that, at first reading, would seem to refer to creation but, after a second reading, brings Christians clearly to mind. This option has some appeal; it will be brought out further in discussing James 1:19-27.

James 1:12-18 challenges us to withstand the trials life presents without flinching in our faith, without undermining the character of God, without distorting the true nature of the universe, without denying responsibility for our own temptation and our own sin. It invites us to see by looking at ourselves that God is responsible for all the good in our lives and that He is not connected at all with any evil that befalls us. Each of us should take some time to do what Johnson Oatman suggests in his hymn:

Count your blessings, name them one by one.
Count your blessings, see what God has done.

CHAPTER TWO

A Proverb Expanded

James 1:19-27

James's opening concerns were about living. He wrote about how to make the most out of life despite the adversities that come our way. Not only do we need to seek God's wisdom and to maintain a positive attitude toward God, James also recommends that the difficulties that come our way can and should be used to help us to mature spiritually.

James 1:19-27 is also about living. The emphasis is no longer on overcoming adversities, however. Rather, the emphasis has shifted to recognizing, valuing, and putting into effect what a Christian has received from God: "the word." James surprises and perhaps confuses us by using a proverb on which to anchor his thoughts. The confusion lies in the fact that, at face value, the proverb says nothing about the word of God. Yet we can see that the three parts of the proverb provide the structure for the section. Verses 20 and 21 expand on the third part of the proverb, verses 22-25 on the first, and verse 26 on the second, with verse 27 providing a summary and conclusion. The importance that James attaches to this proverb is evidenced further by the fact that its three parts introduce the broad concerns of chapters 2 (correctly hearing the word), 3 (the difficulty of controlling the tongue), and 4 (the damaging effect that angry speech has on the church).

The Proverb (1:19)

Everyone gets angry. When we do get angry, we usually end up saying things that we later regret. Often what causes our regret is new information. After we have calmed down, we hear better. We hear something different from what we thought we heard before we blew up. We think, "If only I had tried harder to listen to what was really said or intended, I would not have embarrassed myself or caused undue hurt to the person who bore the brunt of my anger." It is precisely this scenario to which the proverb in James 1:19 speaks when it says, "Everyone should be quick to listen, slow to speak and slow to become angry." If we would just make more of an effort to understand others and to hold our own tongues in check better, we could lessen significantly our moments of regrettable anger.

To call James's presentation of this advice a proverb is to recognize its catchy punctuated phrasing, its parallel structure, and its contrasting choice of words. It has been carefully crafted for easy memorization. This is seen more easily in the literal translation of the New American Standard Bible and the Revised Standard Version, which render it, "Let everyone be quick to hear, slow to speak, and slow to anger." The proverbial nature of the statement is further evidenced by the use of the word *everyone*. A proverb usually makes observations or gives advice about living that can be applied universally, even across cultures. That is precisely the point of this statement: its primary application is aimed at all of us because we have all made the mistake that it presumes. We all would do well to follow its advice. If we did, it would make our lives better.

Proverbs that are concerned about listening, speaking, and anger are common in the wisdom literature of James's time. In Hebrew wisdom literature, like the book of Proverbs, there are words of advice that advocate listening, controlling speech, and controlling anger.[1] Similar advice can be found in literature outside of the Bible, too. However, nothing is known of a source, whether Hebrew, Greek, Egyptian, or from Qumran or Philo that combines all three concerns into one concise statement as it appears in James. Therefore, it is quite possible that James has coined this proverb himself, whether for his preaching or his teaching, and then decided to incorporate it into this epistle.

As already mentioned, the placement of this proverb here is critical, not only to the immediate context, but to the broad context of the entire epistle. The importance of this proverb to James is indicated further by the way it is introduced. The direct address, "my

---

[1]Listening: Proverbs 5:1, 2; 6:20-22; 15:31; 19:20; 22:17, 18; controlling speech: Proverbs 10:8, 10, 19; 13:3; 17:28; 18:2; 29:20; controlling anger: Proverbs 10:12; 12:16; 14:17, 29; 15:18; 16:32; 17:27; 20:3; 29:11, 22.

dear brothers," is a feature James uses nine other times (James 1:2, 16; 2:1, 5, 14; 3:1; 4:11; 5:7, 12) to emphasize a transition in thought. By the attention-getting imperative, "take note of this," James conveys that we should read the proverb as double underscored and boldfaced.

A proverb, like a joke, is supposed to be self-explanatory. Because of this, James does not attempt to explain it. However, if we analyze the proverb, we can see that each of the three parts can stand on its own as wise advice. Yet James ties them together. In doing this, the emphasis progresses toward the third part: being quick to listen and slow to speak will prevent outbursts of anger. We also notice that a meaningful relationship exists between the first and second parts of the proverb as well: being quick to listen can help us control our speech. So the last part of the proverb is dependent on the first two, the second on the first, and the first indispensable to the two parts that follow it.

The primary application of the proverb is to human relationships generally. However, it is not hard to see in this context that James wants us to pick up a second application—a spiritual application. From this perspective, "quick to listen" refers to hearing God and His word of truth and then obediently translating it into deeds (James 1:18, 21-25). Listening to God, of course, is a recurring Biblical principle.[2] Being "slow to speak" refers to the important Biblical idea of being still before God and talking to Him with appropriate reverence.[3] David is a sterling example of this (Psalm 38:12; 40:1; 52:9; 62:1), whereas Job is a bad example (7:11; 34:37; 35:16; 38:2; 40:4, 5; 42:3-6). Lamentations 3:25-29, an unfamiliar passage to most of us, words this principle better than any other passage:

> The Lord is good to those whose hope is in him,
> to the one who seeks him;
> it is good to wait quietly
> for the salvation of the Lord. . . .

---

[2]See Deuteronomy 5:1; 6:3, 4; 9:1; 20:3; 1 Samuel 12:14, 15; Jeremiah 7:24-27; Amos 3:1; 4:1; 5:1; Micah 1:2; 3:1; Zechariah 7:11, 12; and Malachi 2:2).

[3]Psalm 37:7, 34; 40:1; 52:9; 62:1; 69:4; 119:114; 130:57.

Let him sit alone in silence,
for the Lord has laid it on him.
Let him bury his face in the dust—
there may yet be hope.

Irreverence for God in prayer is rebuked in James 4:3. It was also hinted at as the underlying problem in James 1:6-8.

From a spiritual perspective, the idea of being "slow to become angry" could be aimed at resisting the tendency to blame God for temptation and sin, which James brought up in James 1:13-15. The thrust of the proverb would thus be to help change the reader's negative attitude toward God into a positive one. In this way, his spiritual decline would be halted and an acceleration in his spiritual growth would begin.

Although small and seemingly insignificant, the proverb in James 1:19 gives us much to ponder. We all need help in dealing with our anger. This proverb gives us a practical remedy we can use in many situations, whether in our relation to God or man. Simply put, stop talking and start listening! If we follow that advice, we will never say things to God or to our fellow man that we will regret. We will be on the road to spiritual maturity.

Anger Demonstrates our Wickedness (1:20, 21)

People are at their worst when they are angry. Tennis rackets are thrown. Batters charge pitching mounds. Shouting matches occur. Fist fights break out. Children and wives get battered. Auto accidents occur. People are raped and murdered. Countries go to war. In James 1:20, 21, the author seizes this easily observed principle to demonstrate conclusively that people are wicked—all of us—and that it is our wickedness that regularly thwarts the ability of the word of God to work in us and through us.

Attached for motivation to observe the proverb in James 1:19, verse 20 tells us why we should not get angry: it goes against the standard God sets for us. In verse 21, James draws out important implications from what he has said so far: that we need to get rid of the evil in our lives, to activate the word within, and to do both in an attitude of humility.

What makes anger—and especially the uncontrolled display of anger in our speech and our actions—wrong, James says, is that it "does not bring about the righteous life that God desires" (James 1:20). It is not productive. It gets us nowhere along the path to spiritual maturity. It is like landing on a square with a chute and sliding from square 87 to square 24 in the popular children's game, *Chutes and Ladders*. Anger—and by this James means the display of anger, especially in our speech but also in our actions—sets us back in our quest to please God with our lives. The word *life* used in the New International translation is not literal, but it is a good attempt to get across the "righteousness" that should characterize our conduct. This righteousness is the objective standard based on His own character by which God assesses our behavior.

Display of anger, then, falls outside the bounds of the kind of behavior that God considers acceptable. There may have been people in James's time who thought that the gods, or God, worked through uncontrolled, emotionally outraged humans. Perhaps some of us think the same as we rationalize our fits of rage. But James says, "No!" There may be ways of channeling the natural, human emotion of anger in positive ways, but actions or words that erupt from unbridled emotion are unacceptable to God. They work against His kingdom, not for it.

James's next sentence, comprising verse 21, begins with *therefore*. This means he thinks what he is about to say follows reasonably from what he has already said. In this instance, he is commanding two things we should do as well as the proper attitude in which we should do them.

His first command, really a preliminary condition to the main command, is, "Get rid of all moral filth and the evil that is so prevalent." The need for this command was established in the immediately preceding statement in verse 20 and the assumption behind it. The reprehensible words and deeds that flow unchecked from anger are a common failing of all men and women. This situation only highlights the moral depravity of us all. So just as we take off all our dirty clothes before we climb into the shower, James says it is critical that we remove everything that makes us unclean morally and spiritually to prepare us for what he will ask us to do in the main command. He goes on to make the point that we are dirty from top to bottom. Every article of clothing is thoroughly soiled. James says that the evil, which we full well know saturates our lives and from which our angry speech and actions derive, must be discarded in order for us to be able to do what is required next.

James's primary concern is contained in his main command: "Accept the word planted in you." We must go all the way back to

James 1:18 to understand where James is coming from at this point. It was there that he last talked about the word (of truth), saying that it was vital to our birth and to our position before God as firstfruits of what He created. I said there that James may very well be holding two ideas in tandem: that of our rebirth as Christians and that of our natural birth. James's additional description of the word as that "which can save you" certainly establishes rebirth as the primary idea. However, the idea of natural birth is included at least as a secondary idea since the Greek word used for "planted" is really an adjective that usually means "innate," that is, something that one has from birth.

Either way, James is concerned here about Christians who have consciously suppressed the word God has placed in them. It may be the knowledge of God, which Romans 1:18-25 says every human has. It may be the gospel—or, in some sense, the Holy Spirit—which every Christian has. But James makes his point on the fine distinction between having or receiving and accepting or welcoming. The implanted word is something that his readers have but which they have not accepted. He is telling them that, even though they may be "firstfruits," they will never reach their full potential for God until they give themselves over completely to His word.

In traveling for colleges, I have stayed overnight in many homes over the years. I can attest personally that many hosts make their guests feel welcome in their homes. For various reasons, other hosts are unable to do anything more than offer the bare minimum for their guests. There is a great deal of difference between these two kinds of hosts. Those who make their guests feel welcome put themselves and their homes at the guests' disposal and are happy to do it. The other host offers a bed and may act put out. James wants us to move beyond just letting God in the front door of our lives to making Him feel welcome anywhere in the house. We need to accept Him wholeheartedly. James says this is imperative to our spiritual welfare.

Interestingly, in 1 Thessalonians 2:13, Paul says that the Thessalonians have done what James is asking his readers to do:

> And we also thank God continually because, when you received the word of God, which you heard from us, you accepted it not as the word of men, but as it actually is, the word of God, which is at work in you who believe.

James directs that acceptance of the implanted word should be done "humbly." Our need for an attitude of humility was established in James 1:19. *Arrogance* is the unwritten word assumed in that proverb. It is inflated self-opinion that makes us unwilling to hear God or our fellow men, that makes us think we should talk when others shouldn't, that gives us the audacity to lose control of ourselves and yell at others or thumb our noses at God. A humble attitude, therefore, is not only mandatory when we make God the Lord of our lives; it is also required in the preliminary step of cleaning the evil out of our houses. That's what repentance is.

Most translations are not able to cope with this subtle point. They join the idea of being humble with that of accepting the implanted word, just as the New International Version does. Nevertheless, James's wedging of the prepositional phrase "in humility" (a more literal rendering than the New International Version's "humbly") between the two main clauses of this verse is intentional and makes good sense.

Even though you may have professed Christ, are you sure you have given yourself over completely to God? Is your life totally open to God's voice, His word? It is all too easy to become satisfied with where we are in our spiritual journeys. In these verses, James has told us we have farther to go if we have not welcomed the implanted word into every nook and cranny of our lives.

True Hearing of the Word Results in Doing (1:22-25)

Most parents have learned not to expect positive results from requests made of their children while the children are watching television. That placid "Yes, Dad" means their brains have put their mouths on automatic in order to keep the parents happy while their conscious beings are focused on the television program. They will not remember or even acknowledge a commitment made under such duress.

Our ears are marvelous instruments. They are built to receive all the sounds that go on around us. Like satellite dishes, they must be directed and tuned to be effective. Our minds adjust our ears to hear what we want to hear. Unlike a radio or television, we can accommodate background noises. We can hear many more than two things at once; but, in order to hear well, we must focus on one dominant sound at a time. James is trying to convince us to do something similar with our spiritual ears in James 1:22-25. He wants us to tune our ears exclusively to the word implanted by

God in us and, even more importantly, to allow that word to govern the way we live.

In this passage, James supplies the spiritual application for the first part of the proverb (James 1:19), but more particularly he elaborates on what he intended in James 1:21, when he said the implanted word should be accepted. Essentially, he specifies that we must listen obediently to it. If we do so, it should be observable in our actions. If its influence cannot be seen in what we do, then we are suppressing it and our spiritual state is immature at best; at worst, it is counterfeit.

With the dual command in James 1:22, James makes distinct the two kinds of hearing that a person can have. There is the kind by which we "merely listen" without being affected by what we hear. He says "not" to listen to the word that way because this will result in self-deception. Normally, a person is deceived by an enemy who does so quite purposefully. Here, James suggests the absurdity of a person's knowingly playing a trick on himself. Maybe Donald Duck or Pee Wee Herman can accomplish such a feat as this, but no sane human being can.

In what way does James think such a person deceives himself? It must be about his salvation, which is referred to in the final clause of verse 21. Although he should know better, he thinks he is saved. He has the word inside; he may even listen to it occasionally; but it is not the dominant frequency to which he is tuned. This word is not having an influence on the way he lives. Thus, James counterbalances his negative first command with the positive, and crucial, second command: "Do what it says!" More literally, he asks us to be "doers of the word." This should be the primary occupation of all Christians. We may be doctors, lawyers, teachers, journalists, bricklayers, plumbers, auto mechanics, office workers, cashiers, or bus boys, but we should all consider our job as doers of the word the one that really counts. James's emphasis is supported by Romans 2:13 and Luke 11:28.

In James 1:23 and 24, James presents an analogy to convey the absurdity of being a hearer but not a doer of the word. He says such a person "is like a man who looks at his face in a mirror and, after looking at himself, goes away and immediately forgets what he looks like." Now that is absurd, and the absurdity is magnified when we look more closely at how James phrases it. First, although the New International Version does not include it, James specifies that the origin of the man's face is "from birth." (The

King James Version, the Revised Standard Version, and the New American Standard Bible convey this idea with the word *natural*.) It is the same face that this man has been looking at since childhood. It is not as if he has had skin grafts because of an automobile accident or an illness that has somehow altered his appearance. Second, the verb translated "looks" and "looking" in the first two clauses accents the idea of a careful, even studious, observation. Third, he forgets "immediately." It is not a matter of hours, perhaps not even of minutes. But he turns, walks away from the mirror, and he has already forgotten what he saw. So this man examines intently his very own face in the mirror, but within seconds he could not even pick himself out of a police lineup. That, of course, is absurd. We may forget dates, places, people's names, and examination questions, but we do not forget the most important part of our own appearance!

In verse 25, James applies his analogy to the matter at hand: hearing and doing. It is straightforward in its essence: a person who is truly hearing the word God has planted inside him, who has accepted that word into all the rooms of his life, will not "forget" this when it comes to his behavior. It will not somehow get lost from inside to outside. If God's word is this much a part of his being, as it should be, then it becomes an unforgettable part of the person's identity. The tie with who he is cannot be severed. If his actions are consistent with who he is, God will be pleased and bless him. If his actions are not consistent, his credibility as a believer is questionable.

James does throw us some curves in this verse. First, he surprises us with his change of terms. He replaces "the implanted word," which he first called "the word of truth" in James 1:18, with "the perfect law that gives freedom," or, more literally, "the perfect law of liberty." The change from "word" to "law" becomes understandable when we realize that James is talking about the internal and external aspects of the same thing. He had been talking about God's influence on us from its internal aspect, so he used "word" to convey that. Now, he wants to emphasize God's influence on us in its external results on our behavior, so he switches to "law." Consistent, mature Christian living means obeying the word of God. In that sense, it is law.

Why he describes this law as "perfect" and as the source of "freedom" is much more conjectural and more complicated. With *perfect,* James may be trying to make us retrace our steps back to verse 4, where he calls the "perfect" work of perseverance our "perfect," or complete, maturity. (The New International Version does not translate the word literally in James 1:4, but see the New American Standard Bible, the Revised Standard Version, or the King James Version). Obedience to God's word is integral to this accomplishment. With the word *freedom,* James may be presenting God's law as a contrast to the sin and death contemplated in James 1:13 and 14, or even to the prison of self-deception raised in James 1:22. Most likely, though, he is looking forward to James 2:8-13, where the "law of freedom" is interchangeable with the "royal law." There he explains the royal law as, "Love your neighbor as yourself." This law, or principle for living, is rightly described as giving freedom because it is self-regulated. One polices himself. It's simple, too. He doesn't have to know a myriad of laws and their application, as a judge does. In the Christian system, Jesus says this law encompasses all moral law (Matthew 22:39; Mark 12:31-33; Luke 11:25-27). It is truly freeing, too, since God's word working in us helps us be responsible in our application of it. It is a partial fulfillment of Jeremiah 31:33.

James gives us yet another surprise with his choice of the verb here. He does not use the same verb as the one he used back in verses 23 and 24, with its connotation of studious looking. Rather, he uses a word that often refers to a quick glance at something, as in 1 Peter 1:12. (Like many translations, the New International Version's "looks intently" unnecessarily alters the normal meaning of this word.) The point of choosing this word in this context may be to offer maximum contrast with the long look in the mirror noted earlier: even a brief look at the perfect law of freedom can be effective. James adds that he "continues to do this" to achieve the assured results of consistently "not forgetting what he has heard, but doing it."

The final item to note is not so much a surprise as the others, but it is interesting. It can't be seen in the New International translation, but a more literal translation (New American Standard Bible, Revised Standard Version, King James Version), rather than talking about what he does, describes what kind of a person results from looking at the perfect law and staying with it. The New American Standard Bible speaks of his being "an effectual doer" rather than "a forgetful hearer." Even more literally, he is a "doing doer." James uses an adjective that is synonymous to the noun to create this striking emphasis.

Are you a "doing doer," or are you a "forgetful hearer"? If we set up a ten-point scale with "doing doer" the highest and "forgetful hearer" the lowest, how would you rank yourself? James presents these two opposites as if a person cannot be both. Logically, James is correct. A person should either always respond to the word of God or he should not. In reality, though, we all know that sometimes we hear and do what God wants, and sometimes—for whatever reason— we just don't.

Our task, then, if we want to grow as Christians, is to live in a way that is more and more consistent with the will of God expressed to us, not only in the Bible, but also by the word James says God has placed within us. For most of us, this is a slow and difficult process. But James has given us fair warning in these verses that, if we do not move in this direction, our salvation itself is at risk.

Personal Speech Reveals Authenticity of Religion (1:26)

In our speech, we reveal a great deal about ourselves. Our accents reveal from what parts of the country we come. A nasal accent indicates the Northeast, a broad drawl the West, a soft, lilting drawl the Southeast, and flat accent the Midwest. Our grammar usage may exhibit the educational level we have achieved. Good grammar, or at least an awareness of it, usually signifies a college education or a bright high-school graduate; poor grammar, a below-average high-school graduate or a dropout. Our vocabulary divulges educational and social standing as well as our interests, jobs, hobbies, and favorite TV shows and authors. Our speech is as much a part of our personalities as our faces are, but it has the capacity to tell the world much more. Our thoughts, our motives, our worries, our joys, our likes, our hates, our jealousies, and our fears can all be communicated by speaking. So James is right on the mark when he asserts, in James 1:26, that the tongue is a reliable gauge of true spirituality.

This verse is a spiritual expansion of the second part of the proverb in James 1:19, but it also relates to verses 22-25. James offers observable data for determining whether he or she is more a "doing doer" or a "forgetful hearer." He further exclaims that, if there is no effect on what he says or doesn't say, then his profession to be a Christian is fantasy.

The key word in this verse, used as an adjective and as a noun (and again as a noun in verse 27) is *religion*. With the introduction of this term, James widens his appeal beyond Christianity. He states a principle that applies equally to all religions and to all religious devotees. If a religion does not affect an individual positively at the personal level of his speech, then whatever value it might have is not observable to society at large. In effect, "his religion is worthless." There may be other outward acts that are characteristic of that religion, and there usually are, but those acts don't count when evaluating a religion as one among others. Offerings, prayers, and religious garb may be nothing more than show, but a person cannot fake his personal, everyday communication with others. A religion that has truly affected someone will prevent his hurting others with gossip, slander, deceit, mockery, perjury, and anger. His speech will be beneficial to others; it will encourage and help them.

James's point, though, is not so much to help us evaluate religions as to examine religious devotees, mainly ourselves. The religion in question must be influencing the personal life of the person professing it, or he is wasting his time. Not only is the religion worthless to him, but also he is worthless to the religion. His bad example makes others think it is worthless. So much the worse for Christianity if he claims to be a Christian. Perhaps without knowing it, he is negative advertising for the religion he says he believes in. As in verse 22, James asserts here that "he deceives himself." This is true because, when asked, he would say he was a Christian, Moslem, or Hindu, but his life betrays this. He thinks he is one, but, in reality, he is not if his religion does not help him "keep a tight rein on his tongue."

This is a verse we all might like to overlook because of the guilt it causes. Controlling our tongues is so very difficult. We all have got into trouble over things we have said. We all have hurt people. We all have said things we wished later we could take back. James 3 will expand on just how difficult it is to control our tongues. But when we think about what James has said in this verse, we know he is right. Our speech is where the rubber of our religion meets the road of real life. If we have been Christians for a while, we rarely sin in our actions, except perhaps by omission, and could reply similarly to the rich young ruler (Matthew 19:20). However, it is difficult to be so confident if we look at our speech because, in fact, it is here that we sin the most. Let us resolve to give God control of our mouths. Let us be convincing publicity to the world that Christianity is effective and real.

Benevolence Without Contamination Is the Goal of True Religion (1:27)

It is easy to describe religions by their rituals and their architecture. Mosques, cathedrals, synagogues, and meeting houses are clearly different, and they say distinctive things about the religions that meet in them. Lying prostrate in prayer toward the East five times a day, mass, a cantor, and preaching are distinctive of certain religions. We could describe the typical Christian church in the fellowship with which I am affiliated as meeting in a nice but plain building, worshiping with revival songs, extemporaneous prayers, and topical sermons, observing the Lord's Supper each week, and immersing all its members. But do these external trappings we often use to describe religions tell us anything about the actual value of them? Too often, we act as if they do, but we are wrong.

James knows that people tend to confine religion to going and doing something at a particular location with people of like mind. That's the reason he pulls something of a surprise by what he says in James 1:27. When he signals that he is going to expound on what makes a religion "pure and faultless," a first-century reader would assume he is going to say something about how one goes about making sacrifices, vows, or prayers at the temple. But he says nothing about these things. This is not to say that he doesn't think these things have their place, but rather that, for too long and for too many people, such things have obscured the more important function of religion affecting real life. Verse 27 summarizes James's emphasis in verses 19-26, that the implanted word must activate their daily personal behavior. He jolts his readers to attention with his two examples of how a Christian ought to express his religion: in benevolence toward the underprivileged and in personal morality.

The first expression James names of "religion that God our Father accepts as pure and faultless" is "to look after orphans and widows in their distress." This is not a new idea. It appears frequently as a theme in the Old Testament.[4] In fact, Isaiah 1:10-17 condemns Israel for observing the external trappings of Judaism while ignoring the plight of the widows and orphans. Psalm 68:5

---

[4]Exodus 22:22; Deuteronomy 14:29; 24:17-22; 27:19; Jeremiah 5:28; Ezekiel 22:7; Zechariah 7:10.

reveals the compassion God has toward the underprivileged in society when it says that He is "father to the fatherless, a defender of widows." Nor is James the only one to mention it in the New Testament. (See Acts 6:1-6; 1 Timothy 5:3-16.) God's concern for orphans and widows, then, is real. Those who have the implanted word should have the same concern and do something to alleviate their plight.

Giving money alone for benevolence does not cover what James has in mind. The verb *look after* assumes physical effort and contact. The New American Standard Bible translates it "visit." We are expected to go to see them, to administer God's love, not just with money, but also with the encouragement of conversation and personal presence. It is to be faith in action. Of course, widows and orphans are only representative of all those who are disenfranchised by a particular society.

The second expression of Christianity James wants to encourage is "to keep oneself from being polluted by the world." The New International translation is a much-needed improvement over the King James and Revised Standard Versions. The latter have "from the world," giving the wrong impression that James does not want us to have any contact with the world. James does not want us to keep away from the world, but rather to remain unaffected morally and spiritually by our involvement in it. Helping those who need help, the first active expression mentioned, necessitates rubbing shoulders with the evils of the world. James is concerned that we do not become stained or contaminated in our growing relationship with God by the elements in the world that seek to draw us away from Him.

We are not automatically protected from these things just because we are serving God, and we are naive if we think we are. Our personal morality must be a priority. We need to take precautions for it to remain so. Most of us do not have the public exposure of a Jim Bakker or a Jimmy Swaggert, but we all are subject to similar pitfalls, to the detriment of both ourselves and God if we do not heed this verse. God must be the one who influences our life, not the world, which does not listen to Him, does not repent, and, in fact, opposes Him and those who serve Him with its every ounce of effort. This is a critical aspect of true religion.

In this verse, James transforms the whole of Christian life into worship of God. With our lives, we give Him praise, offering, and prayer. Formal worship is an organized expression of people who have given their lives over to His service. It is not to be confused with real religion, which is lived out everyday. Perhaps many of us are guilty of compartmentalizing our "religion" into religious acts of attendance and ritual and have felt content with that. If so, James's teaching in this verse and in this whole section should be taken as a warning to stop playing games and get serious with our Christianity—a warning we need to heed. That's what James wants: to get us on the track toward real spiritual growth and maturity. If Christianity is not involved in our real lives, we need to change to make ourselves constantly attuned to the word God has planted within each of us.

CHAPTER THREE

The Royal Law

James 2:1-13

In moving on to chapter 2, James does not veer from his ambition to change the way we live. In the first chapter, he has talked about how to overcome obstacles and use them for our spiritual maturity (verses 1-18) and detailed the means by which we should live and the effect this should have on us (verses 19-27). Now, in the first thirteen verses of chapter 2, he provides embarrassing evidence of our need to change. Our tendency toward favoritism, he argues, dramatizes one way among many in which we break the royal law, and not just a little, but to smithereens! He still wants us to realize that our faith must show and our maturity must grow to be worthy of the name Christian.

James's remarks about favoritism are made in four distinct sections. In verses 1-4, he describes a hypothetical situation that illustrates the general problem of favoritism he sees in the church. In verses 5-7 and 8-11, he presents two reasons favoritism is wrong. Finally, in verses 12 and 13, he summarizes by drawing general life principles from what he has said.

Favoritism Encourages Discrimination (2:1-4)

I don't know why it is, but we Americans are too easily taken up with the superficial and the showy. Perhaps it comes from our relative wealth compared with all the rest of the world or our consumer-oriented economic system. Nevertheless, we love parades. We get excited by the two weeks of hype that precedes the Super Bowl game. Loud, obnoxious car commercials actually get us into the showroom. Americans celebrate physical appearance for its own sake in beauty pageants and in vacant-headed movie hunks and starlets. An athlete like Michael Jordan becomes a superstar celebrity not just because he can shoot baskets but because he can do it with such style. As a rookie for the Chicago Bears, William Perry's image as "the refrigerator" could make him a celebrity before he even cracked the starting lineup.

Superficial assessment of people may be accented in American culture, but it is certainly not new or restricted to our own land. It is as old as man, and it very likely was a genuine problem in the church of James's day. It clearly tagged their spiritual immaturity, so James brings it to their attention here by his opening statement, "My brothers, as believers in our glorious Lord Jesus Christ, don't show favoritism." If such directness doesn't affect them, James's docudrama recreating a situation similar to happenings in their own churches surely will. What must dismay James is that, as recently as ten years earlier, Christians in Jerusalem—himself included—lived together in a remarkable atmosphere of economic sharing and mutual support (Acts 2:44-47; 4:32-38).

As far as James is concerned, being a Christian and showing favoritism are mutually exclusive. Literally, he says we must not "have" our faith "with favoritism." It's like telling a child he cannot have ice cream with ketchup. He may think it sounds great, but we parents know better. The ketchup will ruin the ice cream. Likewise, favoritism will nullify faith. The Jerusalem Bible brings this incompatibility out well with "Do not try to combine faith . . . with the making of distinctions."

The word translated "favoritism" by the New International Version is translated "partiality" by the Revised Standard Version and "snobbery" by the New English Bible. Literally, it is a compound word meaning "receiving the face." It describes what happens when we depend on external circumstances such as physical appearance, economic status, or race to evaluate people. In the Old Testament, the equivalent Hebrew word is applied to civil justice (Leviticus 19:15; Psalm 82:2; Proverbs 18:5), as in the advice to judges in Deuteronomy 1:17, which says, "Do not show partiality in judging; hear both small and great alike." The basis of this principle is that God does not show favoritism (Deuteronomy 19:17). The principle of God's impartiality in judgment carries over to the New Testament (Acts 10:34; Romans 2:11; Galatians 2:6; Ephesians 6:9; Colossians 3:25), but James is unique among the New Testament writers in applying this principle to ordinary human relationships.

By the heavily weighted *in our glorious Lord Jesus Christ,* James implies that favoritism is improper for Christians because, like God, Christ will not show favoritism when He judges us. This is the second and last time James refers to Jesus directly, although he does so numerous times indirectly using "Lord" (James 5:7, 8, 14, 15) or "Judge" (James 4:12; 5:9). As in the first reference in James 1:1, James honors Jesus with what Christians would consider His full title, complimenting "Jesus" with "Lord" and "Christ." But he adds one more word that has puzzled interpreters for ages. It is not actually blended in so nicely as the New International Version has it. It appears almost as an afterthought, following "our Lord Jesus Christ" and literally translated, "of the glory."

Four main suggestions are given to explain what James intends us to understand by putting this word here. Some suggest that it modifies *faith,* yielding "glorious faith." Others suggest that it acts as an adjective modifying the whole phrase, as in the New International Version's "glorious Lord Jesus Christ." Still others suggest that it modifies *Lord,* as in "Lord of glory" (1 Corinthians 2:8), an idea accepted in many translations including the King James, Revised Standard, and Today's English Versions. Finally, a few take it as a separate noun describing Jesus as "the glory."

Given the position of the word, I think it is most likely that it refers somehow to the person of Christ, which eliminates the first suggestion. I also think that James is trying to do more than boost his reference to Jesus with some general ascription to honor, which eliminates the second suggestion. I do think James is trying to identify Jesus with God by this word, so I would accept either of the last two suggestions. I like the last the best because it does this in the most unmistakable terms. For a Jew in James's time, *the glory* meant nothing other than the presence of God (Exodus 16:10; 33:18, 22; 2 Chronicles 7:1-3; Isaiah 6:1; Ezekiel 8:4; Haggai 2:7-9; Zechariah 2:5). Thus, John 1:14 says that in the Word, Jesus, we have "seen his glory, the glory of the One and Only." See also 2 Corinthians 4:6.

In James 2:2-4, James goes on to detail a hypothetical situation of favoritism that he feels is a fair representation of events that have taken place in the churches. We can tell this because the *you* in "if you show special attention" and in "have you not discriminated among yourselves" is plural. His concern, of course, is that they should not make divisions among themselves based on superficial matters such as the way one dresses. The attire worn by the first visitor to their meeting signals not just wealth but status. A "gold ring" and "fine clothes" may indicate that James has in mind a Roman nobleman and politician of some rank. A more literal rendering of *fine* is *shining,* and it possibly refers to the kind of shimmering white toga they wore. The poor man comes in "shabby clothes." His clothes are not just ragged; they are filthy, just the opposite of the first visitor. This man is not a hard-working man, either. He is down and out, destitute, a bum. He offers the very starkest of contrasts to the first visitor.

These two men are both strangers to the gathering, first-time visitors, perhaps Christians, perhaps not. What kind of church meeting they have come to is not important. Even though James does use the word for "synagogue," it is highly unlikely that he has in mind a Jewish meeting at the synagogue. Almost certainly, it is a Christian meeting at a house-church or in the open air. It is assumed that both have come with positive intentions, yet the nobleman is fussed over and escorted to a seat of honor while the poor man is curtly given a choice between two places of dishonor, where he will sit on the floor or remain standing.

It doesn't matter whether either of the two men is a Christian or not because outward apparel dictated how they were treated. That is the sin. Based on this and this alone, one man was accepted into the fellowship and the other was not. Or perhaps one was being courted to become a Christian, and no one cared whether the other one became one or not.

The terrible thing is that we do the same thing in our churches today. We look at people walk in the door and say to ourselves, "Now, they would be good members," simply because they *look* like a nice, white, middle- (or upper-) class family. We want the basketball star in our church to be president of the youth group and the cheerleader to be the vice president. We want the local politician, the doctor, the lawyer, the millionaire businessman, and the prestigious athlete in our church. We want our church to be in the spic 'n span suburbs, away from the squalor of the city and, more importantly, the grungy people who live there. When we think and act like this, whether it be at church or in our daily contacts with people, James says we violate our faith. We sin—not only against our fellow man, but against our God and our Christ. We prove our spiritual immaturity and our need to allow the implanted word to work in our lives. We "judge" our fellow man unfairly, "with evil thoughts," when we form opinions about people based on outward appearance alone.

In Favoring the Rich, We Side With Our Natural Enemy (2:5-7)

The old adage, "Money corrupts," is true. Money does give wealthy individuals the means and the opportunity to do such things as finagle their taxes and to take advantage of people who have less money and less power. From the beginning, Christianity has been a religion of people without power. "The crowds," the nameless in Jewish society, adulated Jesus. They dogged His trail wherever He went. No wonder. They knew He cared about them as no one else did and that He could do something about their situation. Mary's song (Luke 1:46-55), although spoken to God, duly announces the thrust of Jesus' ministry when she says:

> He has brought down rulers from their thrones
> but has lifted up the humble.
> He has filled the hungry with good things
> but has sent the rich away empty (Luke 1:52, 53).

Jesus himself, at His inaugural sermon in Nazareth, expresses similar thoughts (Luke 4:18, 19):

> The Spirit of the Lord is on me
> because he has anointed me
> to preach good news to the poor.
> He has sent me to proclaim freedom for the prisoners
> and recovery of sight for the blind,
> to release the oppressed,
> to proclaim the year of the Lord's favor.

He said he would reverse their position (Luke 6:20): "Blessed are you who are poor, for yours is the kingdom of God." He said very few of the rich would would be in His kingdom (Matthew 19:24; Mark 10:25). Jesus was crucified by the powerful. Christians were persecuted by the powerful (Acts 4:1-3; 13:50; 16:19; 19:26-31).

For these reasons, James's criticism of the church for catering to the powerful and the wealthy is completely justified. They are on the wrong side. God has been, and always will be, on the side of the poor. They betray Him and His cause when they sell out to the rich. They demonstrate that they do not hear the voice of God.

When James asks in James 2:5: "Has not God chosen those who are poor in the eyes of the world to be rich in faith and to inherit the kingdom. . . ?" he assumes his readers know Jesus' teaching in Matthew 5:2 and Luke 6:20. He also assumes that his readers remember what he himself said in James 1:9-11. Finally, he assumes that the readers know the answer is an indisputable yes. The Biblical record, both Old Testament (e.g. Job 34:25-29; Proverbs 14:31;

28:6-11) and New (highlighted above), is clear. This is not to say that all the poor are automatically saved and all the rich condemned. Rather, it is an observation of reality: the poor are more inclined toward God than are the rich. In the spiritual long run, poverty is a distinct advantage despite the present misery it may inflict. James purposely qualified his question with the idea that God promises the kingdom to "those who love him" in order to demonstrate the vital place of spiritual realities in the general principle he is articulating. A person must trust God and act accordingly, whether rich or poor.

Having established the principle that God is on the side of the poor in James 2:5, James opens verse 6 with a stinging accusation: "But you have insulted the poor." The *you* is indeed emphatic in the Greek. If he had been preaching, I can just imagine a stirring voice, a pointed finger, and haunting eyes as he spoke that word. He wanted the church to feel as David must have felt when the prophet Nathan said, "You are the man!" (2 Samuel 12:1-7).

As he continues, James reveals the true irony of the situation he is addressing: the readers themselves are counted among the poor and have suffered at the hands of the rich. He asks, "Is it not the rich who are exploiting you?" As Christians living in defiant cultures, they had no doubt felt the sting of social and economic bias many times—and perhaps violence, as well. To prove his point, though, James brings up two distinct forms of persecution he is sure they have endured from the rich.

Again, he uses rhetorical questions as points of emphasis. First, he asks: "Are they not the ones who are dragging you into court?" (James 2:6). The question assumes that the rich are initiating civil suits against these Christians who are among the poor and that there is malicious intent. They are trying to take over farmers' fields and people's businesses unjustly. James assumes the courts are tilted in favor of the rich. Consider the Biblical example of Jezebel's conniving to get Naboth's vineyard for Ahab (1 Kings 21). The exploitation here is not so much because they are Christians, but because they are poor. Regardless, he wishes to remind them of the sneaky tactics of the rich that they have witnessed firsthand.

Second, he asks: "Are they not the ones who are slandering the noble name of him to whom you belong?" (James 2:7). This action of the rich is directed at the people in the church because they are Christians. The word that is translated "slandering" by the New International Version is translated "blaspheme" by the Revised Standard and the New American Standard Bible. Blasphemy usually classifies actions that insult God. We normally speak of slander to describe insults toward people. The situation James sketches assumes that the insults are being hurled at the Christians, so calling it slander seems right. However, when we consider that the verbal abuse comes because they are Christians, they aren't the only ones who are offended. Literally translated, the phrase here is "the good name spoken over you" and refers to the name "Jesus Christ" when they were baptized. It is the name they now bear of one who is sinless. So it is legitimate to say that Christ is being blasphemed when people who wear His name are being taunted. It may also be that James thinks the very act of hauling innocent Christians to court, as depicted in James 2:6, publicly defiles the name of Christ and is, therefore, blasphemous. Either way, James wants to jolt their memory of the malicious evil of the rich, not only toward them but toward their Lord.

So James's first reason for not showing favoritism, especially to the rich, is that the rich perennially have been against God and His people and have demonstrated themselves to be against Christ and His church.

Most of us don't think of ourselves as either poor or rich, so we may have a difficult time relating to what James has just said. We think of ourselves as middle-class. But we must remember that "middle class" is only a very recent phenomenon in world history, resulting from the industrial age and democracy. In James's time, there were only two economic classes of people: poor and rich. All but the aristocracy and a few successful merchants were among the poor. We also need to face squarely the fact that, in terms of world economy, middle-class Americans must be counted among the rich. Think about how the comforts of life you enjoy must affect your spiritual growth and your witness for Christ.

Favoritism Betrays the Law of Love (2:8-11)

Parents know this to be true. Good parents make every human effort to love their children equally. My wife and I have twin sons. We never do something for one without doing the same thing or near equivalent for the other. We are careful about this, whether it is a matter of Christmas gifts, birthday gifts, or such everyday matters as offering food at the table, tickling or hugging them, or giving praise. We cringe when others publicly exalt attributes of one without also saying something complimentary about the other. To us and to most parents, making one child feel less loved than another seems an obvious perversion of love. Playing favorites is not loving. James brands it sin.

Although this axiom is apparent to us, it was not so clear to the people to whom James was writing. Not showing favoritism was one among thousands of rules in the Old Testament that was to be observed, but, as I have already mentioned, primarily applied to judges. The same was true with "loving your neighbor as yourself." It, too, was one among thousands of principles in the law. Jesus raised love to be the governing principle for all behavior (Matthew 22:37-40; Mark 12:31, 33; Luke 10:27). James exposes favoritism as a heinous violation of this principle. His case for this is made in James 2:8-11. It comprises his second reason Christians should not show favoritism toward the rich.

James calls Leviticus 19:18 "the royal law" (James 2:8) because Jesus established it as the key ethical principle for His kingdom. James is not the only one who understood this. Paul also understood and taught that Jesus had simplified Old Testament law to the principle of love (Romans 13:8-10; Galatians 5:13-15). In fact, Leviticus 19:18 has the distinction of being the Old Testament verse most quoted in the New Testament (nine times, adding Matthew 5:43 and 19:19 to the passages so far noted). In James 2:12, as in 1:25, James identifies the royal law with the law of liberty, and my comments in 1:25 include the explanation that the freeing aspect of the law of love probably has to do with the fact that it is self-regulated and operates internally rather than being imposed externally as is the case with most laws.

By the inclusion of the word *really* along with the conditional form of the sentence ("If . . . "), James offers us a contrast, not only to what the rich are described as doing in James 2:6 and 7, but also to what the church has been described as doing in James 2:2 and 3. Neither of these descriptions even remotely encompasses loving actions. In James 2:9, James states squarely what he thinks the church has done by its actions, again joining the conditional word *if* with a contrasting word, *but*. He says, "You sin and are convicted by the law as lawbreakers." He goes on to explain why this is so in verses 10 and 11.

Here James draws an analogy with Old Testament law, using a commonly accepted principle taught by the Jewish teachers of his time. Essentially, his point, as that of the rabbis, is that breaking a part also breaks the whole. In our modern world, in which we depend on mechanical devices, we understand this principle all too well. When the fuel filter is clogged, the car will not run. When the fuse is blown, the light won't turn on. When Freon leaks out of the air conditioning system, the whole house gets hot. James makes the point to his readers using Old Testament law as an analogy: "For whoever keeps the whole law and yet stumbles at just one point is guilty of breaking all of it." As an example, he then mentions two of the Ten Commandments, adultery and murder, and goes on to admonish: "If you do not commit adultery but do commit murder, you have become a lawbreaker." Breaking one part of the Ten Commandments, which itself is a part of the law, amounts to breaking the law.

Interestingly, it is likely that James chooses these two items from the Ten Commandments to illustrate his point because Jesus himself joined them to the principle of neighbor love when He quizzed the rich young ruler in Matthew 19:18 and 19. You may notice that their order in James is reversed from the way Jesus gives them there and from their order in Exodus 20:13-15 and Deuteronomy 5:17-19. What you may not know is that their order in James is the same as their order in the Greek Old Testament (the Septuagint), known to be the standard Old Testament text of early Christians. No doubt, James was quoting that source.

In this section, then, James tells his readers that not showing favoritism is a part of the law of love, which Jesus taught as the all-encompassing ethical principle for His followers, just as not committing murder is part of the Old Testament law for Jews. When we show favoritism, as those to whom he is writing have, we break Jesus' law. We sin. We demonstrate our immaturity in Christ and our need to grow up.

We cannot help liking some people more than others, and it is silly to deny that we do. But James is not concerned with whom we choose for friends. He is concerned with how we treat people we don't know. He is concerned about our tendency to berate people who are of a different race and our inclination to ignore the elderly and the handicapped. He is irate that we trip over ourselves to make a good impression on the rich and famous, the beautiful and athletic, blinded by the superficial just like everyone else. Why, O why, can't we remember how it feels to be treated as inferior when people in the world have treated us Christians the way they have? As individuals and as churches, we have some serious repenting to do in this area. May the Lord help us to hear His voice clearly and stop us from the sin of favoritism.

Our Actions Will Be Assessed by the Standard of Love (2:12, 13)

Freddie's father tells him not to get into the cupboards or he will be spanked. With a hand in the Cheerios box and crackers strewn around the floor, Freddie is caught. Even before the promised punishment is inflicted, Freddie begins crying. Why?

Let's change the picture slightly. Suppose the next day, Freddie's father is home with him all day and knows that he has not been into the cupboards. His mother comes home and asks Freddie, "Did you get into the cupboards today?" This time, Freddie stands tall, chest out, face beaming, and says, "No, Mommy." Why?

What's the difference? The first time, Freddie is guilty and knows it. He has been caught red-handed. He also knows his father always carries out punishment he has forewarned and that the ensuing spanking will be painful. The next day, having successfully obeyed, Freddie knows he is innocent. He even has a witness. So he is proud of himself, as he should be, and confidence buoys his answer like a fishing bobber.

In James 2:12 and 13, James concludes his argument that favoritism is wrong by suggesting a working principle for life. He introduces his view of judgment and suggests how we might be able to approach judgment with confidence rather than with fear. His advice, given in James 2:12, is this: "Speak and act as those who are going to be judged by the law that gives freedom." Negative and positive motivation for doing so follows in verse 13.

The New International Version's translation passes over an adverb that precedes *speak* and is repeated before *act*. It is a word that means "in this way" or "like this." The New American Standard Bible and the Revised Standard Version translate it, "So speak and so act." By employing this word and repeating it, James emphasizes that the advice that follows is to influence our manner of living, both speaking and doing. We can see from this and from the actual advice, which involves "the law that gives freedom," that this passage (James 2:1-13) is within the scope of James 1:19-27. James gives evidence here that implementation of the earlier passage is vital.

What kind of judgment does James have in mind? He appears to assume a general assessment of all individuals, including believers, similar to what Paul talks about in 2 Corinthians 5:10: "For we must all appear before the judgment seat of Christ, that each one may receive what is due him for the things done while in the body, whether good or bad." Jesus also speaks of this in Matthew 25:31-46. Since

54

James suggests that the "royal law," which he calls the "law of liberty" in this verse, will be the standard of judgment, he agrees with the other New Testament writers in assuming that Christ will be the judge, and the judgment will occur when He returns. This same assumption also lies behind James 4:12 and 5:9.

The negative motivation James supplies for diligently applying the law of love in our lives is this: "because judgment without mercy will be shown to anyone who has not been merciful" (James 2:13). Background to James's point here certainly includes Matthew 5:7, "Blessed are the merciful, for they will be shown mercy," and the already mentioned Matthew 25:31-46, where "whatever you did for one of the least of these brothers of mine" is the standard of judgment. In Matthew 25, those who did not show mercy were dealt with mercilessly, despite their protests of ignorance. Clearly, James wishes to conjure up the same image of fear and remorse that comes too late in that passage. Those of us who ignore James's warning will receive an awful, eternal lesson in God's impartiality.

The positive motivation to live by the law of love is that "mercy triumphs over judgment!" The word *triumphs* implies not only victory over judgment but confidence and even boasting in the face of judgment. Like the boxer at the weigh-in who voices his confidence of victory because he knows he has trained properly for the match, the person who has shown mercy by demonstrating in words and deeds his love for others, because he has followed his trainer's directions, can approach judgment with confidence and even joy. He can look Jesus square in the eye and say, "I've done what You asked, Sir." This is his eternal moment of victory.

Will we greet judgment with tears of sadness or of joy? Will we be like Freddie on the first day, afraid because of our guilt and failure, or like Freddie on the second day, glowing with confidence because we have done what we have been asked to do? James says, if we show favoritism based on the superficial, we break Jesus' law of love. If we break the law of love, its standard will condemn us in judgment. If we live by it, its standard will reward us in judgment. If we are not doing a very good job of loving our neighbor in words and deeds, we need to listen to the word of God within, which is waiting for us to pay attention. Put more simply, James is saying we need to change, we need to give up our spiritual childhood for spiritual adulthood.

CHAPTER FOUR

The Partnership of Faith and Works

James 2:14-26

Having shown that we are not living as we should and that we can do better, James launches into a theological discussion on the relationship between faith and works. He has already stated (James 1:19-27) that our faith needs to be more than talk. He has also shown (James 2:1-13) that our faith is seriously flawed if it allows us to display favoritism. Now he must interact with those who have been led to believe that behavior is not relevant to faith. If he cannot prove this theological point, all that he has said so far falls apart. There is no reason to improve our speech and our deeds to be more loving toward others if it can be maintained that such things have nothing to do with our position before God.

James's thesis is that faith and works are members of a mutual, binding partnership in which both cooperate to justify a person before God. He thinks it is unhealthy and Biblically wrongheaded to separate those two vital entities in a believer's life. He argues his thesis through an illustration (James 2:14-17), a reason (James 2:18-20), and two Biblical examples (James 2:21-24; 2:25, 26).

Illustration: Workless Faith Does Not Satisfy Needs (2:14-17)

In everyday life, we gauge value by performance. If we buy a can opener that doesn't work, we take it back. If we take our car to be repaired but it comes back with the same problem, we question the ability of the mechanic and probably take it to someone else next time. If we hire a secretary who claims to type seventy words per minute but later find out she can only do thirty, we will probably fire her. A person or a product must be able to do what is claimed or credibility is lost. Not only that, but the work that needs to be performed does not get done.

57

In James 2:14-17, this principle of performance is applied to the matter of faith. By constructing a hypothetical illustration, James shows that faith requires performance. Christian faith demands the application of the law of love. Words alone are not sufficient fulfillment of loving one's neighbor. James sets the stage for this illustration, and really for the entire discussion of faith and works, by posing two rhetorical questions: "What good is it, my brothers, if a man claims to have faith but has no deeds? Can such faith save him?" (James 2:14).

Both questions assume a negative response. No, it does no good if a person has no behavior to back up his profession of faith. No, that kind of faith is not saving faith. In terms of James 2:13, how can a person "triumph over judgment" if he has performed no loving deeds of mercy? James does more than just assume answers to these two questions, though, because he is most likely trying to deal with some people in the church who actually think that, when it comes to faith, performance has nothing to do with acceptability. The illustration in James 2:15-17 backs up the negative response to the first question, and verses 18-26 argue that the answer to the second question must be no.

In James 2:15, James presents the picture of a needy person who is "without clothes and daily food." This does not mean that the person is naked and has absolutely no food, but that he is poor, reminding us of that poor person who was mentioned earlier, in James 2:3, whom the church discriminated against. He may have one beat-up toga as an undergarment, but he probably has no outer garment with which to keep warm. He does not have sufficient food to get through one day, and this situation of malnutrition has probably gone on for a long time. The difference from the earlier poor man is that this hypothetical person is a "brother or sister," meaning a fellow Christian. If he approaches another fellow Christian for help, what should the response be?

In James 2:16, James assumes there is only one acceptable Christian response. Jesus' law of loving one's neighbor especially requires that sustenance and warm clothing be provided a Christian brother or sister. Instead of stating the obvious, though, James pictures a response that is patently unacceptable: "Go, I wish you well; keep warm and well fed." When we hear these words, we may imagine a scowling Ebenezer Scrooge blurting out sarcastically to people collecting for charity. However, James need not have in mind the callous, insincere words of a heartless pagan. The phrase "Go, I wish you well," or more literally, "Go in peace," is a common Hebrew way of bidding farewell (Judges 18:6; 1 Samuel 20:42; 2 Samuel 15:9), which has become abbreviated in contemporary Jewish speech to the familiar "Shalom." There is no indication that it was ever used in sarcasm, for it includes the theological assumption that God will watch over the person, like our "God bless." Similarly, "Keep warm and well fed" is probably a well-meaning expression that God will supply the physical needs of the person.

You see, the verbal expressions are expressions of faith, albeit faith that is insufficient, but sincere faith nonetheless. The person really believes God will take care of the needy. But James's rhetorical response hits the nail on the head: "What good is it?" It may be a faithful response in a purely theological sense, but it is not the response that the law of love calls for in this situation. He must *do* something for the person in need. He must make himself the instrument of God's love.

James does not insult his readers by supplying the obvious answer to the question posed in verse 16. Instead, he moves ahead to draw the conclusion to his first question now made obvious by his illustration. "In the same way," he says, "faith by itself, if it is not accompanied by action, is dead." What he means is that faith, no matter how well-intentioned or theologically attuned it may be, might as well not exist if it does not result in loving deeds when they are called for. The impression given when there are no actions is that there is no faith. A bitter protest to the contrary will not sway an impartial observer. It is like the early frontier days in America, when people were actually buried alive because their feeble pulse and other vital signs could not be detected as they are today by modern medical techniques. They looked dead, so they were treated as corpses. A person with faith that is so feeble that it is unobservable is in the same dreadful situation spiritually.

It is hoped that none of us looks like a spiritual corpse. It is also hoped that none of us is so naive as to think that we demonstrate the credibility of our Christian faith by things so simple as church attendance and having the "right" answers in a Sunday-school class, although, unfortunately, we sometimes act that way. Perfect attendance and exhaustive Biblical knowledge do not make up for failing to apply Jesus' law of love in our everyday lives. We need to make ourselves willing instruments of God's love whenever life gives us the opportunity. That means we must work to satisfy people's needs.

Reason: Even a Non-Christian Can Have Workless Faith
(2:18-20)

When we are doing some serious thinking, sometimes we begin to verbalize the problem out loud. We walk back and forth muttering arguments and counter-arguments to ourselves. This can be very helpful. A student studying for an exam will do well, for example, if he can pose what the possible essay questions will be and then talk through or write out his answers. A courtroom lawyer will increase the odds of success if he or she can anticipate the strategy and the lines of questioning the opposing lawyer will take.

James does something like this in James 2:18-20 in order to present a reasonable argument for his case that works and faith must be a partnership and, particularly, that works dare not be left out. In the first sentence of verse 18, he briefly poses the retort someone might make to what he has said about faith and works so far. Then, from the remainder of verse 18 through verse 20, he rebuts the objection. This type of argumentation is often called knocking down a straw man, but this is so only if the opposing point of view is formulated unfairly. James does not do this. He is responsible in presenting an opposing view that very likely has actual proponents in the church.

So James 2:18 begins, "But someone will say, 'You have faith; I have deeds.'" Imagine the speaker as a cagey philosophy professor who makes the suggestion with a knowing twinkle in his eye. The young student activist may stand and present an impassioned plea for a cause he thinks everyone should adopt. Yet the professor nonchalantly shrugs his shoulders and explains that the student certainly has a right to his own opinion, but he has offered no compelling reasons why his enthusiasm for the idea should be imposed upon everyone else. To each his own opinion. God loves and accepts all His children. To some He gives the gift of faith; to others He gives the gift of works. It makes no difference in the long run, as long as we are all part of the family and appreciate each other. We can compare 1 Corinthians 12:4-11 and Romans 12:3-8, which speak in these terms and contain "showing mercy" and "faith" as gifts of the Spirit.

As we look at James's initial response, we can see that the hypothetical objector views both "faith" and "deeds" as equally satisfactory expressions of Christian faith, and it doesn't even matter to him who is assigned what. Both parties are thought to have faith, but one has a distinct advantage over the other. Deeds can boldly challenge faith: "Show me your faith without deeds!" because he knows it can't. It's like saying "Show your cards!" in poker when you know the person does not have the cards to win. In this case, there is *nothing* to show. On the other hand, the challenger proudly holds four aces; he can say, "I will show you my faith by what I do." The person with deeds is in a superior position because with deeds he can demonstrate faith, too. The person with faith only can't demonstrate anything, not even that he has faith.

In James 2:19, the person with faith-demonstrating deeds further challenges the person with faith only. Attempting to condemn by association, he compares the latter's situation with that of demons. As awful as demons are in their work against God and His kingdom, they do believe some of the central tenets of Christian faith. He brings up monotheism and, with words steeped in irony, says: "You believe that there is one God. Good! Even the demons believe that—and shudder."

Of course demons believe in the oneness of God! They know who their opposition is! They know it is not some of the crazy and ridiculous things that people believe in like idols, mantras, or the New Age. They believe in God, and they believe in Jesus Christ, too, for that matter. There is no reason to think that their beliefs are anything but real and sincere. What is wrong with their faith is patently obvious, however. The actions of demons defy their faith, rendering it null. Demons, despite believing as we do, will not be saved but will be damned. The person whose faith is void of complementary actions, James indicates, is in the same position as the demons—hardly good company to be in.

The fact that the demons "shudder" signifies that the demons at least know they're damned and respond with appropriate fear, knowing that God condemns them. As bad as this is, James implies that it is at least a notch better than the person with faith only who doesn't know he is condemned but naively thinks he is saved.

It is interesting to note that the theological tenet with which James chose to make his point is more than just a belief held by Jews and Christians. It is the opening part of a prayer called the "Shema," recited twice daily by Jews then and still today. It is taken from Deuteronomy 6:4, "Hear, O Israel: The Lord our God, the Lord is one." What follows this is not only the command to "love the Lord your God with all your heart and with all your soul and with all your strength," but also insistence that these commandments be written in their hearts, on their foreheads, over their doors, and on their gates, and are to be taught to their children. Praying the Shema daily

61

became a critical part of following these instructions. The idea of God's oneness, despite the concepts of Christ's divinity and the role of the Holy Spirit, is maintained by Christianity, and it provides crucial grounding for a number of significant New Testament ideas found in 1 Corinthians 8:4-6; Galatians 3:20; Ephesians 4:6; and 1 Timothy 2:5.

James feels so confident that his reasoning is irrefutable that he addresses his hypothetical opponent as "You foolish man!" in formulating yet another rhetorical question, which appears in James 2:20. Like the master swordsman who has just flipped away the sword of the cocky novice swordsman, James wants to know if his defeated opponent is now ready to learn from the victor and offers to teach him. Having been shown the necessary partnership between faith and deeds, is this opponent now open to further Biblical evidence to the fact? And so, James says, "Do you want evidence that faith without deeds is useless?" In other words, he says, "Do you want further evidence?" or, "Are you finally willing to let me show you?" By this rhetorical question, James not only wraps up verses 18 and 19, he looks ahead to the Biblical evidence he wants to present in verses 21-26.

James also makes something of a pun with the word *useless,* which translates a Greek word for work that has been negated, something like 7-Up's putting *un* on *cola* in their advertising. "Useless" is un-work. So, literally, James is saying "Faith without works is unwork." Of course it is! It's two ways of saying the same thing! Faith that has no action has no action. It is useless because it is never exercised. It becomes so fat and lazy it cannot move. Even if faith is there, it makes no difference because no one can see it.

I can say I am a great golfer, just as long as I never play. I can put on my Arnold Palmer golf shoes, my St. Andrews Golf Club pullover, and get out my Jack Nicklaus clubs and golf bag. I can even join Hilton Head Country Club, visit it regularly, talk intelligently with my friends around the bar, and react with enthusiasm to the stories of those coming into the clubhouse from their rounds of play. If I only do these things and never golf, though, I am not a great golfer. I am not any kind of a golfer. I am an imposter. And if I really think I am a golfer, I am deluded. The same goes with being a Christian. I can put on the right clothes, go to the right church, carry the right Bible, say the right things, cry or laugh at the right times, get along great with everyone; but, unless I exhibit love when it is called for, James says I am an imposter. He is trying to shake us out of our delusion that we are saved if we are not. One would hope that he has shaken some of us enough to change.

Biblical Example: Abraham's Works Were Integral to His Faith (2:21-24)

Some things must stay together in order to be what they are. If the engine and the cars are separated, they are not a train. Horses that are separated are no longer a team. Clowns, marching bands, and floats are not a parade unless they are together. A pile of bricks is not a wall. We can think of entertainers who illustrate this principle, too, like Laurel and Hardy, Hope and Crosby in the "Road Shows," Amos and Andy, Simon and Garfunkel, Dick and Tom Smothers, Chip and Dale, and a host of others. They are just not the same when they are separated.

This bond is the same one James is trying to secure for faith and works. He attempts it from a Biblical basis in James 2:21-24 by examining the most critical instance of faith in the Old Testament. By tackling Abraham and Genesis 15:6, he is saying that faith and works are inseparable and always have been, despite the fact that some people are now saying the contrary. Once separated, their ability to bring about salvation is gone. Faith is not faith if it is separated from works.

James begins in verse 21 with yet another rhetorical question: "Was not our ancestor Abraham considered righteous for what he did when he offered his son Isaac on the altar?" Unlike the rhetorical questions in James 2:14, this one anticipates a nod of approval. This is not so only because of the way he asks it, but also because it contains common, traditional Jewish theology. Abraham's offering of Isaac is presented in Genesis as the ultimate testimony to his faith and the linchpin in securing his relationship to God. That's the reason the more literal translation "justified by works" (Revised Standard, New American Standard, and King James) as opposed to the New International Version's "considered righteous for what he did," does not really present a problem, even though James actually mentions only one deed. It was commonly understood that Abraham's offering of Isaac climaxed a lifetime of faithful acts toward God. Philo, a first-century Jewish writer, said exactly that in his book *On Abraham* (line 167).

Some may wonder why James, a Christian, would speak of Abraham as "our ancestor" or, more literally, "our father." However, we must remember that James was a Jew and that the vast majority of the people to whom he wrote, as well as the vast majority of the people in the church at that time, were Jews, too. Abraham was their forefather. But he is also the Christian's spiritual forefather. Paul says in Romans 4:16, "He is the father of us all," meaning Abraham is the father of both circumcised and uncircumcised who have faith. Galatians 3:6-9 makes the same point.

Some may also want to get technical about the fact that Abraham did not actually sacrifice Isaac. However, even though the work in that sense was never completed, emotionally and spiritually the task was done when Abraham raised his knife (Genesis 22:10). At least, that is the way God saw it: "Because you have done this and have not withheld your son, your only son, I will surely bless you" (Genesis 22:16, 17).

James's question in this verse, then, upholds the Jewish theology of his day. The question's key concept, contained in the verb *considered righteous* or, more literally, *justified,* verifies this as well. In the Old Testament, God is seen as the judge who renders verdicts on the lives of people based on what they have done (1 Samuel 12:7; Isaiah 43:9, 26; Micah 6:11). Likewise, in Matthew 5:20, the "righteousness" that "surpasses that of the Pharisees," required of Jesus' disciples who desire to "enter the kingdom of heaven," assumes a measurable improvement in conduct. Matthew 12:36 and 37 says straightforwardly: "But I tell you that men will have to give account on the day of judgment for every careless word they have spoken. For by your words you will be acquitted, and by your words you will be condemned."

So James's proclamation that Abraham was justified because of his works is standard Jewish thinking corroborated by Jesus' own teaching. Paul's teaching runs along different lines, and I will discuss the substantial differences between Paul and James in conjunction with James 2:23 and 24.

In verse 22, James draws out the critical teaching from the life of Abraham, the one whose faith and works are unquestionable: "You see that his faith and his actions were working together, and his faith was made complete by what he did." His main point is that both faith and works are vital. They are partners that cannot be separated without destroying the desired result, acceptance by God. The New International translation gets this across, but it does obscure a subtle but important point enhanced by the New American Standard Bible's literal translation, "Faith was working with his works." Consistent with the implication of James 2:18, James depicts works as the senior partner and faith as the junior partner. Yes, they work together, but work is in charge.

Picture not so much a senior executive and a junior executive, but a trainer and a boxer, a coach and his star player, a teacher and his best student. Works uses all its abilities to help faith reach its aspirations, to make faith attain its highest potential. And, just as the potential of the coach's star athlete is much greater than his own, the long-range accomplishments of faith outdistance what works can do. On the other hand, faith cannot get off the dime without works. It needs to be "made complete," or "perfected." We can gather from this final verb that, although James argues theology here, the practical need for Christian maturity remains his underlying concern.

In James 2:23, James recites Genesis 15:6, "And Abraham believed God, and it was credited to him as righteousness," asserting that "the scripture was fulfilled." He does not mean by this that Genesis 15:6 is a formal prophetic utterance. However, Genesis 15:6 does anticipate Genesis 22. God's assessment of Abraham as righteous was vindicated by the climactic event of Isaac's offering. God's telescopic eye saw that Abraham's belief in Genesis 15 was real and that it included the ability for the kind of action—of which the offering of Isaac would be premier—necessary to complete it. James views Genesis 15:6 as a caption under Abraham's entire life of faith.

James adds to the Scripture citation the information that Abraham "was called God's friend." As far as James is concerned, this seals his point. Abraham secured a lasting relationship with God. He was accepted, or, in terms of the question posed in James 2:14, he was "saved" because of works and faith. You will notice that the New International Version, in agreement with most translations, does not enclose this statement with quotation marks. The reason for this is that no Old Testament passage refers to Abraham precisely in these terms. Even though the New International Version does translate 2 Chronicles 20:7 and Isaiah 41:8 in such a way as to refer to Abraham as God's "friend," its editors are smart enough to know that the word used in those two passages really means beloved. That is close enough for the sense of what James says to be proper, but it is not a quotation, and the fact is that Abraham is specifically called "God's friend" by a number of Jewish writers outside of the Old Testament. Regardless, no one in James's day would contend that this was anything but a true depiction of Abraham's relationship with God.

In James 2:24, James states his conclusion from this Biblical incident: "You see that a person is justified by what he does and not by faith alone." Here James demonstrates that he is not trying to pump up the value of works at the expense of faith. Rather, he is trying to defend the value of works, which some in the church have rejected. James 2:14, and perhaps the whole book to a certain degree, is a reaction against the damage some were inflicting upon the church by teaching that a person *is* justified by faith alone. Such teaching brought development of spiritual maturity to a screeching halt in many people, and still does. It makes some people think that there is nothing for them to do after they become Christians.

The most obvious place to find such teaching is in Paul's letters. Doesn't he say in Romans 3:28 that "a man is justified by faith apart from observing the law" and in Galatians 3:9 that "those who have faith are blessed along with Abraham, the man of faith"? And doesn't Paul cite the exact same passage, Genesis 15:6, not only in Romans 4:3 but also in Galatians 3:6, to prove the opposite point, that faith but not works is necessary in order to be justified?

Unlike James, who took a traditional approach to faith, works, and justification, Paul's observations were new and revolutionary. Paul saw in Genesis 15:6 an eye-opening chronological fact. Abraham was declared righteous by God before he had done anything to make him worthy of such a verdict. All he had done was believe. Because of this, Paul views Abraham as the prototype for Christian faith. Jesus' death on the cross for man's sins does make our works pointless in one sense, and Paul sees that reality of the cross being broadcast from Genesis 15:6. He says in Galatians 3:8: "The Scripture foresaw that God would justify the Gentiles by faith, and announced the gospel in advance to Abraham." Not even Abraham, Paul thunders, was justified by works, for Christ died for his sins.

Paul's frustration was that so many Jews thought they didn't need the gospel and considered the cross irrelevant. They were confident that their obedience to God's law in the Old Testament would be more than enough for God to find their lives "righteous." Paul says no one has a chance on this basis because one violation derails it. Only God's grace allows us to get close to Him. Only Christ's death for our sins makes us acceptable to Him. Paul, then, is looking at salvation from the front end and answers the question, "How do you get in the door?" His answer from that perspective is correct, "By faith in Jesus Christ."

Now James looks at salvation from inside the house. He answers the question, "What does God look at when He assesses your life at the final judgment?" His answer, "Both my faith in Jesus Christ and the deeds I have done that are consistent with my faith," is also correct. When God accepts me into the house, just as with Abraham, He anticipates my worthy participation in the faith, and He expects me to reach my full spiritual potential. That does not contradict what Paul says, nor does it negate his insights on Genesis 15:6. James and Paul each have different concerns that dominate what they emphasize about salvation.

Even if the view of Paul and James on faith, works, and justification can be harmonized, and even if the above explanation of the views of Paul and James is accurate, this does not nullify the probability that James's teaching is in some way a reaction to Paul's teaching. The explanation for this is that Paul's teaching on justification by faith was new and somewhat complex. It was susceptible to distortion to mean that works were not necessary in the Christian faith, since Jesus paid it all. Paul himself acknowledges this vulnerability and attempts to balance his view with arguments similar to those of James (Ephesians 2:10; 1 Corinthians 5:3; 2 Corinthians 5:10; Galatians 5:6). James, then, probably is writing against people who have been influenced by a misunderstanding or a misrepresentation of Paul's teaching.

Given that James is probably writing before Paul has even put pen to paper for any of his letters, he may even be attempting to stop the harmful potential he saw in Paul's early, verbal teaching. Note that he and Paul did have discussions early in Paul's career (Galatians 1:19; 2:9; Acts 15:12-21). James may have seen the danger in Paul's theological separation of faith and works and writes to warn the church not to abandon works, or their spiritual growth will suffer.

How can someone tell whether I am a Christian or not? I can say I believe in Christ, or I can pull out my baptismal certificate, but it's the way I live that shouts the undeniable truth. Despite Paul's invaluable teaching about faith, James will not let us forget that.

Biblical Example: Rahab's Works Demonstrate Her Faith (2:25, 26)

Contrast attracts our attention, and so opposites are often paired: black/white, purple/gold, night/day, love/hate, happy/sad, true/false. In relationships, one's best friends are usually the same gender as he and share many interests with him. However, the person he marries is not only of the opposite gender, but usually has different interests, abilities, and looks from his own. It is these differences that catch our attention.

In order to increase the effectiveness of his point that works are vital to faith, James offers as an example a person who contrasts in every way with Abraham (James 2:25, 26). Rahab is a Gentile, a woman, and a prostitute; her name appears in only two chapters of the Old Testament (Joshua 2 and 6). She contrasts with Abraham in the same way the rich man contrasts with the poor man in James 2:2-4. No one would expect her to be among the "faithful." Yet, there she is. Her faith, as limited as it is (Joshua 2:8-13), is sturdy and real because we can see her work it out in the observable actions of hiding the Jewish spies, diverting the king's police (Joshua 2:4-7), and, as James says, having "sent them off in a different direction" (Joshua 2:15, 16). In fact, she proved it before she professed it! The result is that she enabled the Israelites to capture Jericho, their first victory in their taking of the promised land. In marrying Salmon, she is even listed in Matthew 1:5 as being a factor in Christ's lineage.

Who would have guessed initially that Rahab had faith? But her actions proved that she did. In that sense, she is on equal terms with Abraham. An inseparable union of faith and works occurs in them both. If that is so, it is true for everyone. That is James's point.

So, in James 2:26, James restates as a conclusion what he already said in James 2:17: "Faith without deeds is dead." Although this is the conclusion of his detailed argument, he offers a closing analogy. He says it's "as the body without the spirit is dead." This is an apt analogy. A corpse gives no signs of life. That's the reason we call it dead. Unless vital signs are detected within a few minutes, only one conclusion can be drawn. The relationship of works to faith is just like this. An observer can draw only one conclusion if there are no vital signs of faith detectable. No deeds means there is no faith. Faith and works are an inseparable partnership.

It's easy for us to think our eternal destiny is secure because we believe Christ has secured it for us. It's natural for us to think that because we have done what is necessary to be accepted into the house of God that we can never be expelled. Such a view of eternal security is a perversion of Paul's theology. James's theology about works corrects this. You see, there is no reason to think that, if our behavior becomes unacceptable and we break the rules of the house, God cannot kick us out, just as a father may throw a rebellious teenager out of the house.

However, it is quite probable that, when we profess our faith in Christ, as with Abraham, God can foresee whether our life will be consistent with our profession or will deny it. He knows who His true church is. But, as humans, we do not. We can't anticipate how consistent a new Christian will be, so we accept each one into the church. But we must admit, some of us really are saved; others of us really are not. Some mature and develop as they should; others are stunted in their spiritual growth. What separates us in God's eyes is not our denominations, but our works. Some of us do what God wants us to do in our lives; others don't. Into which category do we fall? We all need to stop relying so much on the false security of our church membership and try to see ourselves as God sees us. This is what James has been trying to persuade us to do in James 2:14-26.

CHAPTER FIVE

The Wise Teacher

James 3:1-18

In chapter 3 of his epistle, James sharpens his focus on one major aspect of our behavior: our speech. He touched on this concern in James 1:19, 20, 26, and 2:12. We can see that he always intended to return to it once he had established his general theological point that the Christian life must include Christian behavior. In James 1:19 and 20, he briefly observed that our angry speech demonstrates that we are smothering the word that God has implanted in our lives. In verse 26 of the same chapter, he asserted that our speech accurately gauges the effectiveness of our religion. In James 2:12, he warned that our words, just as much as our actions, should be guided by the law of love.

Now, in chapter 3, he illustrates just how difficult it is to accomplish this, using the real problem of too many unqualified teachers in the church of his day as a launching-off point. The problem of speech, or of the tongue, certainly is not restricted to teachers, but the problem comes to the forefront when the nature of their profession is considered.

After demonstrating the difficulty of controlling the tongue (James 3:1-12), James discusses how we can discern Heavenly wisdom from earthly wisdom (James 3:13-18). This is appropriate not only for our own spiritual welfare, but also as we evaluate our Christian teachers or ourselves as Christian teachers. We should seek true wisdom as well as to be taught by wise teachers.

The Tongue Cannot Be Controlled Perfectly (3:1, 2)

A child may grow up aspiring to be an astronaut. He reads Buck Rogers cartoons, he assembles model rockets, and he visits the Kennedy Space Center. He memorizes the names of all the famous astronauts like John Glenn, Neil Armstrong, and Sally Ride. Eventually, he goes through the Air Force Academy, gets accepted into the astronaut training program, and finally is selected to be an astronaut. At first, it is everything he dreamed of, and he keeps pinching himself to be sure it is real. As the months become years, however, he learns that being an astronaut is not all glory and honor. An immense responsibility rests on his shoulders, not only for himself but for the rest of his crew, for the space program, and for the entire nation.

When James talks about teachers in James 3:1 and 2, he is worried about people who aspire to be teachers without realizing the grave responsibilities that are involved with the position. Being admired drives their ambition. They forget or don't know that teachers work hard and must be qualified. Teachers in the church have spiritual responsibilities as well as eductional ones. James wants to discourage the ambitious but unqualified from being teachers. So he says, "Not many of you should presume to be teachers, my brothers, because you know that we who teach will be judged more strictly" (James 3:1).

As with the rabbi in Judaism, being a teacher in the early church was a highly respected position. A teacher was the third most prominent person in the church. With the apostle's being a traveling authority, the teacher probably shared the leadership at the local level with the prophet (Acts 13:1; Romans 12:7; 1 Corinthians 12:28; Ephesians 4:11).[5] A teacher's primary job was to transmit the teaching of the apostles and to apply it accurately and faithfully to his local church (2 Timothy 2:2). As in Judaism, some may have thought that, because of the teachers' devotion and service, God would be kindly disposed toward them in judgment. James quickly dispels this notion. In fact, he tells us that just the opposite is true. God will examine them "more strictly," he says, and he includes himself—even as he writes.

Teachers will receive closer scrutiny because they have taken on more responsibility. This is in harmony with what Jesus says in Luke 12:48: "From everyone who has been given much, much will be demanded; and from the one who has been entrusted with much, much more will be asked." It also corresponds with His announcement in Mark 12:40 that the Jewish teachers of the law would be "punished most severely."

---

[5]The office of elder could include all of these: apostles, prophets, and teachers.

A big reason teachers are more at risk, according to James 3:2, has to do with the nature of the task they perform. Teachers talk. In fact, they talk more than most other people. Thus, the abiding principle James recites incriminates teachers more than most and supports his reasoning in James 3:1. Every one of us does "stumble in many ways." And it is reasonable to think that "if anyone is never at fault in what he says, he is a perfect man, able to keep his whole body in check." In the next ten verses, James will be trying to show the validity of this principle, but we can begin to appreciate the sense of it at face value.

The words *stumble* and *is never at fault* are different translations of the same Greek word. Literally, this word means to "trip" or "stumble." When it is used in the New Testament (Romans 11:11; 2 Peter 1:10; and already in James 2:10), it visualizes sin. When we think about it, we know the tongue is the most difficult part of our anatomy to control. Our mind is not always quick enough to stop it. It plays a prominent role in the "many ways" in which we sin. If we could control it, I suppose that would demonstrate that we can maintain control in all other aspects of living. However, being realistic, we know what James is really saying: we cannot keep the tongue from sinning, and we are not, nor can we be, perfectly sinless. That is the foundation for his point about the risk to which teachers expose themselves.

We have all had our favorite teachers, and we know they wield an enormous amount of influence on their students. I remember the high-school math teacher who made me think carefully, the college theology professor who encouraged me to go on to further theological study, and the Sunday-school teacher who gave me my first Bible. Students trust their teachers and can develop deep loyalties.

A teacher in the church is further entrusted by God with eternal truths. Because of this, teachers will be held accountable for the positive or negative effect they have on their pupils. Good teachers impart the truth, and their students grow and develop in Christ. They advance the kingdom of God and will be regarded appropriately. Bad teachers impart falsehood or are sloppy, and their students rebel from the faith or stagnate in it. They will be punished. We need to keep these sobering truths in mind when we appoint our Sunday-school teachers and Bible-study leaders. Teachers can't be perfect any more than the rest of us can be, but they do need to be made aware of the gravity of their task and continue to justify the trust placed in them.

The Tongue's Power Far Exceeds Its Size (3:3-5a)

Think of the power button on your stereo or the ignition key for your automobile, and you have an idea of what James is trying to get across in these verses. He talks about rudders and bits, things that are very small in relation to the energy they control. James says the same thing is true about the tongue in relation to the body, and he presents horses and ships as analogies.

The key verb is in both analogies. The New International Version translates it "turn" for the horse and "steer" for the ship. The New American Standard Bible and New English Bible use the more generic "direct" in both analogies, and the Revised Standard Version has "guide." It is a compound from a preposition that means "with" and a verb that means "bring" or "lead." It is used chiefly in the sense of changing direction. Because "we put bits into the mouths of horses to make them obey us," the rider can tug the reins and the horse stops going one direction to go in the direction the rider prefers. He may take the horse out of the danger of a hazardous ditch or force it into a grueling ride. Whatever, the horse is no longer wild. When the bit is in his mouth, he is entirely under the control of his rider, for good or ill. Likewise, a ship, however big, is at the mercies of the winds and the waves, unless it is "steered by a [comparatively] small rudder wherever the pilot wants to go" (James 3:4). It may sail into the Persian Gulf or into the San Diego port, but, because of the rudder, the captain is in control.

Similarly, the controlled tongue has enormous power. What is important to notice is that James does not stress that the tongue is powerful in itself. He highlights this in the ship analogy when he refers to the "strong winds." The rudder is as ineffective as its size would indicate without the captain to channel its potential into purposeful action. We can assume this about the bit in the horse's mouth, too. It does no good without a rider. In James 3:6, James will answer the question of who controls the human tongue.

In the meantime, James is content to use the horse and ship analogies simply to accentuate the tongue's relative smallness, saying, "Likewise the tongue is a small part of the body, but it makes great boasts" (James 3:5). As it stands, the *great boasts* here functions as a handy contrast to the tongue's small size. The horse and ship analogies demonstrate that such boasting has a solid basis because the tongue's importance far exceeds its size. If we look ahead to the forest fire imagery in the latter part of the verse, the boasting of the

tongue becomes more than a handy contrast. It suggests an unflattering picture of the tongue out of control in its boasting. In this case,
James may be suggesting a subtle contrast with the "tongues" of
horses and ships, which can be controlled perfectly, and the human
tongue, which cannot be.

Anyway, we can all relate to the idea that our words give our lives
direction. We make pledges, promises, predictions, protests, and
other verbal pronouncements that dictate many of our activities.
Some help us. Some get us into trouble. Some just embarrass us. We
must first recognize the enormous capacity of our tongues to control
our lives if we are to get anywhere in corralling it.

The Tongue Is the Most Destructive Force in the Human Body (3:5b, 6)

A hydrogen atom is so small that we cannot see it with the naked
eye. It is the least complex and lightest of all chemicals on the peri-
odic table. Yet, when this atom is split, it releases one of the most
devastating forces known to man. James knows of a more destructive force—though it is just as unassuming. In the second half of
James 3:5 and in verse 6, he outlines the destructive power of the
human tongue.

He begins with a third analogy to help us comprehend the kind of
devastation he thinks compares to that of the human tongue. James
himself separates it from the first two analogies: unlike them, this
one is clearly negative, and it prepares the reader for the scathing
words of verse 6. He says, "Consider what a great forest is set on
fire by a small spark." James continues the size contrast in this analogy as in the others, but the emphasis is now on a spark that has
started a fire raging out of control. It doesn't matter whether the fire
was natural, accidental, or intentional. Anything comparable to the
ship's captain or the horse's rider is purposely absent. The point of
this analogy is to expose the negative, destructive capabilities of a
tongue that is not properly controlled.

After the statement that "the tongue also is a fire" come four
clauses that detail four different reasons this is an appropriate description, at times playing off the picture of the raging fire drawn
earlier. The clauses describe an ever-expanding sphere of harm.

The first clause would be better understood as beginning a new
sentence after "the tongue is also a fire" rather than connected to it
with a comma (as in the New International Version). It has its own
subject and verb, which are included in the Revised Standard

Version's translation: "The tongue is an unrighteous world among our members." This helps, but the verb involved carries significantly more meaning than simply "is." It means "appoint," and the form of the word here can be either reflexive, "appoints itself," or passive, "is appointed."

The first translation conveys the image of a swaggering South American military leader who appoints himself the country's president, corresponding to the description in verse 5 of a tongue that boasts. In this case, the tongue usurps authority and power over the rest of the body because of its strategic position, pushing aside other rightful claims to authority.

The second translation, "is appointed," suggests quite a different scenario. This time, we get the picture of a European monarch who confers authority and power on a prime minister whose party has been duly elected. In this case, the tongue's appointment over the rest of our behavior is legitimate and is probably seen as coming from God. Its role, then, is to be the instrument through which the "world of evil" operates in our lives. Calling this role divinely ordained is simply saying that the way we are is the way God made us.

I favor this second translation, "The tongue is appointed the world of iniquity among our members." As I have already pointed out, James never considers the tongue powerful in and of itself, and not until the fourth and last clause of this verse will he name the actual source of its power. On the other hand, as we have seen in other verses like James 1:9-11, 17, 18, 21, and 2:5, James strongly believes that God ordains what happens in human life. I will draw out the implications of this view of the tongue later.

In the second clause, James expands the tongue's sphere of harm to include another realm. Not only is the tongue infected with evil, it infects the rest of the body. James says, "It corrupts the whole person." Fortunately, the translation is not such a problem, although we need to remember that this is really a dependent clause (no proper verb) revealing one of the consequences of the tongue's role as "a world of evil." The New International Version appropriately translates the words in spiritual terms rather than leaving them in physical terms. However, literally, the word for "corrupts" means "stains" and the word for "person" is "body." The imagery compares to a person drinking a red dye that quickly spreads to discolor every molecule of his body. The spiritual message is that the evil of the tongue contaminates our whole lives, and there is nothing we can do about it. It is a permanent stain.

With the third clause, James moves beyond the sphere of the individual's contamination by the tongue to its ruin of human society. According to the New International Version, he says that the tongue "sets the whole course of his life on fire." The problem with this translation is that James really has already said this in the second clause. Evidence strongly indicates that the key phrase, literally, "the cycle of birth," or perhaps "the wheel of life," refers to human existence on the broadest possible scale—past, present, and future. Thus, the human tongue sets human civilization ablaze. Since James returns to the fire imagery, we may say that, just as a forest fire destroys not only one tree or many trees but the forest as a whole, so our tongues harm not just ourselves, not just those offended, but even society at large.

In the fourth and last clause, James moves beyond the natural to the supernatural. He finally identifies the source of the tongue's evil. He says that the tongue "is itself set on fire by hell." The word translated "hell" is sometimes transliterated as "Gehenna" and designates the place of eschatological punishment (Matthew 5:22; 10:28; Mark 9:45; Luke 12:5). James's use of it here is highly appropriate since it was originally the name of a valley south of Jerusalem once used for pagan fire sacrifices (2 Kings 23:10; Jeremiah 7:31) that Jeremiah pictured as the place of God's punishment upon Jerusalem. Closer to the time of James, it may have been used to describe a place of a constantly smoldering garbage dump outside the walls of Jerusalem. The word almost certainly stands here as a euphemism for Satan. Thus, James is saying that the human tongue is Satan's garrison for dispatching his harmful designs on the individual and on society.

To continue the governmental analogies used earlier, the tongue is a puppet dictator controlled by the head of the military or the secret police. The destructive power of the tongue is Satan's power, not its own. But to incorporate the first clause of this verse, even further behind the scenes is God, who wills all this to be so. Perhaps we could picture Him as the benevolent president in exile knowing the nation will one day grow tired of its corrupt government, overthrow it, and invite him back to suppress the corruption and lead them into peace. Although James does not call for such an ouster to occur in our lives in this chapter, he does so in James 4:7-10. In this chapter and this verse, his purpose is to reveal that our tongues are out of our own control and are the tools of Satan for our harm and to the detriment of mankind. Thus, those of us who teach in the church face a serious handicap: our primary teaching tool serves Satan.

James's words about the tongue are very harsh. In fact, even though the Old Testament, and especially Psalms (50:12; 52:3, 4; 120:34) and Proverbs (19:28; 26:23-26), levels serious charges at the human tongue, nothing else said in the Bible is as uncategorical as what James says here. We hate to admit it to ourselves, I suppose, but we all know from experience that James is right. We all have been hurt by the words of others; we all have hurt others with our words; we all have hurt ourselves with words. Of all the parts of our body, our tongue shouts the loudest that we are sinners, helpless pawns of Satan. Without God and the gospel of Christ, this can never change. And even after we have accepted Christ, we constantly need the Spirit's help to suppress the devil's permanent foothold in what we say.

The Tongue Cannot Be Controlled by Man (3:7, 8)

The best thing about circuses are the animals. Forget the jugglers and high-wire acts. It is the dancing elephants and the lion hugging his trainer that excite me most. The animals at the circus, the seals balancing balls on their noses at water shows, and my dog Cindy shaking hands and rolling over display what James says in these verses. Having said that the destruction of the human tongue is controlled by Satan in verse 6, he has implied that we cannot control our tongues. Now, in James 3:7 and 8, he states this openly, contrasting the situation with man's control over animals.

The New International Version's translation of James 3:7, "All kinds of animals, birds, reptiles and creatures of the sea are being tamed and have been tamed by man," reduces the contrast James intends to exaggerate for effect. In fact, he says, *"Every* kind of animal," as in the Revised Standard Version. The major categories of animals James recites demonstrate his dependence on Genesis 1:26, in which, along with Genesis 1:28, God sanctions man to rule over and subdue them. Man's ability to capture and domesticate animals comes to mind first with the word *tamed.* However, he also probably has in mind hunting and fishing. James repeats the verb in the present and in the past to convey that the divine ordination has always proven to be true, presently is so, and always will be. The Revised Standard and King James Versions' translations of "humankind" and "mankind" reveal the subtle irony in James's repetition of the word *kind* to depict the human race as another of God's creations.

In James 3:8, the other shoe drops. "But," he says, "no man can tame the tongue." As far as James is concerned, this is an eternal truth, and is one of the ironies of life. Man can subdue the wildest and most powerful animals, but the individual cannot do anything to stop the wanton destructiveness of his tongue, a relatively small and seemingly unpretentious part of his own body. James very well may be hinting here that no man can do this apart from God's help. If so, it is no more of a hint than he gave us in the fourth clause of James 3:6 and is secondary to his main purpose as I explained. Given the tie-in to creation in James 3:7 and the definitive nature of his statement here, he probably thinks that man's incapability to control his tongue has been determined by God to be the nature of things.

James completes verse 8 by describing the human tongue in terms reminiscent of verse 6. "It is a restless evil, full of deadly poison." Both descriptions focus on aspects of its evil that make it immune to control. The first conjures up images of a wild animal, quicker and more cunning than all others, eluding all attempts at capture, and ready to pounce. The second accents the potency of the tongue like that of a poisonous snake striking out at others, comparable to Psalm 58:4 and 140:3, and supporting the third clause of James 3:6. But it could also describe the fatal effect on the speaker of a mouth full of poison, comparable to Job 20:12-16, and supporting the first and second clauses of James 3:6. James very likely intends both descriptions to bring Satan to mind, especially as we see him in Genesis 3, thereby supporting the fourth clause of James 3:6.

We probably don't think very much about how often we sin by what we say. That is part of Satan's ploy. But James's teaching should shake us enough to take a stern look at the poison that comes from our mouths. Maybe we should monitor what we say for a few days and record the sins we have committed and the people we have harmed. No doubt, we will be alarmed. Even if we don't do that, perhaps we should take this opportunity to repent and ask forgiveness from those whom we have harmed with our tongues just today.

The Tongue Is Inconsistent (3:9-12)

Like many, I shake my head at commercials that make a product out to be something it isn't. Candy bars are not nutritious. Beer does not insure a good time. Soft drinks don't improve your love life. I am just as turned off by a person who, because he has delusions of grandeur or is just plain deceitful, tries to make me think he is something he isn't. Such a person is a phony, and we all would agree, I think, that he does himself no good in the long run. It is just such a point that James wants to make about the tongue in James 3:9-12.

We must be just as wary of its attempts to be good as its overt acts of evil because its basic nature cannot be changed, nor can its connections to Satan be severed. The best we can do is minimize its harm.

In verse 9, James begins with an illustration—to be followed by three analogies—intended to expose the inconsistency of the tongue for what it is, a sham. He says that "with the tongue we praise our Lord and Father, and with it we curse men, who have been made in God's likeness." Then, from this specific evidence, he formulates the obvious contrast into a general principle: "Out of the same mouth come praise and cursing" (James 3:10). This is a fact of human existence. Our most venerable use of our tongues is to praise God. Our most despicable use of our tongues is to curse a fellow human being. We do both all the time, sometimes with nary a breath taken. However, a subtlety in James's writing must not be overlooked. He notes, from Genesis 1:26 and 27, that the people we curse have "God's likeness." In effect, then, when we curse others, we are really cursing God himself. What does that say about the genuineness of our praise to God? It says that even our best praise is always tainted by the impurity of our tongues. This does not mean that we stop praising God, but it does mean that we should never be so naive or deceived as to think that the motives behind our worship are ever entirely pure. We must never forget the reality of our sin and that our tongues are cunning tools of Satan.

Thus, James concludes this verse by exclaiming, "My brothers, this should not be." This censure actually reveals another glimmer of hope in James's utterly pessimistic view of the tongue. He cannot mean by this that a person should just buckle up and take charge of his own tongue to make it consistently honorable. He just said in verse 8 that man does not have this capability, and his approach all along has consistently personified the overwhelming destructive power that flows through the tongue from Satan. Therefore, although he does not elaborate on how we should actually deal with this despicable situation, he must be assuming we can apply what he said about "receiving the implanted word" (James 1:19-27) and what he will soon say about wisdom (James 3:13-18), and that we can wait for the further directions he will give (James 4:6-10) to repent and rely on the Lord's help.

In verses 11 and 12, James constructs three analogies from nature and then a sharp conclusion based on the first analogy. These are analogies of consistency. They certify that, in the natural order, things do not change their nature. They remain consistent with what they are. James begins with a rhetorical question, a favorite device of his as we have seen previously: "Can both fresh water and salt water flow from the same spring?" The word for "fresh" is actually the Greek word from which we get the word *glucose*. Again, James is trying to accentuate the contrast between good-tasting ("sweet") water and bad-tasting (bitter) water. The answer to his question, of course, is "no." But he attempts to answer this question in verse 12 by posing two more analogies: "My brothers, can a fig tree bear olives, or a grapevine bear figs?" Again, the answer is "no." Trees and plants cannot go against their natures. They can only do what God created them to do. So James draws the only appropriate conclusion: "Neither can a salt spring produce fresh water." Here we see what James was really getting at when he drew the first analogy. A spring cannot make itself over into something it isn't; a bad spring cannot make itself a good spring.

Although it would have been nice if James had drawn his own conclusion regarding the tongue itself, his point must be that the tongue cannot make itself into something it isn't. We can mix the fresh water of God in with the salty water of our tongue, but the bitterness cannot be eliminated. God has appointed it to be a conduit of evil, and that it will remain. We need to respect this reality. That's the reason teachers need to be especially wary. That's the reason we all need to be wary. We must depend upon God's help to reduce the tongue's evil in our lives.

Heavenly and Earthly Wisdom Described (3:13-18)

Teachers are more than information dispensers. They are people who inspire, encourage, correct, and lead us. Their knowledge of teaching techniques is important, but their character and personality often have the greater impact on us. This is true of public-school teachers, Sunday-school teachers, and college professors. Our favorite teachers are the ones we like. The frosting on the cake—one would hope, at least—is that they taught us the subject matter. This is what James gets into when he talks about good and bad wisdom (James 3:13-18). He is not talking about information, but about the moral and spiritual character of those who dispense it. He focuses on this area because he wants to help us distinguish between good and bad teachers in the church, and also because he hopes all of us will set our course to be wise in the way we live. He moves now from the mouth to the heart, from the external expression to the internal motives of speech.

James begins by raising a question to which he will respond immediately (James 3:13), but then he goes on to present further information (James 3:14-18) to help us answer the question for ourselves. "Who is wise and understanding among you?" This is more than a theoretical question. It is a challenge. As he will declare later (James 4:1-4), James doesn't think very many of his readers are wise. This is the first time he has mentioned wisdom since James 1:5, and even there he assumed most of his readers didn't have it. The word *understanding* does not carry the sense of sympathy or consolation, as we might think. Rather, it refers to the knowledge and skill of an expert.

In what is James concerned that they be expert? The Christian faith. He points to this by his response, which reminds us of James 1:22-25 and 2:14-26: "Let him show it by his good life, by deeds done in the humility that comes from wisdom." The Gospels illustrate that this is what Christ did. He demonstrated by His behavior that the source of His humility, expressed in Matthew 11:29, was wisdom—wisdom that comes only from God. It was wisdom "proved right by her actions," as Matthew 11:19 projects. James wants us to follow His perfect example, especially those of us who are teachers.

James contrasts the wisdom he is talking about with what some people think is wisdom in James 3:14-16. By doing this, the true wisdom he describes (James 3:17, 18) will stand out in relief. James 3:14 is framed in the form of advice: "But if you harbor bitter envy and selfish ambition in your hearts, do not boast about it or deny the truth." He is talking about our motives for teaching or leading in the church. Do we want to teach so that we can stand up front and be noticed, because we want to prove that we are better than someone else, or because we need to assuage an inferiority complex? Such desires do not manifest wisdom, but rather foolishness and self-deceit. For such a person to consider himself wise is a pompous lie. He is the farthest thing from it! Yet people in the church continue to be fooled by this. We must endeavor to heed James's warning here.

James flatly denies that this is real wisdom and names its true source: "Such 'wisdom' does not come down from heaven but is earthly, unspiritual, of the devil" (James 3:15). People who operate with such evil motives cannot manifest wisdom. The New International Version's quotation marks around "wisdom" here are highly appropriate because this so-called "wisdom" really isn't wisdom. It is not founded in God and is as fleeting and empty as a soap bubble. Such a beautifully disguised void can come from only one source in this universe, the devil, to whom James has already tied the tongue (James 3:6). The actual word here is *demonic,* as the New American Standard and New English Bibles have, but the end result is the same.

The observable result of this counterfeit wisdom, which is seen in people with such troubled inner motives and ungodly ties, "is disorder and every evil thing" (James 3:16). With this announcement, James prepares us for his unflattering description (James 4:1-4) of the churches to which he is writing. A church with leaders and teachers of this sort will be a mess, a chaotic embarrassment to the name of Christ.

In contrast to the demonic wisdom (James 3:14-16), and to complete his description of wisdom, James gives a list of wisdom's characteristics (verse 17). The preeminent characteristic of a person whose wisdom is "from heaven" (literally, "from above"), is that he is "pure." Unlike his counterpart, his motives are as clear as the mountain air. There is no evil polluting his words. Instead, he is "peace-loving." He is at peace with himself, and he promotes harmony among people, the opposite of the disorder mentioned earlier. (James will expand this characteristic in verse 18.) He is "considerate," a synonym of *humility* in James 3:13. He handles the confrontational and the confused with words of care and calm. He is "submissive," not meaning that he is a wimp or a pushover, but that he listens attentively to another person's point of view and his needs, reminiscent of James 1:19. He is "full of mercy and good fruit," as he exhibits love to people in need. (See James 1:27; 2:13; and Matthew 7:17, 18.) He is "impartial," an antonym of showing favoritism, which James has decried earlier (James 2:1-13). Thus, he doesn't make decisions or deal with people based on superficial factors. Finally, he is "sincere." The New International Version translates in a positive sense a negated form of the word "hypocritical," which means that his actions back up his word (cf. James 1:22-25; 2:14-26). He practices what he preaches, or teaches, as the case may be.

James concludes his description of wisdom with a curious proverb emphasizing that the person who is wise conducts himself in a peaceful manner. This cannot be gleaned easily from the New International Version, which switches the subject and the object to achieve the translation: "Peacemakers who sow in peace raise a harvest of righteousness." A literal translation would read: "The fruit of righteousness is sown in peace by those who make peace." The *fruit of righteousness* is the subject, not the object, of the proverb. James uses this term as a substitute for *wisdom* in order to relate to the way he began his discussion of wisdom (James 3:13), stressing there that wisdom is demonstrated by good conduct. Saying now that "the fruit of righteousness," or wisdom, is to be "sown in peace by those who make peace" highlights the mention of humility in verse 13.

So James rounds out his discussion of the wise teacher by providing a little proverb that challenges us to practice what wisdom we might have in the proper manner. Nothing other than an attitude of peace and a motivation of achieving peace is appropriate. Teaching or anything we might say that produces anger or division in the church is not wisdom. Its results bear witness against itself. Therefore, let us use this proverb as an instrument to help us be wise for the benefit of the church. Let us be wary of our tongues, as this chapter has so forcefully reminded us, but let us be wise teachers, sharing with others by our character of life and by our words the wisdom of God himself.

CHAPTER SIX

Being God's Friend

James 4:1-17

In contrast to the peace endorsed at the close of chapter 3, chapter 4 opens with scenes of war. In James 3:14 and 16, James described envy and selfish ambition as attitudes of non-wisdom, which result in strife. Now he will talk about selfish desires and pleasures and how they not only tear apart the church but also propel us into such a spiritual decline that a serious strain is put on our once-healthy relationship with God. James considers the people in the churches to whom he is writing to be at a spiritual crossroads. They must choose who is going to dominate their lives, the world or God. Are they going to be self-seeking like everyone else, or are they going to serve God as they have been called to do? He sees only one remedy to their predicament: start over with a clean slate. They must repent. They must change the way they are living if they are going to be God's friends.

The problem is diagnosed in James 4:1-4. Verses 5 and 6 provide the critical, Scriptural background that points to the solution. Then James hammers out the remedy in a series of ten stinging commands (verses 7-10) and provides specific rules of thumb for relating to a fellow Christian and for making future plans, both of which are grounded in remembering God's sovereignty (verses 11-17).

Pugnatiousness Reveals Hostility Toward God (4:1-4)

Every spring at Lincoln Christian College, the students have a "skip day," a day of fun to break the monotony of academic routine. When I was a student there, this event always featured tug-of-war contests over a mud hole. The competition was between dorm floors, and I have fond memories of F-1's being undefeated in these competitions. The key to winning, we discovered (but didn't tell anyone else), is momentum, coordination, and a strong anchorman. At the start signal, the team members must begin tugging first and tug in unison to a cadence until they win. James considers Christians to be in a spiritual tug-of-war. The big problem is that many of us, including those to whom he is writing, are on the wrong side. Our T-shirts say "God's army," but any observant spectator can see we are pulling on the side with those whose T-shirts read "World's Pleasures." If we stay on that side, James asserts, we will lose because God is anchorman for His team. He is infinitely stronger than the anchorman for the other team—Satan.

James begins by asking two rhetorical questions, the second one supplying the answer to the first: "What causes fights and quarrels among you? Don't they come from your desires that battle within you?" (James 4:1). The words *fights* and *quarrels* are military expressions for *wars* and *battles*. James means to dramatize the seriousness of the widespread verbal squabbles that are enlisting proponents in the churches. The cause he discloses may come as a surprise. We might have expected him to name a theological issue like faith and works, a behavioral problem like the tongue, or even a supernatural influence like Satan. But he doesn't do this. He pins the blame squarely on us.

The irony is that he presents the situation as an internal battle within the individual that spills over into our relationships with our Christian family. A further irony is that the combatants have the same sponsor. The New International Version labels this "desires," an internal yearning, but the word is really *pleasures* (the same as in James 4:3, which the New International Version does translate "pleasures"), representing the objects of desire. It is the word from which English gets the word *hedonism*. Various self-indulgent pleasures, then, are wrestling to gain the upper hand in us. This preoccupation with pleasures is affecting the way we treat one another.

James describes what these warring pleasures cause us to do (James 4:2, 3). The first thing we do is damage our fellow Christians. He describes a frustrated desire for some pleasure, "You want something but don't get it," which results in murder, "You kill." The most common motive for murder, in fact, is greed. Here, though, James thinks of murder not with a knife but with words that cut to the heart. Some warring words occur in the heat of battle, like cursing, ridicule, or insults; others occur behind the lines, like gossip, slander, or even perjury (which actually can lead to death). James has already alluded to the tongue's capability to inflict "death" (James 3:8). This dreadful image of the tongue is supported in the Old Testament (Job 20:12; Psalm 10:7-10; 64:4-6; Jeremiah

9:8), especially by Proverbs 12:6: "The words of the wicked lie in wait for blood," and Proverbs 10:6: "Violence overwhelms the mouth of the wicked."

James highlights his accusation about the verbal murder occurring in the Christian community by repeating comments he made before about the war going on within and the war that results without. So he reiterates: "You . . . covet, but you cannot have what you want. You quarrel and fight." This puts the focus on what lies in the center: murder.

The second thing these warring pleasures cause us to do is to stop praying. He says, "You do not have, because you do not ask God" (James 4:2). His charge assumes that God is our loving provider (as in James 1:5 and as proclaimed by Jesus in Matthew 7:7). However, he does not mean that a functioning prayer life obligates God to provide us everything we ask, especially if we have the wrong attitude (as James 1:6 and 7 affirms). The problem exposed here is a total collapse of healthy spiritual dependence on God. Some of us are so preoccupied with pleasures that we have forgotten about God.

The third thing warring pleasures are causing us to do is related to the second but is worse because it involves not just ignoring God, but insulting Him. Some of us actually have the audacity to spend what prayer time we still have asking God to supply us with these self-indulgent pleasures. He says, "When you ask, you do not receive, because you ask with wrong motives, that you may spend what you get on your pleasures" (James 4:3). God, who gives us all the good things we need in life (James 1:17), certainly is not going to feed our insatiable need for pleasures that are driving us away from Him, wreaking havoc in us and in the church. Even to think that He would exhibits how poorly we understand God.

Based on such incriminating evidence, James makes a last-ditch effort to shake us up from our spiritual collapse. He wants us to see that, if any of us have been so foolish as to make pleasures our priority, then not only is our former relationship with God null and void, but we have become His enemy! He says, "You adulterous people, don't you know that friendship with the world is hatred toward God? Anyone who chooses to be a friend of the world becomes an enemy of God" (James 4:4). Precedent for using the term *adulteresses* for people who have betrayed God by becoming spiritually bankrupt is established by Isaiah 54:5-7; Jeremiah 2:2; 3:30; Hosea 2:2-5, and by Jesus in Matthew 12:39; 16:4. Also, the church is considered the bride of Christ (Ephesians 5:22-33). Hankering after the pleasures of the world does surely violate our confession and baptism in the same way as a wife's affair breaks her wedding vows and consummation with her husband. Just as divorcing couples often become enemies, so our choosing to live with the pleasures of the world makes us God's enemies. Both are jealous for us. We must choose one or the other. James speaks of this as our last chance to ditch our lover, who loves us only for our bodies, in order to return to the arms of the One who truly loves us for who we are.

In these verses, James hits on an everlasting problem for us. They didn't have computer games, water parks, shopping malls, fitness clubs, sun beds, *Playboy* magazine, or cocaine, but the carnal nature of man, which lives life only for the self-seeking fun it can provide, still exercised itself even in his time. It lured God's people away from Him then, and it always will.

Perhaps some of us are in its clutches right now. It can happen so easily in our contemporary American society. We have become contentious with people we used to consider friends. We have stopped praying except for things we want. Hear what James is saying! If this describes you, you are about to lose your closest friend. You have already betrayed Him, but He will take you back if you come now.

God Grants Grace Upon Grace (4:5, 6)

Sports commentators sometimes praise athletes by saying they have natural ability. What they imply by this is that there are skills that people learn and that there are certain abilities that we inherit. A great athlete usually has inherited physical prowess that disciplined practice and coaching have honed to near perfection. It is no surprise that the sons and daughters of great athletes often become excellent athletes, too. Two "gifts" are involved: the natural talent and the opportunity for good coaching. This amounts to gift upon gift, or grace upon grace, because both are really blessings from God.

In this section, James finds in Scripture a greater grace and a lesser grace. The greater grace involves the opportunity God gives us to repent, and is based on Proverbs 3:34. The lesser grace is the natural inclination of our spirits toward God, based on Psalm 42:1 and 2 and 84:2, with 119:20, 131, and 175 offering further support. His point is that those who are pursuing pleasure rather than God are squandering their natural gifts, just as potentially gifted athletes sometimes ruin their bodies by drugs, alcohol, or overeating. The natural gifts should cause us to seek God. However, we may be wasting the greater gift, too. Having committed ourselves to God through confession and baptism, we may have become friendly with the world and turned our back on God. But, praise God, the "greater" grace earns its label because it always stands ready to be activated. We can repent and recommit ourselves to God, who stands ready to receive us with open arms like Hosea, who took back his adulterous wife (Hosea 3:1), or the father in the parable of the prodigal son (Luke 15:20).

It is a fairly straightforward task to find that James 4:6 quotes Proverbs 3:34: "God opposes the proud but gives grace to the humble." However, it must be explained that he is quoting from the Greek translation of the Old Testament, called the Septuagint, which all but the Jewish scholars were using by New Testament times. So the verb *opposes* is correct even though our Old Testaments (which translate the Hebrew rather than the Greek) may have *mocks* or *scoffs*. This is a common theme of the Old Testament,[6] which comes to light not only here but also in James 1:9-11, in 2:5, and also in 5:1-6. First Peter 5:5 also quotes Proverbs 3:34. For James, spiritual attitudes are being contrasted: the arrogant, who thumb their noses at God in pursuing their pleasures, and the contrite, who admit their sinfulness. If we read ahead to verses 7-10, we can see that James intends this Scripture to help motivate us to repent.

The task of determining James's Old Testament reference in James 4:5 is anything but straightforward, not only because he has only snatched a few key words and then paraphrased the theme of Psalms 42 and 84, but also because most translations are not done in such a way that the relationship with these Psalms can be recognized. The sentence actually can be taken a number of ways, but the way I am going to suggest is the only way that qualifies as some kind of grace or blessing and can be traced to an actual Old Testament reference.

The New International Version's translation, "Or do you think Scripture says without reason that the spirit he caused to live in us envies intensely?" is like most translations (for example, the King James, Today's English, and New English Versions) in making our natural spirits that God gives us the subject. This is the most natural way to understand it. But how can its tendency toward envy be in

---

[6]Psalm 18:27; 34:18; 51:17; 72:4; 138:6; Isaiah 61:1; Zephaniah 3:11, 12.

any way a blessing or a grace from God? James has just spent the last four verses blasting whoever gives in to such a self-indulgent approach to life as God's enemies! Also, as I indicated, there is no Old Testament text to support this translation.

The Revised Standard Version tries to solve the problem by making God the subject: "He yearns jealously over the spirit which he made to dwell in us." This comes close to something like a grace in response to what James has described in verses 1-4 and, with "yearns," does provide a more accurate rendering of the verb. However, the words translated "jealousy" are really *with envy,* and the Old Testament, understandably, never associates such a trait with God. It doesn't even use the all-too-human emotion of yearning when speaking of God.

The solution lies in taking what I believe are the best parts of both translations. This gives us something like the following: "The spirit that he has caused to live in us yearns with envy." For what does this spirit yearn? It yearns to have a meaningful relationship with God. The Jerusalem Bible, the only one to translate the passage in this sense, reads: "The spirit which he sent to live in us wants us for himself alone."

What "spirit" is this that yearns in this way? It is possible that James means the Holy Spirit, but it is more likely that he has in mind the residue of God's image placed in us at creation (Genesis 1:26, 27), to which he has already alluded in James in 1:18, 21 as one aspect of the implanted word of truth. Why is it envious? It is envious, and justly so, of those people who have fulfilled its need and are faithfully living out their commitments to God in Jesus Christ. It is the spirits of those Christians who have left a meaningful relationship with God that James is trying to call forth and hopes will yet save these backsliders from everlasting separation from God. Psalm 42:2 says, "My soul thirsts for God," and Psalm 84:2 says, "My soul yearns, even faints, for the courts of the Lord."

Some of us may be in the same tragic predicament as that in which James's first readers were. Maybe we have been cavorting with the world to the point that we have forgotten all about God, even though we may still be in the church. God's candle may be barely flickering somewhere down a deep cavern in our lives. But the grace is that God does not allow us to put it out. He created us to find fulfillment only in Him. His second grace is made available by the work of His Son, Jesus Christ, on the cross. It waits patiently, lovingly, for our return.

90

Repent and God Will Befriend You (4:7-10)

Many of us find it difficult to admit we are wrong. "I'm sorry" does not not come from our lips easily. Just as watching thousands of murders on television each year has numbed us to the horrors of death, self-centeredness can blind us to the tragic results of our sins: people who have been maimed, perhaps scarred for life, by hateful, thoughtless things we have said; a loving God who has been scorned. James says there is only one solution: to look on our bloody sin until it cuts us to the quick and causes us to repent.

This section contains ten commands. The first and the tenth commands, "Submit yourselves, then, to God," and "Humble yourselves before the Lord," are synonymous, echoing the Scripture cited in James 4:6. James's challenge to repent immediately, then, is the main point. By sandwiching eight commands in between these two, James attempts to specify what he thinks is involved in true repentance. The promises connected to the second, third, and last commands reflect God's grace mentioned in verse 6.

The second command, "Resist the devil," is the necessary complement to the idea of submitting to God. Just as friendship with God and the world are mutually exclusive, so withstanding the onslaughts of Satan is the flipside to pledging loyalty to God. When he knows the arsenal of God stands behind, he has no choice: "he will flee from you."

The third command, "Come near to God," dramatizes a further reaction to Satan's approach. If one is to maintain a healthy distance from Satan, he must move toward God. The wall created when pleasures of the world are pursued vanishes into thin air when a face turns toward God. A returning sinner can be assured that God's love and protection will reach out: "and he will come near to you."

The fourth and fifth commands are about cleaning up our lives. "Wash your hands" emphasizes the external changes that are required. We must straighten up our behavior. We may need to say "I'm sorry" to people whom we have hurt. Unlike Lady Macbeth, we can wash the blood off our hands. "Purify your hearts" emphasizes the internal cleanup that is required. Our hardened hearts must be softened and restored to proper working order so that we can again care about others and about God. "Sinners" and "double-minded" are what we are until our spiritual scrubbing is completed, sinners who have tried and, not surprisingly, failed at loving God and the world at the same time.

The sixth, seventh, and eighth commands, "Grieve, mourn and wail," draw attention to the fact that true repentance involves our emotions. Children often cry when they are disciplined, not so much because of the spanking, but because they realize they have let their parents down. Similarly, we should be upset and show it when we realize just how far away we let ourselves get from God. This is an important part of our repenting. Joel (2:12), Jesus (Matthew 8:12; 22:13; 24:51; 25:30), and James again (5:1) speak of repentance in these emotional terms.

The ninth command, "Change your laughter to mourning and your joy to gloom," expands on the seventh command and parallels a remark by Jesus in Luke 6:25. James pictures sneering, overconfident laughs of arrogance and hollow joy. We must look squarely at our old lives and cry at the horror of it all, like the picture of Dorian Gray that mysteriously acquired the debauchery of his life-style. What we did to God and others, and consequently to ourselves, should not be hidden. Seeing it will bring us to our knees.

Finally, the tenth command, as previously stated, reaffirms the emphasis of repentance in the first command. However, the promise attached to it, "and he will lift you up" (which comes from Jesus himself—Matthew 23:12; Luke 14:11; 18:14), closes out this section by stipulating the penultimate grace of God. Those who submit to God will not only set Satan running and have a meaningful relationship with God now, but they are promised a permanent relationship with God forever.

Repentance is supposed to be a major element in our initial conversion. Too often it is not, perhaps because becoming baptized after being raised in the church does not seem like such a big deal. Even when adults join the church, we often slide over that nasty part about repentance. James serves notice that repentance is critical for a person to get right with God, whether for the first time when he becomes a Christian, or for the hundredth time after falling away. This may be something some of us need to do today to untangle ourselves from the clutches of sin that is driving us away from God.

A Judgmental Attitude Toward Others Insults God (4:11, 12)

Being critical of others is so easy. We just watch and wait because people are sure to slip up sooner or later. We can then criticize them to their faces or behind their backs. Either way, for some perverted reason, it seems to make us feel better about ourselves. Feeding our ego this way is condemned by Jesus when He says, "Do not judge, or you too will be judged" (Matthew 7:1; Luke 6:37). The same theme is applied by Paul (Romans 2:1; 14:4; 1 Corinthians 12:20) and Peter (1 Peter 2:1; 2 Peter 2:12; 3:16), and is frequently disapproved of in the Old Testament (Leviticus 19:16; Psalm 50:20; 101:5; Proverbs 20:13).

And James, grounded by what Jesus said and by the Old Testament, adds his censure (James 4:11, 12). He does so because slander and related sins of speech have become a major problem for many in the church of his day. He already brought this to light in James 4:1 and 2 as evidence of sin, and he called for repentance in James 4:7-10. Now he wants to respond specifically to that problem and help motivate people to control this kind of sinful behavior. After the initial reprimand, "Brothers, do not slander one another," James accomplishes this in four unique and carefully reasoned steps.

In the first step, James reasons that, when we speak against someone, we put ourselves in the position of judge over the law. Swiftly, he puts slander under the broader rubric of judging: "Anyone who speaks against his brother or judges him speaks against the law and judges it" (James 4:11). Of course, it is totally inappropriate for us to judge a brother, or fellow Christian, and James is right: slander is a type of judgment. Instead, as family, we should love one another and stand united against attacks rather than attacking one another. Also, as brothers and sisters, we do not have the right to make the rules of conduct. We are equally under their authority.

In his second step of reasoning, which completes verse 11, James argues that evaluating the law puts us on the wrong side of the bench: "When you judge the law, you are not keeping it, but sitting in judgment on it." As defendants, so to speak, we have no authority to rule on the appropriateness or legality of the law. Our judgment necessarily will be biased, and the black robe we put on does not belong to us. As citizens of God's kingdom, we are under the law, not above it.

In his third step, James firmly lays down the key plank in his argument: "There is only one Lawgiver and Judge, the one who is able to save and destroy" (James 4:12). God designed the law, and He administers it. These are basic Biblical principles. Yet we must not overlook the fact that James may also have Christ in the back of his mind. After all, Christ's principle of loving our neighbor, emphasized in James 2:8 and brought to mind by the use of *neighbor* at the end of this verse, and His words about judging one another (Matthew 7:1) are the relevant "laws" in this context. Jesus is most likely the Judge in James 5:9. Probably drawing on what Jesus himself says (Matthew 25:31-46; John 5:19-29), other New Testament writers are not bashful about speaking of Christ's role as Judge on God's behalf.[7] Yet, one key New Testament passage obligates us to maintain God's priority in judgment generally and also in this verse. James's assertion that the "Judge" is "the one who is able to save and destroy" is undoubtedly based on Jesus' own assignment of judgment to God in Matthew 10:28 (Luke 12:4): "Do not be afraid of those who kill the body but cannot kill the soul. Rather, be afraid of the One who can destroy both soul and body in hell."

James's fourth step of logic, concluding verse 12, comes in the form of yet another rhetorical question. It is masterfully designed to remind us just how out of place we really are when we speak against someone and thus rewrite the law. He asks, "But you—who are you to judge your neighbor?" Today, we would say, "Who do you think you are?" The audacity, the pomposity, the blasphemy even, of sitting in God's chair is a serious offense, which most of us would never consciously presume to do. That is exactly how James expects us to react. From now on, he wants us to keep in mind how terribly we are offending God when we talk about a fellow Christian, or anybody, in a critical or slanderous way.

James is not trying to prevent us from honestly evaluating one another or even reproving one another. We need this in order to grow and develop spiritually and in other ways as well. Critiques of this sort are done out of love and concern. The kind of criticism he is talking about is done out of spite, anger, arrogance, and disdain. The intent is to hurt someone, with words substituting for an actual weapon. Sometimes, the feeling can be close to murder, as James called it earlier (James 4:2), and this reminds us of how Jesus related anger to murder and lust to adultery in Matthew 5. Let's vow not to use words as weapons to harm the people around us. Rather, let's use our words carefully, as instruments of love and encouragement.

Pretentious Arrogance Is Sin Against God (4:13-17)

One of the keys to being productive human beings is planning the next hour, the next day, and the upcoming year. Quite rightly, we make goals and projections for accomplishments, the sooner on the

---

[7]See 1 Corinthians 4:3-5; 2 Corinthians 5:10; Romans 2:6; 2 Timothy 4:1, 8; 1 Peter 4:5.

schedule, the more specific. I have planned to write this section of the book you are now reading during the next hour or two. I plan to write chapter seven next week. I plan to submit this manuscript next month. I plan to complete commentaries on James and the Epistles of John within the year. Planning is the shiny key to accomplishment in any field or endeavor.

From a spiritual standpoint, we normally consider planning good stewardship. We would hardly consider it sin, much less blasphemy. Yet James 4:13-17 says—in no uncertain terms—that it very well could be. Planning, especially successful planning, James reasons, can arise from arrogance and be considered boasting. Sustained success can make us forget about God and foolishly think we control our own destinies. It is one way in which the pleasures of the world can take us away from God.

James begins with a sharp rejoinder, "Now listen," which brings us up short. Then he singles out the businessmen from among us and puts in their mouths words they might very well say as they plan a new marketing venture: "Today or tomorrow we will go to this or that city, spend a year there, carry on business and make money" (James 4:13). He mentions no specifics really, not the date, not the city, not the kind of business, not the amount of projected profit. This statement is a blank form that could be filled in with details by any real businessman.

James goes on to remind us that all our plans are contingent. We are blind regarding the future, and, when it comes to eternity, our significance is minute. He cajoles, "Why, you do not even know what will happen tomorrow. What is your life? You are a mist that appears for a little while and then vanishes" (James 4:14). Although translations of this do differ, the New International Version rightly agrees with the Revised Standard and King James Versions in formulating the second clause as yet another rhetorical question. His answer is visual. We are a pale morning fog, a puff of smoke, a wispy cloud; hardly noticeable, unsustained, insignificant. James puts us in our place against the backdrop of the universe. He bursts our balloon of arrogance to bring us down to earth with a more realistic perspective of ourselves.

With that in mind, James imposes an amendment to the statement he put in the businessman's mouth (James 4:13) that properly acknowledges our frailty: "Instead, you ought to say, 'If it is the Lord's will, we will live and do this or that'" (James 4:15). By the way this is phrased, we can see that James used businessmen to represent a widespread problem. We all need to view our future as contingent upon God, no matter what it is or who we are. Whether we recognize it or not, He is in control of what happens. Especially as Christians, we insult God when we live as if He were not. We must stop this, even if it means literally inserting "if the Lord wills" into our regular vocabulary. This practice is exhibited elsewhere in Scripture: Acts 19:21; 1 Corinthians 4:19; 16:7; and Hebrews 6:3. Surprisingly, though, it is a Greek custom begun by Socrates rather than a Jewish custom that James and the early church appear to have adapted for Christian use.

"As it is," or without accounting for God's will in the matter, "you boast and brag. All such boasting is evil" (James 4:16). Here James assesses how serious a problem the statement in verse 13 is. The problem is attitude. The plans being uttered are swaggering predictions of self-accomplishment and personal success. They are boasts. A more literal translation, like that in the Revised Standard Version or the New American Standard Bible, identifies the attitude: "You boast in your *arrogance*." All pride and boasting is not wrong. We can boast of what God has done through us, as James encourages in James 1:9 and as Paul does in Romans 5:2 and 3; 1 Thessalonians 2:9; and Philippians 2:16. However, boasting in God's face (whether we know He is watching or not) is not only evil, it is blasphemy. As we plan for success, we set ourselves up as god over our own schedule if we do not acknowledge His sovereignty.

Finally, James concludes this section with a principle that, at first, seems a little out of place: "Anyone, then, who knows the good he ought to do and doesn't do it, sins." The idea of sinning by omission may be applied broadly to many situations in our lives. The presence of such a warning here must mean that James intends for us to apply it to what he has just said about not ignoring God's sovereignty over our lives when we are making plans. We may have been naive before, but we no longer have any excuse. It is wrong to snub God in our planning, but it is now also sin to snub James's explicit warning to stop doing this. Now that we know better, we must change.

To our believing grandparents, "If the Lord wills" came naturally out of their mouths when they talked about tomorrow's or next week's plans. In Scotland, where I lived for a time, verbal announcements of this evening's services or next Lord's Day's almost always were prefaced with "If the Lord wills." It may sound negative or puritanical to our modern ears, but I think we may have discarded a good speech habit that we should seriously consider reinserting into our talk. It may be the very aid we need to keep ourselves conscious of God's role and interest in our lives.

This chapter has told us how to be God's friends. The principle is reasonably simple: we need to respect Him for who He is. This is the basis for any friendship. Because He is God, we need to show respect and include Him in our plans for the future. Showing the respect He deserves will help us respect others He has created and loves when we talk about them. Proper respect for God will influence how we pray. It will influence the manner in which we conduct ourselves as we serve Him in the church. It will bring us to our knees in repentance when we get uppity and think we can do better without Him.

CHAPTER SEVEN

Closing Concerns: Suffering

James 5:1-20

James does not conclude his epistle as Paul and most other New Testament writers do. He does not say, "Good-bye," or, "See ya soon," as we would expect in modern correspondence. James gives closure to his epistle in a different way, which resembles what we see in 1 John. The ending is like a matching bookend to the beginning. In chapter 5, James returns to the style and the subject matter that characterizes James 1:1-18. He does not explain the connections between condemning the rich (1-6), recommending patience (7-11), honesty (12), and prayer (13-18), and rescuing a backslider (19, 20) any more than he explained the reasoning for going from section to section in chapter 1. However, we found there a connecting string: adversities in life and how to deal with them. Likewise, we find here a complementary theme, and it is the same as before: sufferings in life and how to deal with them.

Suitably, in contrast to the rather harsh tones of censure that have dominated the epistle, especially chapter 4, James's closing remarks seem to sympathize with his readers for the predicaments life imposes upon them. He can be sympathetic in chapter 5 because the problems addressed are coming from outside the church. Christians are the victims rather than the criminals, and he wants to help them, mostly in spiritual ways but also in physical ways.

Those Who Take Advantage of the Poor Are Condemned (5:1-6)

We could cut out this section of James and place it in Isaiah or Amos, and it would fit right in. Isaiah (13:6) warns Babylon, "Wail, for the day of the Lord is near." Amos (8:3, 4) wags his condemning finger in the faces of wealthy Hebrew landowners who cheated the poor laborers and declares, "In that day . . . the songs in the temple will turn to wailing. Many, many bodies—flung everywhere!" In Luke 6:24, Jesus says, "But woe to you who are rich, for you have already received your comfort. Woe to you who are well fed now, for you will go hungry. Woe to you who laugh now, for you will mourn and weep." James has already warned the rich of their precarious position (James 1:9-11), he has accused them of blasphemy (James 2:7), and he has chosen successful businessmen to typify our disrespect for God's sovereignty (James 4:13-17). But in none of those places did he condemn them in such irreversible terms as he pronounces here.

The fact that James opens his attack on the rich with "Now listen, you rich people" (James 5:1), similar to the way he opened James 4:13, should not be taken to mean that he is still addressing the church as he was there. Here, he sets his sights on the rich as a class; he is not concerned whether a particular individual within the class might be a Christian or not. We would hope, though, that no declared Christian is guilty of the indictments James sets out. He pictures the vast majority of Christians to be among the mistreated: "the workmen" who are "crying out against" the rich, "the harvesters" whose "cries . . . have reached the ears of the Lord Almighty" (James 5:4), the "innocent men" who were "condemned and murdered" by the wealthy (James 5:6).

Perhaps the best Old Testament example of an "innocent," or "righteous," person who did not resist unjust execution is Naboth (1 Kings 21). As a part of Jezebel's plot, "scoundrels" falsely accused him of blasphemy, and he was stoned so that Jezebel could take his little vineyard and give it to her husband, King Ahab.

In the New Testament, we come upon the archetype of all who are victimized by the powerful, Jesus. False charges were trumped up as the most innocent of all men sat silently before His executioners, and He was crucified. The fact that the word *innocent* (more literally, *righteous*) is in the singular and that the telling phrase *who were not opposing you* (more literally, "He does not resist you") is also singular suggests that James may very well intend to bring Jesus to mind as the readers contemplate their own sorry situations. Jesus, then, becomes the role model for those who suffer unjustly, and especially for the poor who suffer at the hands of the rich. James encourages us to continue trusting God even in the worst of adversities because we know the good that was accomplished through the outrage of Jesus' suffering.

After representing the reaction of the rich to the misery that awaits them as weeping and wailing (James 5:1), James graphically portrays the particulars of their coming judgment. In order to convey the certainty of their doom, he makes it seem as if they have just watched these things happen before their very eyes, like some kind of torture or like watching themselves on television: "Your wealth has rotted, and moths have eaten your clothes. Your gold and silver are corroded" (James 5:2, 3). This part of their punishment conveys an excruciating reality to them: their possessions are worthless in eternity. The yield of their fields, their fine clothes, and their valuables are spoiled.

What they have spent their entire lives accumulating (at the expense of others, James informs us in verse 4) is not only futile but is pictured as the instrument of their own destruction: "Their corrosion will testify against you and eat your flesh like fire." The New International Version loses the visual relationship James sees between fire, which is red and destroys wood, and "rust," which is red and destroys iron, by replacing *rust* with *corrosion,* which is black or green. On the other hand, the translation is correct in that it employs the proper word for the decay of metals like gold and silver.

With the last sentence of verse 3, James levels the first of four charges against the rich: "You have hoarded wealth in the last days." Not only have they put their faith in things rather than God, they have been oblivious to God's timetable. Like the rich fool of Jesus' parable (Luke 12:13-21), he has acquired and acquired, but he has allowed everlasting joy to slip through his fingers. As James reminded us earlier (James 4:14), life gives us no guarantees in terms of days or years or even hours. The last days are not some time in the distant future. They are now, for each of us. To spend today gathering items that may stop us from crossing over into eternity rather than developing our spiritual character, which carries us across, is indeed foolish.

James's second charge is packed with real-life drama and is based on the stipulation in Hebrew law that a laborer be paid at the end of each working day (Leviticus 19:13; Deuteronomy 24:15; Malachi 3:5). In fact, when James says, "Look! The wages you failed to pay the workmen who mowed your fields are crying out against you," and, "The cries of the harvesters have reached the ears of the Lord Almighty," he purposely echoes Deuteronomy 24:15, which says to pay a hired man "before sunset" or "he may cry to the Lord against you." Even today, the vast majority of people in the world purchase tomorrow's food for their family with today's earnings. Not receiving what they have earned creates a spiral of unjust hardship that the wealthy cannot understand. Such delays in payment are one way the wealthy attain their profits in the first place. But James affirms that the Lord hears the cries of anguish from the poor, and He who commands Heaven's armies, as *Almighty* expresses (1 Samuel 17:45), will annihilate those who take advantage of them.

James further charges that the rich have been living "in luxury and self-indulgence" (James 5:5), and he surely believes that they have heartlessly stepped on the bony hands of the poor in the process. Therefore, the last day for them will be a "day of slaughter," as pictured in Isaiah 30:25; Ezekiel 7:14-23; and Revelation 19:17-21.

James's final charge against the rich (James 5:6), as I have already suggested, involves conspiracy and perjury. In terms of beleaguered Christians, it recalls James 2:6, 7. Because the wealthy are also the powerful in society, they can and do manipulate the courts, the banks, and the police to serve their interests at the expense of the poor who have no resources to fight back. The end result of this, for some—for Naboth, for Jesus—is death. However, James's entire thrust has been to encourage the disadvantaged Christians to take courage and trust in God because His judgment will be fair, for them and for the rich.

Anyone reading this who feels as if he is living under someone's boot heel should take heart and find hope. The oppressors of the world, whether they be white landowners in the South, factory owners in the North, business tycoons, roving gangs in the inner city, a military dictator in Central America, or just a local employer, will ultimately receive their due. James reaffirms this unwavering Biblical theme. If someone reading this is responsible for people working under him or her, whether as an owner of a business or as a supervisor, heed James's warning. Treat your people with respect, fairness, and thoughtfulness.

Be Patient and Do Not Gripe Against One Another (5:7-11)

We live in a society that does not know very much about patience. In contrast to Europeans, who routinely wait in line, or "queue" as the British say, without complaint for most services, we Americans expect quick service, and we do not like to wait in line. The boom in self-service enterprises, quick shops, and fast-food restaurants is ample evidence of our love affair with speed. But when we are put into situations where we have to wait—perhaps in a restaurant, in a department store, or at the doctor's office—we can become easily distraught. If we don't voice our complaint to the manager, we often at least commiserate with others near us. It is this very human trait of complaining when we become impatient that James addresses when he advocates patience and silence to those who are victimized by the powerful.

James's use of *brothers* when he admonishes, "Be patient, then, brothers, until the Lord's coming" (James 5:7), assures us that he is now speaking to fellow Christians who are either being persecuted because of their faith or are simply among the poor who are tyrannized by the rich. Either way, he bases his counsel of patience on the assumption that Christ will administer the justice of the Lord "Almighty" (James 5:4) and usher in the "last days" (James 5:3). They can be confident that the oppressors will get their due when He comes. In the New Testament, "the Lord's coming" is a common theme of hope for Christians (1 Corinthians 15:23; 1 Thessalonians 2:19) and dread for unrepentant sinners (Matthew 24:37-39; 2 Thessalonians 2:8).

James's agricultural analogy reminds us that our patience will be rewarded. God's promises will come to pass just as certainly as the rains come to Palestine in October and May, the beginning and the end of their planting season. God actually did utter a promise to give the Israelites "autumn and spring rains" (Deuteronomy 11:14). James's readers, most of whom were scattered from Palestine (see the introduction, "Getting Acquainted With James"), will have experienced the yearly fulfillment of this promise.

James 5:8 appeals to us to be patient like the farmers, and adds a note of encouragement, "Stand firm, because the Lord's coming is near." *Stand firm,* which is more literally translated, "strengthen your hearts," is intended to contrast with the rich who, literally, "fattened [their] hearts" for slaughter (James 5:5). Lean hearts, toughened by living through grueling experiences, should be ready and eager for the Lord's coming. James adds that His coming "is near," which should further quicken the heartbeats of those of us who anticipate Christ's return. The New Testament teaches that Christ's return is always "at hand" because it can come to pass at any time.[8] Whether or not He comes tomorrow, we must live today as though He may.

Wishing to reinforce his prohibition against scurrilous remarks among Christians (James 4:11, 12), James says, "Don't grumble against each other, brothers, or you will be judged. The Judge is

---

[8]See Mark 13:32-37; Romans 13:11, 12; 1 Thessalonians 5:1-8; Hebrews 10:25; 1 Peter 4:7.

standing at the door!" (James 5:9). Under the cast of the Lord's impending return, such behavior is all the more out of place. Language like "against each another," "you will be judged," and "The Judge is standing at the door!" certainly recalls James 4:11 and 12 and, in turn, Matthew 7:1. That Christ is the judge in mind, rather than God, is apparent from the immediate context, which concerns His return, and from Matthew 24:33; Mark 13:29; and Revelation 3:20, in which Jesus is the one at the door. The imagery of standing rather than sitting implies that He is getting ready to open the door, further underlining the nearness of the time. Picturing Him just on the other side of a door shows His proximity to us and implies that He can overhear our conversations. If we really believed this, we would be sick about ourselves and clean up our acts. That reaction is what James is counting on.

In verse 10, James finally uses the word that links the various thrusts of this chapter together: *suffering.* He gives two prominent "example[s] of patience in the face of suffering" that come easily to mind to anyone familiar with the Old Testament: almost any of the prophets and Job. Jesus saw His disciples as being in the line of the Old Testament prophets and warned them about similar persecution (Matthew 5:12). Who can help but think of Job when recalling what he endured: the killing of his family, the loss of his wealth, the shame of his appearance, but most of all the devastating, wrongful judgment of him and the searing comments made to him by his "friends"? The prophets, too, were ridiculed as well as mistreated by their people. Just look at Jeremiah (7:27; 18:18-23; 20:1-27; 26:12; 37:16, 21; 38:6). James commends the prophets and Job to us as role models because of their character and because God verified their trust. Prophets stood by their words, and prophesies came to pass. Job never cursed God, and he was rewarded with much more than he ever lost. James uses a key word, *perseverance,* in connection with both Job and the prophets, which links this passage with James 1:1-18, especially verses 2-4 and 12. Because they persevered under trial, they were "blessed." And James probably means to imply that they are models of wisdom. Regardless, they illustrate magnificently that "the Lord is full of compassion and mercy" (James 5:11), especially toward those whose patient suffering is a steadfast witness to His faithfulness toward them. He wants us to take this enduring truth to heart in our own varied high-pressure situations in life.

Most all of us at one time or another suffer unjustly, not necessarily because we are Christians, but because of the various situations in which our lives place us—our job, our family, our neighborhood, or our economic or social status. Maybe it's the color of our skin, our gender, our size, even the way we talk. James counsels us how to handle the anger, the self-doubt, and the depression. He warns us not to give in to the self-defeating tendency to grumble and complain, especially to fellow Christians. Rather, he says, "Hang in there! You can count on the fact that the Lord knows your situation and will handle it fairly when He comes." So let's resolve to trust God and stick it out.

Be Honest (5:12)

Cicero, the great Roman orator and lawyer of the first century B.C., admires a story he has heard about early Athens. He relates the story in a letter *(To Balbo)* and says there was once a well-respected member of the community who was called upon to give testimony in a trial. But when it came time to swear the oath to tell the truth, the jury protested that it wasn't necessary. Cicero says, "The Greeks did not wish it to be thought that the credibility of a man of proven honesty was more strictly secured by a ritual observance than by the truthfulness of his character." This is precisely what James is getting at when he says, "Above all, my brothers, do not swear—not by heaven or by earth or by anything else. Let your 'Yes' be yes, and your 'No,' no, or you will be condemned" (James 5:12). He thinks the honest character of Christians should be so evident to those who know them that their word can stand alone without being propped up by oaths of truthfulness.

James 5:12 strikes us as coming out of the blue. It does not seem to follow from verse 11, nor is it taken up in verse 13. Rather, it seems like a rock in the middle of a stream, with the theme of coping with various types of suffering flowing all around it. Yet James begins the verse with, "Above all," which means he considers it the last and most important in a string of admonitions. If so, James must see it as climaxing his condemnation of speech sins. James probably considers swearing the most serious among these because a broken oath directly involves God in falsehood. As a named accomplice, His own character is defamed. This is much more serious than indirectly slandering Him by criticizing someone else, the sin involved in James 4:11 and assumed to be the same in James 5:9.

How might swearing relate to suffering? The kind of oaths James is talking about would be used primarily by a person doing business with someone else. If they are poor and desperate, Christians may be tempted to use oaths to fend off creditors or to obtain credit for food and other necessities. People still do that today, saying, "I promise I'll pay you tomorrow," knowing full well only a miracle would make it possible. In James's day, people would swear in God's name or, more likely, use a customary substitute like the ones James mentions. Other substitutes—Jerusalem, the temple, the gold in the temple, and a person's head—are mentioned by Jesus (Matthew 5:33-37; 23:16-22) when He attacks the same penchant in first-century Palestine for using oaths to sponsor deceit rather than for guaranteeing truth.

In fact, the language (Matthew 5:33-37) by which Jesus calls for His disciples to abstain from making personal oaths is strikingly similar to what we see in James. The key slogan there is: "Let your 'Yes' be 'Yes,' and your 'No,' 'No'; anything beyond this comes from the evil one" (Matthew 5:37). Many translations, like the New International Version, translate them exactly the same despite their slight differences.[9] Regardless, we can see that James's heavy emphasis on eliminating oaths from the Christian life-style carries on Jesus' bidding.

It is important to understand that when James and Jesus talk about swearing, they do not mean cursing, as we sometimes do. They mean using God's name or an unaccepted substitute to signify truthfulness or credibility. Neither does James or Jesus mean that we should refuse to make oaths when civil or legal convention requires them, as in being a witness in court. Rather, the concern is about personal oaths that a person might volunteer when doing business or in replying to probing questions from a distrustful friend or family member. This hits us all. Our job as Christians is to establish personal credibility as witnesses to the trustworthiness of God and the gospel of Jesus Christ. If we are going to wear the name, we must take care not to deface it before the world.

Earnest Prayer Is Powerful—So Pray (5:13-18)

Jewish teaching uses one word to summarize all that is necessary for God to hear the prayers that people direct to Him. That word is *kawwanah,* and it stands for sincerity, devotion, submission, and focusing on God. The rabbis say that, as long as *kawwanah* is present,

---

[9]Matthew 5:37 is, literally, "But let your word be yes yes, no no, for anything beyond this is from the evil one."

God hears. The person's location does not matter; he can be in the synagogue, in the field, or even in bed—God still hears. James tries to teach a similar truism in this passage: that, in whatever circumstance a Christian might find himself, prayer to God is an appropriate and meaningful response.

James concentrates on a variety of stressful circumstances in the passage, like illness, but he spotlights joyous situations as well. He consciously picks up the theme, only marginally maintained in verse 12, by asking a question that focuses on one of the words that he used to describe the prophets in verse 10: *suffering*. Although the New International Version phrases the question, "Is any one of you in *trouble*?" (James 5:13), the word used here is really the same as the one used in verse 10. The New International Version is right to expand the sense somewhat, though, because James surely means suffering in the widest possible sense, whether from mistreatment by the rich, social ostracism because of the faith, physical illness, or spiritual decline. James's admonition, "He should pray," teaches that petitioning God for help when we are in trouble is always part of the remedy we need. He will always give us strength, if not deliverance.

Whereas the first question and response cover the negative situations in life, the second question and response cover the positive situations in life: "Is anyone happy? Let him sing songs of praise" (James 5:13). Our good experiences should cause us to look to God as much as our bad experiences. We can actually sing or simply utter words of appreciation to our great God, who is responsible for all good (James 1:17). By commenting on the two extremes, James exhibits that there are appropriate responses to God to fit all our moods and conditions.

James then selects a practical incidence of suffering among people in the church to demonstrate his point about prayer's effectiveness. In doing so, he asks a third question, "Is any one of you sick?" (James 5:14) and makes a long and fairly involved response that extends through verse 16. Certain aspects of his response, like the elders, the oil, and the role of sin, puzzle us. Yet the thrust is convincing because it confirms what we still experience in the church today: "The prayer offered in faith will make the sick person well" (James 5:15). Most churches pray every Sunday for their members who are ill, and we witness the positive results. James seems to reflect customary church practice of his time in saying that the person who is sick should "call the elders of the church to pray over him and anoint him with oil in the name of the Lord." When we think about it, this is not so different from our practice of the minister's visiting those who are hospitalized or bedridden and praying with them. We don't usually administer oil, but we do offer words of encouragement and faith in the name of the Lord during the visit.

James's mention of oil in this context is the basis of the Roman Catholic deathbed sacrament of "extreme unction." Biblically, however, oil is applied as medicine (Luke 10:34), is associated with healing (Mark 6:13, but in exactly what sense we don't know), and in symbolizing spiritual consecration (Exodus 29:7; 40:9; 1 Samuel 16:3; Hebrews 1:9). It is unlikely here in James that the oil means anything more than to signify that the sick person gives himself over to God, since James states clearly that "the Lord will raise him up" in response to prayer. The oil, at best, is incidental. The faithful intercessory prayer moves God (or James could have Jesus in mind here) to restore the ailing person. It is this point that he repeats in verse 16, "The prayer of a righteous man is powerful and effective," and then illustrates with Elijah in verses 17 and 18.

When James brings in the element of the sick person's sin, "If he has sinned, he will be forgiven" (James 5:15), he is doing no more than admitting that no one but Jesus and perhaps the guilty party has the ability to separate sin from sickness (Mark 2:1-12; John 9:2, 3; 1 Corinthians 5:5; 11:27-30). James's advice intends to cover the possibility that the Christian's ailments may arise because of sin, but it doesn't presume either way. As a practical matter, those who attend to the sick should still provide opportunity to talk and, perhaps as a result, confess and repent.

James issues a principle in verse 16 that widens the burden of responsibility for dealing with sin beyond the individual and the minister to the congregation as an entire body of people who trust each other and care for each other. He says, "Therefore confess your sins to each other and pray for each other so that you may be healed." Again, James does not presume to suggest anything more than the spiritual reality that unconfessed sin can encumber healing. He knows, therefore, that if people in the church are communicating with one another on a spiritual level, "discipling," as we call it today, there should be no unnecessary barrier to the healing potential of prayer on anyone's behalf should they become ill. This is a preventive measure that is good advice to us in any context. Interestingly, the sacrament of confession to the priest for Roman Catholics derives from this verse, the priest not representing the people, oddly enough, but God.

Although James speaks of a "righteous" person's prayer having impact with God, he does not mean that a person must be perfect or in any way superhuman, and certainly not a specially chosen "faith healer." Prayer power is available to anyone who trusts God. He draws attention to this when he uses Elijah as an example of someone who prayed effectively, saying, "Elijah was a man just like us." The story he recounts about Elijah (James 5:17, 18) is based on 1 Kings 17 and 18. However, James fills out the story with three reasonable assumptions: that Elijah prayed at the beginning and at the end of the drought, that the drought lasted "three and a half years," and that "the earth produced its crops" afterward. To us, this may not be the most prominent exhibit of effective prayer in Elijah's life. We would think of Mount Carmel first (1 Kings 18:16-46) or the widow's multiplying flour and oil (1 Kings 17:7-16). However, James wants a picture of intercession and restoration that corresponds to praying for the sick. So he chose Elijah's prayer that restored a devastated land.

Most of us feel guilty about our wimpy prayer lives, and James tells us that we should. Regular, even routine, communication with God is essential to our spiritual development, not to mention the beneficial effect that it can have on the people for whom we pray. Prayer is a key factor in a vibrant church—not just meaningless repetition of generalities, but specific, thoughtful, worshipful prayers of faith offered in petition and praise. We need to know one another and care about one another to be truly effective in prayer. So let's stop feeling inadequate or self-conscious. Let's begin praying as we know we should.

Restoring the Christian Dropout Is Valued Service (5:19, 20)

In the summer of 1989, a Memphis teen received local notoriety as a hero because he saved a little four-year-old girl from drowning. He seemed surprised by the attention the television news reporter gave him when she pressed him for details of what happened. He simply responded, "I saw her on the bottom of the pool and pulled her out." Most of us wouldn't think twice about diving into a pool or bashing open a wrecked vehicle to rescue someone in serious trouble. Yet we are often reluctant to do the same when people are in spiritual trouble. Perhaps they are being led astray by a religious charmer who undermines Biblical teaching. Maybe they are caught in a web of moral indiscretions. Maybe they have just stopped coming to church because they are being lured by the pleasures of the world. Luckily, there are a few spiritual heroes among us who notice when people are fading away and will quietly, without fanfare, go and talk to them and eventually carry them home, rescuing them from certain spiritual and eternal death. This is what James is pushing for us to do as he brings his letter to a close.

For the tenth and last time, James refers to his readers as "My brothers" in order to underline his loving relationship with them as he makes his final point. Of course, we in the church today are also his brothers as we listen to his counsel. He pleads for us to care about those of our number who "wander from the truth." The truth he speaks of is Christian truth, the gospel, which works itself out in both theology and behavior. He has in mind people who have departed from the truth as he has tried to present it in this letter. In many ways, we can see James's teaching as an attempt to correct people who have gone off course either in theology or in behavior. He himself has tried to be one who will "bring back" such people.

Perhaps the people James has in mind have been enticed by heretical teaching or a bad influence of some type; perhaps they have simply been careless about their Christian lives. Regardless, they bear full responsibility for their choices or non-choices, and they are in big spiritual trouble. James reminds us as he concludes the letter: "Whoever turns a sinner from the error of his way will save him from death and cover over a multitude of sins" (James 5:20). Restoring someone who is spiritually ailing is even more critical for the church than restoring someone who is physically ill, a topic James just left (James 5:13-18). This is so because the death contemplated here is spiritual, everlasting death, not just physical death. What is at stake is a person's eternal existence, not just his physical health. The sins that will be covered when such a person is restored to a vibrant Christian life-style are his nearly fatal sins of apostasy. He can come back anytime as long as his physical health holds up, but even that may be in question here. The Christian who goes out and rescues people who abandon the truth can also expect a reward from God, and that may be suggested here as well.

So James ends his letter trying to enlist a volunteer rescue force, a special commando unit, to join him. Nominal Christians need not apply. The participants must be the mature, committed, growing Christians James has been trying to train throughout his letter. The assignment will be to seek out Christians who are in spiritual trouble, restore them to spiritual consciousness, and bring them back into the church. The pay is minimal, but the job will bring its rewards in self-satisfaction and in knowing one has served his Commander-in-chief faithfully and well.

We all need to be a part of this force: alert, concerned, active on behalf of the family of God. We ourselves may need help someday, and maybe one of those people we helped salvage from the refuse will be on the lookout for us.

Perhaps this letter from James has jolted us enough to try again to serve God the way we know we should.

Part Two

Principles of Perseverance

1 Peter, 2 Peter, Jude

Commentary by Paul K. Carrier

Getting Acquainted With 1 Peter

Late in his life and ministry, Peter went to Rome, which was often called "Babylon" by Christian writers.[10] So, when it is indicated by Peter that he was in Babylon (1 Peter 5:13), he was more than likely referring to Rome. Being in Rome, then, at the time of this writing, the date being about A.D. 64, Peter was eyewitness to the beginning stages of Nero's persecution of Christians. He was aware that it would likely spread out into the provinces in greatly increasing severity. The slander against the Christians from the government, the police actions, and the social pressures were already beginning. It was in A.D. 64 that Nero took direct action against the Christians, blaming them for his own madness.

As the churches in northern Asia Minor received this letter from Silvanus (Silas) in late 64, the persecution was spreading to their area. Many would find their commitment to Christ put under severe stress. They would be threatened with imprisonment, or even death, simply because they were followers of the Christ. They would have to consider their own safety and that of their families. Their businesses would be boycotted, and they would face financial ruin. Some would even begin to doubt the reality of the idea that God was a God of love. They would doubt His strength and power against Roman might. They would doubt His concern for their well-being. In other words, they would consider denying their faith and departing from Christ.

Peter wrote this very important letter to encourage them to remain faithful in the midst of persecution and stress. To deny Christ was

---

[10]See Papias (via Eusebius), for example. Many scholars also believe the references to Babylon in Revelation 17 and 18 are references to Rome, codified to protect the author.

and is the ultimate sin. It is the only sin that causes us to lose our salvation relationship.

Peter himself was martyred in this severe persecution in A.D. 67, so he was writing this letter out of his own emerging experience as well as his insight into where history was going. Christ had warned the disciples about such persecution, and now Peter was passing these warnings on to his fellow Christians. Even though Paul had established the Christian beachhead in Asia Minor, Peter felt a strong pastoral kinship with them. Many of them were Jewish Christians, and Peter was their "hero" among the apostles.

Does this letter apply to twentieth-century Christians? Indeed, it applies in its most literal interpretation to Christians in certain areas of the world where imprisonment and death are threatened every day. It also applies in principle to all Christians as they face the stress of being maturing disciples in the midst of the secularism and humanism that dominates our culture. Many "intellectuals" hold Christians to ridicule in the academic setting. Christians who are serious about their faith are openly degraded in literature and cinema. This subtle stress is no respecter of age groups or socioeconomic class. We are tempted at times to give in, to deny, to pull back.

This letter also applies to Christians who face the severe difficulties of life itself. The stress of family disintegration, job loss, physical disability, spousal or child death—each is a part of real life that occasionally causes us to have times of severe doubts and questions regarding God's love and concern.

Yes, the principles of 1 Peter apply to any time in the flow of human history. Even now. Even here. Even to you and me.

Peter seeks to answer two basic questions: (1) Why should Christians remain faithful to Christ in the midst of stress? (2) How can we remain faithful? In this section of this devotional commentary, we shall see a number of "principles of perseverance" from the pen of the beloved apostle Peter.

CHAPTER EIGHT

Living Hope

1 Peter 1:1-12

Principle 1: You Are Chosen (1:1, 2)

Nero was blaming the Christians for burning Rome. They were his scapegoats. After a strong public relations campaign against them, he began outright persecution of the Christians. Thus, the Christians became social, political, and economic outcasts throughout the Roman empire.

In the first verse, Peter calls his readers "strangers." They were strangers in the Roman culture, "aliens" (New American Standard Bible). There was, and is, a sense in which Christians are aliens wherever they live and whenever they live. We are different in our worldview, our life-styles, our moral choices, and our life relationships. The world does not accept the dynamic Christian, just as Christ predicted (John 15:18-20; 16:1-4, 33). In the case of the Jewish Christians in Peter's day, they were double aliens, being Jews by nationality and Christians by religion. Nero had used the Christian doctrine of Hell, and the real or symbolic "fire" of Hell to accuse the Christians of bringing fire judgment against Rome.

In this section, Peter will give the Christians a "why" principle—a reason they should remain faithful to Christ in this period of stress. Why should we remain faithful to Christ? For the same reason Peter urged the Jewish Christians in his day to do so: because we are "chosen." In Deuteronomy 7:6, Israel is called God's chosen nation. They were His people to whom and through whom He would communicate His truth. Even today, God may still have some plans for Israel (as many scholars believe is alluded to by Paul in Romans 11). However, the church, made up of Jews and Gentiles, is now God's "chosen nation," a title Peter uses for the Christians (1 Peter 2:9). Most certainly, the Jewish Christians would quickly understand this phrase, so Peter used it to point out to them, and to the Gentile Christians, that the church is now the "chosen race."

In the next verse, 1 Peter 2:10, Peter says, "Once you were not a people, but now you are the people of God. . . ." The church is a "new people," a "new nation," a "new chosen race"—"chosen" by God! Christians have this in common, in spite of cultural differences—we are "chosen."

The Plan

First, Peter indicates we are chosen as a part of God's plan. He uses the word *foreknowledge* (1 Peter 1:2). This means something is known before or planned ahead. God planned the church and the whole idea of salvation in Christ beforehand. We are now God's chosen people because God planned that we would be His chosen people. In 1 Peter 1:20, Peter says that Christ was "chosen" from the beginning, "before the creation of the world." But He did not finally appear until these last days. God planned it ahead of time! Even before sin entered the experience of man, Christ was "chosen" to be the "lamb of God" to take away sin.

There are at least two views of this idea of the foreknowledge and foreordination of God. One is that God chose us individually to be His "elect," His "chosen ones." Further, according to this view, He chose some to be saved and some to be lost. This means that God knows who will be saved because He chose certain to be saved. In this view, foreordination (predestination) precedes foreknowledge—God chooses individuals to be saved; therefore, He knows who will be saved.

The other view, simply stated, is that God planned to send Christ into the flow of history to redeem man from his lostness, and that He planned to save those who would believe. This view holds strongly to the free will of man, yet accepts the sovereign God's planning for man's salvation ahead of time. It holds that God planned to save man through Christ, and those who become the "chosen" are those who choose to believe—to accept His offer of grace. This view seems to take into account the total teachings of Scripture more than the Calvinistic view stated earlier.

The point to those under stress is this: we are a part of God's plan! Having accepted Christ, we are now "special" in that we are God's people, the "chosen nation."

The Provision

Peter goes on to point out God's provision for our being His chosen ones. He says we are chosen for "sprinkling by his blood" (1

Peter 1:2). We were once aliens in our relationship to God. We had sinned against Him. We had denied His authority in our lives. We were not God's chosen ones, but were rather His enemies. God's provision to change this relationship was the shedding of Christ's blood on the cross. When we accept Him and the sacrifice He made (the shedding of His blood) on our behalf, then we receive the "sprinkling of blood" (the benefits of His sacrifice) in our lives.

In the Old Testament, "sprinkling of blood" was a symbolic ceremony in three different situations. When a leper was declared to be free of leprosy, "clean," he went through a cleansing ceremony in which the priest sprinkled blood on the leper and on the altar. It symbolized cleansing (Leviticus 14:2-7). Second, at the ordination of a priest, a lamb was killed and its blood was sprinkled on the altar and on the priest (Exodus 29:1, 10-21). Finally, at the feast of Atonement, the priest would sprinkle the blood on the mercy seat and on the altar in the tabernacle to effect the forgiveness of the sins of the people (Leviticus 16:11-19).

So, the sprinkling of Christ's blood accomplished our forgiveness and our cleansing and makes us priests! This is God's provision for our being "special"—the chosen ones. Hebrews 10:22 states we can approach God with confidence because we have had our "hearts sprinkled to cleanse us from a guilty conscience," and "our bodies washed with pure water," as symbolized in baptism. Our hearts are clean—no more sin! We are special.

The Presentation

Peter talks about the "sanctifying work of the Spirit" (1 Peter 1:2). This is not an emotional experience—a "sign" that we are one of the chosen. Some say we must have some dramatic emotional experience to prove that the Spirit has set us apart for salvation. Nowhere is it indicated in Scripture that the Spirit gives us warm feelings, bright lights, or an audible voice speaking words to indicate our acceptability. In Paul's conversion, the Lord spoke and appeared in the form of a bright light to make him an eyewitness of Him after His resurrection so that Paul could be an apostle (see Acts 1:21, 22), not as a usual "conversion experience."

In John 16, Jesus told the disciples that the Holy Spirit would be the revealer of truth to them and to the world. In 1 Corinthians 12:3, Paul indicates that no one can conclude that Jesus is "Lord" except by the Holy Spirit. In 1 Peter 1:23, Peter indicates that the "seed" by which we experience the new birth is the "living and enduring word of God." This Word about Jesus and from Jesus is given by the Holy Spirit; this Word is the source of our new life in Christ; it is the truth that causes us to conclude that Jesus is Lord. So the Holy Spirit works, among other ways, through the truth revealed in the Word about Jesus, to "set us apart" to faith by our own acceptance of the truth of the Word. The Holy Spirit thus "presents" us to God for the reception of the benefits of the sprinkling of Christ's blood so that we can become chosen!

The Proposition

Peter says that we are chosen "for obedience to Jesus Christ" (1 Peter 1:2), which is our part of the whole process of being "chosen." Christ sprinkled, or shed, His blood; the Holy Spirit presents the truth about Christ, His claims, His sacrifice for our sins through the Word; and we do our part by responding to the command to believe in Christ.

God's proposition is that we ourselves choose to obey Christ by believing in Him and making Him "Lord" of our lives. Initially, we declare our faith in confession and are baptized to give outward expression of our posture of obedience. Our response to this proposition issues forth in a lifelong attitude of submission to His will in every aspect of life. This is principle number one—we remain faithful to Christ because we are His "chosen" ones. We are chosen by God's *plan,* His *provision* through Christ, the Holy Spirit's *presentation* of the Word, and our accepting God's *proposition* by obeying Jesus Christ.

Principle 2: You Have an Inheritance (1:3-5)

Hope is the key to the second principle that Peter presents to encourage the Christians to remain faithful to their Lord. We persevere through hard times because of hope: we have hope of something better yet to come! As Paul says, "In this *hope* we were saved" (Romans 8:24). Why should we persevere under stress? Because we have an inheritance worth obtaining! It is worth it. It is worth forbearing any persecution or stress our enemies—or life itself—may throw at us.

Heirs by Propagation

Peter says, "God . . . has given us new birth into a living hope" (1 Peter 1:3). We are born into a parent/child relationship with God, by His instigation, through Christ. And one of the results of this new relationship is that we become "heirs of God." We have an inheritance, promises from God, a living hope.

The basis of this new birth into God's family is "his great mercy" (1 Peter 1:3). *Mercy* indicates that God did something for us that we did not deserve. He went beyond justice. Forgiveness was involved. We had sinned against God and thus alienated ourselves from Him. We were enemies of God, strangers to His family, aliens to His nation by our own wrong choices. This broken relationship was not pleasing to God, for it was opposed to His purpose for us. He made possible a new relationship by offering us a new beginning—a new birth, as it were. This new birth relates us again to Him and gives us an inheritance.

This provision is through Christ's death and resurrection. Peter says we have this hope, "through the resurrection of Jesus Christ from the dead" (1 Peter 1:3). The two elements of the provision are the death and resurrection of Christ. His death was to pay the price for our sins, and His resurrection was to overcome death for us. It is through what God did in Christ that we begin life all over again in a new family relationship with God. It is through this that we have the inheritance promised us.

It is interesting to note in 1 Peter 1:23 that the author identifies the "seed" that gives life in the new birth process as the "living and abiding word of God." In his Gospel, John points out that Jesus was and is the "Word" of God (John 1:1, 2). The truth about Jesus is given in conceptual form through the ministry of the Holy Spirit (John 16). We come to conclude that Jesus is Lord through that "Word-giving" ministry of the Holy Spirit (1 Corinthians 12:3). This conclusion that Jesus is Lord is called "faith," which Paul says comes from hearing the Word (Romans 10:17). So the new birth conception takes place when the seed of the truth about Christ, given by the Spirit, is planted in our minds through the hearing (or reading) of the Word. If we accept that truth with our intellect, emotions, and will, then we are conceived (or, more in keeping with the analogy, begotten) of the Spirit. When faith is fully developed from the initial (what we might call the "embryo") stage to full vital development, it breaks forth from water in baptism, just as a physical embryo, when it is fully developed, is born from water. Jesus alludes to this in John 3:5 when He uses faith ("born of Spirit") and baptism ("born of water") together.

God has given us this new life! Our sins are all forgiven! We are in a new, inheritance-receiving relationship to God!

Peter describes this new inheritance in some beautifully pic-turesque ways. He says first that it comes from being born into a "living hope" (1 Peter 1:3). Two ideas are implied in this phrase. It is a hope that will forever remain alive. Also, it is a hope of liv-ing—of living forever! It is based upon the fact that Christ lived after His death in His resurrection. In that Christ lived, we too shall live. In that He lives forever, we too shall live forever. Our hope in-volves living.

Peter's next description of our inheritance in Christ is that it "can never perish" (1 Peter 1:4). It will not rot or decay, and it is not sub-ject to a successful attack. Our future will not decay and it cannot be taken from us. It will not be taken from us by God, and cannot be taken from us by Satan. Read Romans 8 and John 10:27-29. It is clear that God will not change His mind about our inheritance, and that no one is strong enough to snatch us from God's hand. Our new Father's love is eternal, and our relationship is secure. Of course, we can run away ourselves. We can decide we do not any longer believe and do not want to remain in the relationship. We can deny Christ's authority in our lives and leave Him. But God won't quit, and no one else can take us away. That's security. It's worth persevering to be secure eternally.

The third descriptive phrase is "never . . . spoil." To the Jews, the temple was "spoiled," or "defiled," if a Gentile entered, for Gentiles were "unclean." Daniel prophesied an "abomination" (Daniel 9:27; 11:31; 12:11) that he connected to a time when the Gentiles would enter the temple and destroy it. But there will be nothing unclean or unholy in our future. No unclean thing or person will be there. No sin will be there. Satan will not be there. No death or disease will be there. Our future is free from sin, fear, and death.

The fourth phrase is "never . . . fade." On special occasions, we give our spouses roses. They are beautiful and express our love. But, in a few days, their beauty fades and the flowers wilt. They are no longer expressive of beauty and love. They fade away. Our future, on the other hand, will be beautiful forever; it will not change.

Finally, Peter says our inheritance is "kept in heaven for you." When something is "kept," it is guaranteed, and it is yet to come. God's promises are guaranteed and yet to come. Note that they are in Heaven, God's home. They are in Heaven because they are from God. Also implied here is the fact that we will be in Heaven as a part of our future. Christ assured His disciples that He was preparing a place for them to be with Him in the future when He said, "I am going there to prepare a place for you. . . . I will come back and take you to be with me" (John 14:2, 3).

I will persevere because this kind of future is worth waiting for. It is worth having, for it will not burn like Rome; it is not subject to attack like Palestine; it will never, like any thing else, lose its beauty and luster. When we face the severe times in life, we must remember the promises!

Heirs With Protection

In this family relationship, we are not only born to receive a promised inheritance, we are also protected! Peter says we "through faith are shielded by God's power" (1 Peter 1:5). As fathers protect their children, so God protects us.

From what does He protect us? From rejection by our culture? No. Does He protect us from outright persecution, imprisonment, or even death for the faith? No. Does He protect us from disease, job loss, family stress, and the other negative aspects of life in the flesh? No. What does this mean, then? It means He makes it possible for us to stay in Him—to keep our sonship relationship in Christ—in spite of whatever opposition we face. Paul wrote that He will not allow us to be tempted beyond what we are able to bear (1 Corinthians 10:13). He also notes that God gives a way of escape and/or the ability to bear the stresses of life.

How are we protected by God? There are many ways, but here Peter focuses on His protection that is "through faith." It is by faith that we cling to the truth about God's everlasting love for us, even when we are seemingly ignored by Him. In Romans 8:35ff, Paul indicates that such experiences as tribulations, distress, persecution, famine, nakedness, and death are not indications that God has quit loving us, as some might interpret them. Paul assures his readers that God's love is steadfast. So we are protected by such truths in the midst of persecution. Having faith means believing God—trusting Him to tell the truth, to keep His promises. It is this faith that protects us from falling away from Him.

Other ways God protects us are through the presence of the Holy Spirit in our lives and the fellowship of other believers. Romans 8 indicates that the Spirit's ministry in the life of a believer helps him overcome the flesh, assures him of sonship and his inheritance, helps him pray, and gives assurance of God's love. The writer of Hebrews points out the value of fellowship with other believers when he exhorts his readers to assemble together as the stresses of being a Christian close in, and as we look forward to Christ's return (Hebrews 10:25).

As earthly fathers protect their children, even more so does our Heavenly Father protect His children. He protects us by His power, by His Holy Spirit who indwells us and is constantly with us, and through the fellowship of our family members—the church. What could offer more assurance than the knowledge that the God who made the world and all that is in it is our very own protective Heavenly Father?

Principle 3: Glory Follows Suffering (1:6-12)

Undoubtedly, many of the Christians receiving this letter were wondering whether God still loved them, or whether any of what they had believed was true. They were suffering physically, socially, emotionally, and economically. Now they were beginning to suffer spiritually. They were facing doubts. So Peter introduces his third principle for perseverance: glory follows suffering.

The Reality of Suffering (6)

The Christians receiving this letter knew that the suffering about which Peter was writing was real—it was indeed a reality in their lives. Nero had begun to imprison them for simply believing. He had them put to death, at times in excruciatingly painful ways. Some were fed to lions in arenas; others were rolled in pitch and set afire as human torches. Many were crucified like Christ. They had their businesses boycotted by their fellow citizens, thus losing their livelihood. They were disowned by their families, a problem especially common among the Jewish Christians. Parents were separated from their children. Their suffering was multidimensional; they experienced every possible form of human suffering, "all kinds of trials" (1 Peter 1:6).

In twentieth-century American culture, our suffering is not so blatant. It takes the form of cultural stress rather than outright persecution. Pseudointellectuals mock us for holding to ideas they say were created by primitive man to explain the unexplainable. We are cast in extremely negative light in literature, cinema, and even in television sitcoms. It is tempting to stay at the nominal level of our spiritual development where we pose no threat to our humanistic culture; to simply remain silent except when we are in concourse with other believers. Suffering and stress are real, whether blatant or subtle.

124

These sufferings—theirs and ours—are much like the suffering of our Savior. He faced ridicule and rejection. He even suffered family alienation for a time. People around Him were thankless and disrespectful. Most did not believe Him. He suffered physically to the point of painful death. He suffered a sense of separation from the Father. Peter indicates that this suffering of Christ was predicted by the prophets (1 Peter 1:10, 11). He also points out that they predicted as well His glory "to come." In the case of Christ, suffering was followed by glory.

In Philippians 2:5-11, Paul gives a beautiful summary of Christ's suffering when He gave up the rights and glory of being in Heaven in complete, divine communion with the Father to become a man. He gave up His rights as a man and became a servant. He gave up His right to life and died ingloriously on a cross. Then God exalted Him! After suffering—real suffering—came glory.

It was reality in Christ's teaching, too. Jesus had warned, "A servant is not greater than his master." His followers were warned that they, too, must suffer: "If you would be my disciples you must deny yourself, take up your cross, and follow me."

Suffering was also real in Peter's life when he wrote this letter, and as they later read the letter. Within three or four years of the writing, Peter was crucified like Christ (in A.D. 67) for his faith. To our knowledge, all of the apostles, save John, died as martyrs.

The Reasons for Suffering (7)

It is easy to misinterpret these stresses and trials. One who is suffering can readily draw the conclusion that God has deserted him or that He never was there. One might conclude he is being punished because his sins are greater than those of other Christians. Realizing this possibility, Peter states some positive reasons for suffering.

Purification. Just as fire burns out impurities in precious metals like gold, Peter says, the stress of our trials produces purity of faith. It also causes spiritual growth. For instance, our physical muscles grow stronger when they are put under the stress of severe exercise. They are put under "fire." Relationships, at times, grow in the midst of stress. We realize that love is still there even in severely negative circumstances. Every time we make it through a crisis in our marriages, we become more assured of our ability to stay together no matter what may come. We appreciate life more when we face the stark reality that we may lose it. So our faith is purified and strengthened by the stresses we encounter.

Genuineness. A second and related concept is found in the phrase "proved genuine." Here the benefit is the knowledge that faith is real and lasting. In suffering, we see that God keeps His promises, but only if we "hang in there." God knows how strong or weak our faith is without testing us. We are the ones who benefit from the testing that proves the genuineness of our commitment. Each time our faith survives, we become stronger and more assured of it!

When we lose a spouse or child to death, we go through severe stress on our faith. It is only after we are through the ordeal that we realize God's power and presence to its fullest, for we made it! We are through it and are still believers. He has seen us through it all.

Value. The third reason for suffering is that we see our relationship to the Lord is "of greater worth than gold." We had a family in our church go through the trauma of the father's going through a heart transplant operation. Today their faith is more precious to them than before, by far! Not only is it stronger, it is emotionally more precious. It takes a more dominant place in their patterns of thought and emotions.

Through suffering, we realize that our relationship to God through Christ is our most precious possession. We can take it with us into eternity. And it empowers us to survive anything right now.

The Reward of Suffering (8-12)

Because we believe, we have rewards, and the first reward mentioned by Peter is joy: we "are filled with an inexpressible and glorious joy" (1 Peter 1:8). Joy is a present reward that sees us through suffering. There is the joy of knowing we are loved and accepted by God—the God who made the universe. There is the joy of knowing we have worth in His sight. We are worth enough for His Son to die in our place. We have the worth of being called into His service. He has called us to salvation, but also to service. We are needed by God to fulfill His work in the world. That brings joy. There is the joy of succeeding in His service. The joy of winning someone to a saving knowledge of Christ is overwhelming. This joy permeates all of life and lasts even through the stress times.

One reason this joy is so enduring is seen in the word *glorious.* We "are filled with . . . *glorious* joy." We have a down payment of the glory that shall be ours later. The Holy Spirit's presence in us is God's promise to bring us to the glory of His presence eternally (Ephesians 4:30). We are also full of glory in that we are full of the hope of future complete glory. We shall see Him as He is, and be like Him, John writes in his epistle (1 John 3:2). Such hope makes our joy even greater.

Another reward, implied here, is the future reality of glory that shall be ours at the resurrection of believers. Peter describes this as being "the goal of your faith, the salvation of your souls" (1 Peter 1:9). We shall be fully saved at Christ's return for His own. It will be a time and space event. In Romans 8:18-25, Paul states this same principle of suffering followed by glory. He says, "Our present sufferings are not worth comparing with the glory that will be revealed in us" (Romans 8:18). He says we "wait eagerly for our adoption as sons, the redemption of our bodies" (Romans 8:23). Our spirits go to God at death, and our bodies to the grave. At Christ's return, He will bring our spirits with Him and raise our bodies in new form, an incorruptible form. Our spirits and new bodies will be reunited, and we shall live and reign forever with Him. We shall be like Him. We shall see Him and serve Him. That will be glory! (See 1 Thessalonians 4:13-18.)

Again we say, "It is worth it." Even the suffering is worth it because of the glory to come.

Persevere!

CHAPTER NINE

Growing in Holiness

1 Peter 1:13—2:3

Principle 4: You Are Holy (1:13-16)

Peter's fourth principle of perseverance tells both "why" and "how" to persevere. Why should we persevere in the midst of stress? Because we have been declared to be holy by the God who has forgiven our sins through Christ. How are we to persevere in the midst of stress? By living the holy life-style on a constant basis in spite of that stress.

For some reason, we often think of holiness in a bad light. Some think holiness is offensive piety, or that to be holy is to go around with a "holier than thou" attitude. Some such "holy" people recite religious platitudes, dress in certain patterns, abstain from anything that brings joy, and judge all who do not agree with them. Others think holiness is a charismatic extreme; they equate holiness with emotional displays like shouting, leaping, ecstatic speech, and contemporary miracle-working. Neither of these extremes is a part of what Peter teaches here.

There are two concepts of holiness in the New Testament. One is that we are declared to be holy—set apart—by our acceptance of Christ and the forgiveness of sins (cf. Romans 6:11). We are then "sanctified," "holy," or "saints." We are set apart as children of God, forgiven of sins, going to Heaven. The other concept has to do with our response to this declaration of our being holy. Since we are declared to be holy through God's grace, we should live in a holy manner (cf. Romans 6:12ff). We live in a holy, set-apart manner to glorify God, not to obtain His forgiveness. We already have forgiveness. We do it because we love God and want to do His will. We do it because He has forgiven us. We do it because His Holy Spirit, through the Word and through His indwelling presence, instructs us.

Peter is using *holiness* in the latter sense, referring to the life-style of the Christian. In this case, it is valuable in perseverance.

"Prepare your minds for action," Peter writes (1 Peter 1:13). All our behavior and all of our emotions issue forth from our patterns of thought. Before we can change our behavior or feelings, we must change our thinking.

Peter uses an interesting analogy here. Ancient garb was a robe that was comfortable in the warm climates as well as in cold climates; but they were cumbersome. In order to move with any speed, the wearer had to pull the flowing robe up between his legs and put the excess through his belt. This was called "girding one's loins," and—though not apparent in the New International Version—it is this very expression that Peter chooses here (1 Peter 1:13). The verse might literally be translated, "Gird up the loins of your minds." What he is saying is, "Get your minds ready for action! Put on your thinking caps. Be mentally alert. Get your thinking under the Holy Spirit's control!"

A little later (1 Peter 1:15, 16), Peter sets the standard for holiness: "As he who called you is holy, so be holy in all you do." That means we are expected to be like God! But how do we know what God is like? We know Him through Christ. He came into the flow of history to show us what God is like in terms we can understand. Holiness, then, is conceptually understood to be patterns of thought, emotions, and behavior that are like Christ's.

If we are to "prepare our minds," we must be alert to two things. What was Jesus like, and what did Jesus teach? What was Jesus like under stress? In the Garden of Gethsemane, He sweat and prayed—He felt it. On the cross, He cried out—He felt it. The writer of Hebrews points out that Jesus faced all of mankind's temptations, yet did not sin (Hebrews 4:15). Jesus always remained faithful to the Father. Jesus never retaliated for evil done to Him. He prayed in times of stress. He remembered the words of the Father in times of temptation. He showed His knowledge of Scripture when He recited it in the Satanic temptation. He taught us to forgive those who persecute us, to turn the other cheek.

In order for us to face stress, we must have the mind of Christ. We must think as Jesus wants us to think. In order to do that, we must know the Word through constant study. Remember, all emotions and behavior issue forth from patterns of thought. To be like Christ, we must think like Christ. (See Philippians 2:5ff; Ephesians 4:20ff.) Of course, this has to do with more than facing stress. It has to do with making moral decisions in every circumstance of life. The mind of

Christ is to be the controlling factor of the Christian life. Paul prayed for his readers to be "fill[ed] . . . with the knowledge of his will" (Colossians 1:9). We must know what to do before we can do it!

It is important that our whole worldview be that of Christ. We must discover His view of purpose, of meaning, of future, of morals, of values, of priorities, of responsibility. Our world is throwing opposing views at us in every communicative art. Films, TV, novels, textbooks, music, and lyrics are dominated by humanism (man is god) and hedonism (if it feels good, do it). We need the "mind of Christ" in the midst of this milieu! We must not only stay in the faith, we must stay in the life; we must "walk in the Spirit."

Holy Emotions

Peter also says we are to be "self-controlled" (1 Peter 1:13). To be self-controlled means we can keep our emotions under control. Man's thoughts are in constant warfare between what he *ought* to do and what he *wants* to do. We all have instinctive drives, including sex, hunger, thirst, self-esteem, and self-preservation. In the midst of severe persecution, the self-preservation drive might win over our concept of what ought to be done as taught and modeled by Christ. After all, we must live, mustn't we? Not if it means denying Christ and bringing Him to shame!

Peter calls this proneness to misuse our human drives "evil desires" (1 Peter 1:14). He does not mean that the drives themselves are evil, that they are not to be found in a Christian. We still retain our God-given instincts. They are no longer to be "evil" in the sense that we no longer let them control our behavior and thoughts. Our former misuse of our drives was done "in ignorance." We did not know God's will and the reasons behind it then. All we knew was that we *wanted* to do certain things. And we often went ahead and did them because our consciences were not trained with the mind of Christ to tell us what we *ought* to do instead.

Peter uses the interesting phrase *obedient children* to describe the Christians. Our duty now is to bring our drives under the control of our new minds, of our newly developing consciences. Our new sense of what *ought* to be needs to control our continuing sense of what we *want*. This is a vital aspect of holiness.

Holy Behavior

Holiness finally includes our actual behavior, as Peter states in 1 Peter 1:15: "Just as he who called you is holy, so be holy in all you do." All behavior issues forth from our thoughts and our wants. If our thoughts and wants are controlled by the mind of Christ, our behavior will be like that of Christ as well.

Peter quotes from Leviticus (11:44, 45) when he gives the concluding statement about holiness: "Be holy, because I am holy" (1 Peter 1:16). God is perfectly holy in all of His thoughts, emotions, attitudes, motives, and behavior. He is holy in all of His relationships and values. The goal of the Christian life is to be like God by being like Christ, who modeled God for us in the flesh. Christ never sinned in His behavior. He was tempted to sin, but He made the right choices. Christ never sinned in His behavior because His thoughts and emotions were holy. The bottom line for us is behavior, but the determining factors are our thoughts and attitudes and feelings. Sin is any pattern of thought, emotions, or behavior that is against God's will. Righteousness is a pattern of thought, emotions, and behavior that is within His will.

Why do we remain faithful? We are declared to be holy. How do we remain faithful? By being holy.

Principle 5: You Are Responsible (1:17-25)

The next principle Peter sets forth has to do with accountability. He challenges them, and us, to be faithful and to persevere because we are responsible. We will be held accountable for our faithfulness by our Heavenly Father. On the basic premise that God is our Father through the new birth, we should fear Him and obey Him. We obey Him, among other reasons, because we are part of His family.

Father

Peter begins this section, "Since you call on a Father who judges each man's work impartially, live your lives . . . in reverent fear" (1 Peter 1:17). There are many implications to the term *father* when applied to God, such as source of being, provision, love, authority, and inheritance. The two concepts set forth in this passage have to do with our source of being and with His authority.

As Father, God is our source of physical life. Also, even more important to the Christian, He is the source of our new spiritual life. In 1 Peter 1:23, Peter refers to the concept of "born again" by saying that we were newly born from "seed" *(sperma)* that is "imperishable, through the living and enduring word of God." Birth begins with an act of love where the Father plants the seed. Here the seed is defined as being the word of God. What word? Peter has earlier called attention to the idea of being "redeemed" (1 Peter 1:18), which means the penalty has been paid, the price paid in full. This "word," then, that saves is a word about redemption. Peter points out that the price was not paid with "perishable things such as silver or gold," with things or possessions. He points out further that it was not aided by the "empty way of life handed down to you from your forefathers." To the Jewish Christians, that would mean the rites and rituals of the Old Covenant, plus all that the traditions of the fathers that had been added to them. These saved no one, for they also included the perfect keeping of God's laws, which none save Christ ever kept. Paul admitted after becoming a Christian that the old law only brought him guilt and feelings of guilt (Romans 7:7-24). It was only through Christ's forgiveness that he could be free of guilt.

Peter goes on to point out that the redemption took place through "the precious blood of Christ, a lamb without blemish or defect" (1 Peter 1:19). That was the price that was paid. That was the content of the "word," the life-giving "seed" of the new birth experience. This "word" of redemption through Christ was a part of God's eternal plan. As Peter puts it, "He was chosen before the creation of the world, but was revealed in these last times for your sake" (1 Peter 1:20). Messianic prophecies were fulfilled in Christ Jesus.

Note another aspect of our new birth. Not only was the content of the seed-word important, but so was our acceptance of the word. We needed to respond to the word in order for the new birth to take place. Peter says that, through Christ, we "believe in God, who raised him from the dead and glorified him, and so [our] faith and hope are in God" (1 Peter 1:21). We became believers in order for the birth to take place. Baptism is not mentioned here by Peter, but is in 1 Peter 3:21 in a different analogy. It is certainly a part of the new birth process. It is stated here that God, as Father, is the object of our faith and our hope.

Fear

The Father's authority is the second stress of this section. Peter says He "judges each man's work impartially," so we should conduct ourselves "in reverent fear" (1 Peter 1:17). His authority demands accountability. We are clearly not His children because we have sufficient good works. We are His children through the new birth. We are His children through the redemption of Christ's blood. But, as His children, we are held accountable by the Father for our behavior. He will judge us!

This should not be seen as a contradiction of the doctrine of grace. We are saved, as Paul says, "by grace . . . through faith . . . not by works" (Ephesians 2:8, 9). Yet we will be judged by our works, too, but not for salvation. Paul makes it clear in 1 Corinthians 3:10-15 that Christians will be judged by their works for reward or loss of reward—not for salvation: "If [any man's work] is burned up [judged unacceptable], he will suffer loss; he himself will be saved . . ." (1 Corinthians 3:15).

How we behave under stress will be judged by the Father. How we behave in every circumstance will be judged. We will be held accountable! Later (see 2 Peter 2), we will see that we can go far enough back into the world to lose our faith and be lost again. We are not saved by good works, but sinful works can drag us away from faith in Christ and His lordship in our lives.

Since He is Father, and since He will hold us accountable, as any good father would, we should hold Him in "fear." Fear means respect or awe. He is God; therefore, we hold Him in "awe." We respect His authority. We respect His judgment. We hold His Word in awe—this life-giving, everlasting Word. (See 1 Peter 1:24, 25.) This fear is a vital part of faith. We not only believe in God, we believe God—His Word, His judgments.

Family

The two contexts in which we "fear" and obey God are the world and the church. Peter stresses our obedience in the church by saying, "Now that you have purified yourselves by obeying the truth so that you have sincere love for your brothers, love one another deeply, from the heart" (1 Peter 1:22). Motives are important. Thus our love for one another should be "sincere," "deep," and "from the heart." We should view people the way God views people. God loves by seeing worth, so we ought also to see the worth of others. We should be authentically concerned for others' well-being out of a sincere awareness of their worth. This is instinctive in most earthly family systems. Although they may fight among themselves from time to time, brothers and sisters instinctively value one another. They come to one another's rescue—even in the midst of normal sibling rivalry. Peter calls us "brothers." We are mutually born into God's family. We share Him as Father; therefore, we are brothers. An instinctive, sincere love for one another should emerge.

This love is to be expressed; it is to be "deep" or fervent. We should verbally express it. We should pragmatically express it in such ways as providing food, clothing, and shelter to those in need of such provisions. We should listen to one another and weep with one another. We should rejoice together. Can you see how this would help in stress, this sense of mutual responsibility in a family atmosphere in the church? We must love one another spiritually, emotionally, financially, and physically.

We are responsible to God as Father, who gave us birth. We should respect Him, for He holds us accountable. He holds us responsible for ministering to one another as family.

Principle 6: You Must Grow! (2:1-3)

Peter now builds on the idea that we are God's children. He has set forth some implications of our relationship to God as a father, and to our fellow Christians as brothers in a family. In this brief section, he picks up on the statement in 1 Peter 1:23, where he talks about our new birth into God's family through the "living and enduring word of God," the "seed" that gives us new life.

After we are born, we must grow! Our relationships are with the Father and with our brothers and sisters in His family. But we also have a responsibility to ourselves, and that is to see to our own personal spiritual growth in Him. It is to this responsibility that Peter now calls our attention.

In this section, there are three verbs of exhortation to the readers: "rid yourselves," "crave," and "grow up." Each one is instructive about how we meet this obligation.

Grow in Respect to Salvation

There is more to life than the birth event. I am alive today, not only because I was born in 1935, but also because I grew up and stayed in a pattern of health. Spiritually, there is more to salvation than the new-birth event. There is a whole new way of thinking, feeling, and behaving to be discovered. God is at work in us "both to will and to work for his good pleasure," Paul writes in Philippians 2:13 (New American Standard Bible), and this is in the context of his exhortation that we "work out [our] salvation" (Philippians 2:12.). The substance of the saved life, which began with the new birth, is that God is working in us to remake us, to instill in us a new will resulting in a new work. Just as our natural life is a process of discovery, experience, and growth, so also is our spiritual life. It is a process of gradual growth through intellectual discovery, emotional awareness, and volitional choices, guided by the Holy Spirit. This is what Peter is talking about when he exhorts, "Grow up in your salvation" (1 Peter 2:2). He is challenging his readers to discover the saved life in all of its facets.

Rid Yourselves

Peter points out two aspects of growth: things of which we "rid ourselves" and things we must "crave." A part of the process of maturity is to give up attitudes and patterns of behavior that accompany each stage of our development and to replace them with the more mature attitudes and patterns of behavior that are characteristic of the next stage of development.

The immature Christian has been "born again" but has not fully developed new Christlike patterns of thought and behavior. There remain significant signs of his old life-style and relationships. Two characteristics of this immaturity are pretense and selfishness.

Peter deals with immature pretending by using the words *deceit* and *hypocrisy* (1 Peter 2:1). The Greek word translated "deceit" means "to use a second face." In other words, it means to pretend to be something you are not—to wear a mask. Children pretend; it is a part of growth. But we cannot pretend forever. We cannot simply pretend to be grown up; we must actually become mature. Peter is telling his readers to quit pretending, quit faking it.

The second word he uses to describe immature pretending is *hypocrisy*. This also means mask-wearing, but it additionally implies "answering back." It is a term used in drama to denote wearing the right mask and saying the right lines. It is always used in a context of pretense. Immature Christians are often deceived into thinking that maturity is to be equated with learning the right key words and phrases. They think if they use these basic words and can give the right answers, they are mature. Peter calls that hypocrisy, pretending to be something they are not and saying things they neither understand nor really believe.

Selfishness is another characteristic of the immature Christian, as denoted in the words, *malice, envy,* and *slander. Malice* means evil behavior; *envy* means seeking of one's self, and *slander* is vengeful speech. Children try to get away with breaking the rules. They are selfish and seek their own way. They want everything for themselves. They put down other children to show themselves better in some way. Peter is exhorting the readers to get rid of their evil, self-centered, aggressively destructive patterns of thought and behavior, for they are signs of immaturity.

These patterns destroy our relationships with others. In 1 Peter 1:22, Peter has stressed the importance of a relationship of fervent love for our fellow Christians, love from the heart. We need this to survive the stresses of the Christian life in a lost world.

Crave the Pure Milk of the Word

Not only do we need to rid ourselves of certain patterns of thought and behavior in order to grow, we need also to take in proper nourishment. Newborn babies need nourishment to survive and grow. This is also a principle of Christian survival and growth.

I remember when our children were infants. They sensed their need for nourishment and readily expressed it. They literally screamed for satisfaction of their hunger. But they always tasted the bottle of formula or the baby food before eating it. They took a small swallow or a small bite first. If they liked it, they would eat it enthusiastically. If not, even though they were hungry, they would not eat it. Peter refers to this truth in verse 3: "Now that you have tasted that the Lord is good," you should "crave" the nourishment He provides.

Peter identifies the "milk" we should crave as the "pure word." This is Christ, the living "Word of God" (John 1:1). The title also applies to the Lord's New Covenant teachings. Christ taught His disciples how to live a life that would glorify God. He taught them conceptually and verbally; He taught them by example and role-modeling. The Word of Christ is "pure" in that it is truth, unadulterated truth. It is truth from God, revelation truth. It contains no error, no contamination. It not only tastes good, but it completely nourishes and brings strength and health to the growing Christian. Paul refers to this idea of the empowering of the Word in 2 Timothy 3:16 and 17. He says it is "inspired by God." Paul goes on to point out to Timothy that the Word is good for "teaching, for reproof, for correction, for training in righteousness, that the man of God may be adequate [mature], equipped for every good work" (New American Standard Bible). The eating of the "pure Word of God" is necessary to Christian maturing. A constant, prayerful, careful study of the written Word is how we achieve this element of growth today. We must study what Christ and His inspired apostles and prophets taught about life, relationships, values, and priorities. We must then integrate these principles into our own patterns of thought, attitudes, and behavior. They become an integral part of our personalities, of our characters.

Once the newborn baby has tasted the milk and finds it to be good, he drinks it in with great vigor. My daughter used to put her hand on her forehead, close her eyes, and sweat profusely from the drinking effort. She craved the milk. It tasted good and met her needs. When we first accept Christ as Savior and Lord, we have "tasted" of His goodness. We are assured of His love by His death in our place, His cruel death on a cross. He gave himself that we might live and become "children of God." If there is one thing clear to the sincere newborn Christian, it is the kindness of the Lord. We are drawn to Him by the kindness of the cross, of His love, and of His grace. Now we want more! It tastes good to us, so we want more of His goodness, of His truth, of Him. We crave the pure milk of the Word. It is necessary for our survival and growth in the midst of the stresses of this life. We must be nourished constantly from the Word and move from immature patterns of pretense and selfishness to a genuine life-style of Christlikeness!

CHAPTER TEN

Christians Are Special

1 Peter 2:4-17

Principle 7: You Are Special (1 Peter 2:4-10)

Leaving the analogy of the new birth, the fatherhood of God, family, and growth to maturity, Peter now moves into a section of mixed analogies. The focus of these analogies is that Christians are special people, important to God's purposes in the flow of history. We will see that Peter uses Old Testament analogies concerning the Messiah, and Israel as God's special people. He shows that the church is now the people, the special people, through whom God is working to bring the world back to himself.

Through Christ, God has intervened in history to bring the world back to himself, back to the purpose for which He made us from the beginning. That purpose was to know, worship, honor, obey, and glorify Him as God. We who have responded to Him in Christ are now His special people, whom He uses to bring the rest of the world back to himself.

In this segment of Scripture are three truths regarding our being God's special servants. We shall see that we have come to a "special position" to be a "special people" with a "special purpose."

Special Position

Peter begins this segment by saying we have "come to him, the living Stone" (1 Peter 2:4). We have come to a special relationship with this "living Stone," that is, Christ—the Messiah. We have come to this position with Christ by "trust[ing] in him" and, thus, we shall not be "put to shame" (1 Peter 2:6). Peter reinforces the fact that this position is gained through believing when he says that it is "to you who believe" that "this stone is precious" (1 Peter 2:7).

Christians have come to believe that Christ is the living stone of prophecy. In Isaiah 28:16 and Psalm 118:22, the Messiah is referred to as a "cornerstone." This is not a decorative stone in the corner of a building with the builder's name and date of construction. In ancient times, this was the crucial stone of a building or an archway. In a building, the large "cornerstone" was laid first and all measurements were made relative to it. When building an archway, scaffolding was used to hold up the stones from each side of the arch as it was being built. The scaffolding remained until the final, connecting stone—the "capstone" (1 Peter 2:7)—was put in place. That stone gave the arch its strength; it held it together. Only when this stone was in place could the scaffolding be removed.

Peter points out that the stone that finally became the most important, the "capstone," was often rejected during the construction. It didn't fit anywhere else, so it was cast aside as useless. Only when the builders came to the point of needing that crucial capstone would they realize the ultimate worth of the previously rejected stone. The Christian has come to realize that the "stone" that history rejected and crucified is the "capstone" of life itself. He is the Creator God, the source of life, the purpose of life, the future of life. He is the divine Son of God, the Savior of the world.

The results of our accepting Jesus as the Messiah, the "cornerstone," are twofold in this segment. First, we "received mercy" (1 Peter 2:10). Our sins have been forgiven by the mercy of God. If God were simply "just," we would remain in our lost state, but He is merciful. Second, Peter says we have been called "out of darkness into his wonderful light" (1 Peter 2:9). "Light" is symbolic of truth and morality; of the perfection of God. God has called us into His fellowship through truth concerning Christ and through mercy. He has declared us to have His morality—His righteousness—through the forgiveness of our sins in Christ.

Special People

As a result of the new, special position that we have in Christ, we are declared to be God's people. Peter uses several analogies and concepts from the Old Covenant in describing Christians as God's new special people.

The first concept is "stones" (1 Peter 2:5). In this context, Peter uses the analogy of God as a builder of a new building—a new creation. Christ is the crucial stone in this new creation of God. He is the foundational "cornerstone," the critical "capstone" of the arch. But we also are important to God's plan. The cornerstone is not a building. The capstone is not an arch. All the other stones are required, too. We are the "stones" in God's building.

The tabernacle, and later the temple, were buildings that symbolized God's presence. The Jews offered sacrifices to God in these buildings, and the priests taught the people in their courts. God is building a new "temple" to symbolize His presence in the world: the church. The stones are people who have come to believe that Jesus is Messiah and that God has begun a new creation.

Peter then calls Christians by a number of titles given to ancient Israel (1 Peter 2:9, 10). He says we are "a chosen people" (Deuteronomy 10:15) indicating God's initiative in choosing us in Christ. We did not seek God; He sought us and provided us an opportunity to become His people through His mercy. Peter then calls us "a royal priesthood" (Isaiah 61:6), indicating our ministry of representing God to the world and representing the people to God. In calling us "a holy nation" (Exodus 19:6), Peter indicates the manner of life we are to live before the watching world. We are to model God's righteousness—His morality—before the world by daring to be "holy," different from the world. Then Peter calls us "a people belonging to God" (Exodus 19:5), indicating our acceptance of God's rulership and ownership of our lives. We were once not "a people"; we had no separate identity as a people-group. But now we "are the people of God," a new people-group made of people from all previous people-groups who accept Jesus as Messiah.

Special Purpose

Each of these titles, once attributed to the Jews as God's special people, indicates something of the purpose for our ministries in the world. In addition, however, Peter points out two special purposes in this text that we are to fulfill.

The first purpose is "offering spiritual sacrifices acceptable to God through Jesus Christ" (1 Peter 2:5). This relates to the analogy of Christians as "holy priests." Priests in the ancient temple offered sacrifices for themselves and then for the people. The unblemished sacrificial lambs and doves were offered as sin offerings to God. They took the sins of the people upon themselves, and they were put to death for those sins. Christ is the "Lamb of God" that has been offered for the sins of the world.

In Hebrews, we read that Jesus is clearly the final sacrifice for the sins of the world (Hebrews 7:27; 9:11-14, 24-26; 10:10). If Jesus is the final sacrifice, then what sort of sacrifices do we now offer? Certainly not sacrifices to remove sin; Christ has already done that. But just as the Old Covenant had additional sacrifices, or offerings, given in the worship of God, so the New Covenant includes some sacrifices of its own. There is the "living sacrifice" of our "bodies" (Romans 12:1, 2), our whole beings offered in total submission to God's will. There are sacrifices of praise (Hebrews 13:5). And Paul points out that there are also the sacrifices of those whom we win to Christ (Romans 15:16).

Of course, the ancient priests did more than offer sacrifices. They also taught the people God's law and God's ways. Peter says this continues to be a purpose for God's special people: "that you may declare the praises of him who called you . . ." (1 Peter 2:9). As God's new priesthood, Christians are to proclaim His praises, His power, His holiness, His mercy, and His grace to the world. The Great Commission states very clearly that our task is to "preach the good news to all creation" (Mark 16:15).

Since we are important to God's new creation, His intervention into history to call creation back to himself, we must remain faithful to Him in the midst of the stresses of this world. We are special.

Principle 8: You Are Christians (2:11-17)

Persevere! Be faithful! Why? The world is watching you. This segment of Peter's letter of encouragement deals with both why and how we are to persevere in the midst of stress. Why should we persevere? The world is watching; thus, we should be an example of true Christianity. How should we persevere? By being a constant and consistent example, a real Christian. This was vitally important because of the false accusations of the world that were isolating Christians from the rest of the culture. By their very Christlike conduct, the Christians experienced alienation and isolation from the culture, and this brought rumors and accusations of sin and wrongdoing from those in the world culture.

The Condition of the Christian

In verse 16, Peter reminds the Christians of their newfound "freedom." In the Roman socioeconomic system, there were millions of slaves, many of whom had become slaves because they had incurred huge debts and chose servitude as a means to repay their debts. Unfortunately, many of them would never be able to pay all they owed. They were slaves for life. Many of these slaves, then, were drawn to Christ by the new sense of personal worth they realized through His death for their sins. Peter uses the analogy of being "free" to describe the Christian condition.

142

A Christian is free from several "bondages." He is free from the bondage of sin's consequences. He no longer has the "death penalty" hanging over him, for Christ took his death, his separation from God, by His death. Christians are also free from the law and its condemnation. The law defines sin and accuses our behavior. But Christ died for our sins, thus satisfying the law by paying our penalty. Christians are becoming free from the power of sin as well. Through the power of the indwelling Spirit, we are in the process of overcoming the "flesh" (Romans 8).

These "freedoms" brought claims of being forgiven by God from the lips of Christians. They spoke of having freedom through His grace, even though they were still in economic slavery. Their lifestyles, their moral choices, their values, and their responses to stress were dramatically changing.

The result of these changes was that they were considered to be "aliens and strangers" (1 Peter 2:11). They considered themselves to be different from their cultural surroundings, and their culture also considered them as alien and strange. They no longer participated in the immorality that was so prevalent in the Graeco-Roman world. They no longer participated in pagan worship and practices. They were aliens and strangers, and the surrounding culture was watching them and accusing them.

The world watched for any flaws in these "free slaves," these Holy-Spirit-indwelt "holy people." They would, at times, find real fault because of the immaturity of Christians. At other times, they would make up lies about them. They accused them of breaking up marriages, of sexual immorality in their "agape feasts," of cannibalism in the Lord's Supper, and later of burning Rome in a "judgment of fire." Peter says that the world would "accuse you of doing wrong" (1 Peter 2:12).

The Conduct of Christians

Since the world is watching and falsely accusing, how should Christians behave? How are we to live before our watching world?

Peter says we should "abstain from sinful desires." This has to do with our moral behavior. *Desires* refers to our natural instincts, our drives. Every human being has these drives; sex, hunger, thirst, self-esteem, and self-preservation are some of them. These instincts are not intrinsically evil, for they were given us by God himself. The proper use of these drives is called "righteousness," and their improper use, "sin." Our proneness to misuse these drives is called "the flesh," and to use them obsessively is "lust." Paul fought this same battle with the "fleshly lusts," as he confessed in Romans 7:7-25. The Holy Spirit comes to indwell Christians at conversion (Romans 8:1-17) and empowers us with the resources to battle against the "flesh." Christ not only forgives our sins, He sends the Comforter to help us overcome them! Peter is exhorting Christians to use the power within them to overcome "sinful desires." Our moral behavior "shuts the mouths" of our accusers.

Peter also says to "submit . . . for the Lord's sake to every [civil] authority," such as kings, and to "honor the king" (1 Peter 2:13, 17). Under Roman law, the crime of which Christians were accused was insurrection against Rome and the power of the Caesar. The cult of Caesar worship was evolving in Roman society as a basis for retaining central power in Rome. Citizens were being required to worship Caesar as a God, but Christians, of course, refused. They could not worship any false gods. Peter here exhorts Christians to honor Caesar as king, to obey the law, and to respect governmental authority. They were to respect the "governors" sent by kings (1 Peter 2:14), for they were the keepers of peace and law. They kept order in society. Christians should never be viewed as outlaws! Even today, we must submit to governmental authority and not ever be accused of political revolt (Romans 13).

He also exhorts them to behave as "servants," even though free (1 Peter 2:16). There is a proneness to misuse freedom. Christians might be "free" to do certain things, but the exercise of that freedom might cause Christianity to be misunderstood and rejected by the surrounding culture. So, though free, we must be fully aware of the possibility of being a stumbling block to others and a hindrance to the acceptance of Christ by those in the world around us. Even though "free," we still have responsibility!

The Consequences of Our Conduct

The results of our Christlike behavior will be twofold. First of all, it will "silence the ignorant talk of foolish men" (1 Peter 2:15). Those who were falsely accusing Christians would be considered liars, even by their peers, because of the obvious holiness of the behavior of Christians. Our morality and our submission to governmental order will speak louder than their lies! By heeding the exhortation of Peter in 2:17, "Show proper respect to everyone: Love the brotherhood of believers, fear God, honor the king," we will gain the sincere respect of society. False accusers, in order to be

144

effective, must be believed. Our conduct will make the lies totally unbelievable!

The second result of Christlike conduct before the watching world is found in 1 Peter 2:12: "They may see your good deeds and glorify God on the day he visits us." By our conduct, the world will recognize God's power to change lives. Many will accept Christ as a result. The "day of visitation" is the return of Christ into the flow of history, and many will be in Him because of our conduct! This restates the saying of Jesus in the Sermon on the Mount (Matthew 5:16).

The world is watching those who claim the freedom that is in Christ! They are looking for a way to accuse us. Peter's exhortation is to be an example, to be "aliens and strangers" in the best sense of the terms—to be really different in holiness, an important principle of perseverance!

CHAPTER ELEVEN

Relationships

1 Peter 2:18—3:7

It has often been said that a person is known by the company he keeps. Even more important than the company itself, however, is the person's relationships with others—the way he treats them. How does he treat his family? How does he treat others around him? How does he treat those society considers his superiors? How does he treat those he considers to be subordinate?

Peter is sensitive to this issue. He writes that our relationships with people should reveal our relationship with Christ. The next two principles of perseverance are aimed at keeping the character of our relationships as pure and attractive as possible so that we glorify Christ and win others to Him.

Principle 9: Submit As Servants (2:18-25)

There were two accusations frequently brought against the Christians during the persecution by Rome. The first was that they were rebels against the authority of the Roman government and of Caesar (1 Peter 2:11-17). The second accusation was that they were out to destroy the socioeconomic system of the Graeco-Roman world. To a great extent, the economic system of the time was based upon slavery. Non-waged or low-waged workers were "owned" during servitude by their masters. In Christ, these slaves had found a new sense of worth as equal recipients of God's love and Christ's forgiveness. They had also found a sense of identity with Christ, who himself had come as a "suffering servant" into the flow of history. Thus, Peter gives these words of warning and instruction to the Christian slaves as to how to live in their perilous situations.

The Call to Be Servants

Peter says to the slaves, "To this you were called"—to follow in the steps of Christ, a suffering servant (1 Peter 2:21). This was, and

147

is, true not only of those who were literal slaves, but of all Christians. We are all "servants of Christ," serving Him as our "master" before the watching world.

In verse 18 Peter uses the Greek word *oiketai* for the slaves. This word was most often used for household slaves who had special skills beyond ordinary labor. These slaves often served as stewards or managers of the master's estate, for they were trusted implicitly by their masters.

Most of the slaves in the Roman system, about one million throughout the empire, were debtor slaves. They had become servants because of their debts or the debts of their fathers. They would be "owned" by their masters until the debt was worked out, usually at a very unfair rate of payback. Some of these were military slaves, obtained in Roman conquest. Christians are all debtor slaves of Christ, for we owe a debt we can never repay. We are His servants for a lifetime and for eternity.

Some slaves were voluntary servants. Often, after years of service to a master, a slave would stay on in the employ of a master because of the mutual love and respect between him and the master, or because his wife and children belonged to the master and he wanted to stay with them. He preferred to stay on as a servant rather than go free. In this sense also, all Christians are servants of Christ in that we willingly serve Him because of our love for Him and for the family that belongs to Him, His church.

A third type of servant is the one mentioned in this text, the household servant. There are two major characteristics of household servants. First, they were greatly trusted by their masters because of their character. Second, they were specially skilled. They may have been doctors, attorneys, cooks, or even bankers before becoming slaves. Some were trained in these areas by their masters. All Christians are also this kind of servants in that we are entrusted by God to carry on His work, and we are especially gifted by the Lord through gifts of the Spirit with skills to minister in special tasks in the body of Christ.

Though Peter is dealing directly with literal Christian slaves, the principles apply to all of us who are in Christ, to all of us who serve Him in the world.

Characteristics of Servants

The first characteristic of a servant, by Peter's instruction, is submission (1 Peter 2:18). Once a Christian slave found out his new worth before God and learned of the freedom he inherited as a child of God, he might have been tempted to express this freedom in a tangible way and flee from his earthly slavery. Though literal slavery was against God's will for man, Christian slaves were exhorted not to flee from their masters, but to remain until their debt was paid in full. Not only were they taught to remain, they were taught to be obedient, submissive slaves.

The second characteristic of literal servants, and of Christians as servants, is that we will experience suffering. Peter exhorts them to obey their masters whether they are "good and considerate" or "harsh" in their demands (1 Peter 2:18). The servants must always keep a good conscience, Peter says, and not break Roman law or their master's will. If they suffered, they must not do so for law-breaking, but totally because of the injustice of their masters. Peter says, "If you suffer for doing good and you endure it, this is commendable before God" (1 Peter 2:20). This calls to mind the teachings of Jesus regarding "turning the other cheek" and "returning good for evil," as well as the Old Testament injuction, "'Vengeance is mine,' says the Lord."

Christ is set forth in 1 Peter 2:21-24 as the example of one who suffered unjustly as a servant and thus accomplished a greater good. First, He did not sin, nor did He revile or complain, nor did He threaten His persecutors. Christ trusted himself to the Father, who will judge "justly." He "bore our sins," suffering for the wrongdoing of others. All of this was done for the greater good, providing forgiveness for the lost world.

There was a greater good to be accomplished by submissive slaves. If the masters were to sense that rebellion was the result of their slaves' becoming Christians, they would reject Christ and not allow their slaves to worship Him or talk of Him. But if their slaves were even more submissive, honest, and respectful, the masters would be supportive of Christianity and might even be drawn to Christ themselves.

The last characteristic of slaves inferred here is that of security. Slaves, especially those who had fair masters, were given all that they needed and were considered as having real value by their masters. Peter points out to the Christian slaves that, even if they did not sense security from their earthly masters, they did have security in their Heavenly Master, who had once been a slave himself. Jesus Christ, the suffering servant, suffered for our sins, so we have been "healed" (1 Peter 2:24). We have found our way and are no longer "going astray" (1 Peter 2:25). As Christians, we have returned to Christ, the "Shepherd" who leads and loves, the "Overseer" who protects our souls.

Christianity made slaves into better slaves, and masters into better masters. Eventually, slavery as a socioeconomic system was eliminated—for the most part as a result of the principle of the worth of each individual taught by Christ and His followers. Yet, paradoxically, we who are in Christ are still servants: bond servants, willing servants, and skilled household servants!

Principle 10: Submit in Marriage (3:1-7)

There was a third frequent accusation made against Christians during the Roman persecution of the church. They were accused of destroying Graeco-Roman family life. Remember, the previous accusations with which Peter has dealt have been rebellion against governmental authority (see principle 8) and destruction of the socio-economic system of slavery (see principle 9).

In order to understand this problem, we must take a look at the prevalent cultural notions about family relationships of that time. Among the Jews, a wife was a possession, a symbol of a man's wealth. She had no authority. She could not divorce the husband, and she could not change religions without her husband's permission. Among the Greeks, the wife was to be obedient, stay at home, and basically be silent. She also could not divorce her husband. In the Roman culture, the authority of the husband was absolute, extending even to the point of life and death. A Roman wife could not drink wine, make legal decisions, speak in opposition to her husband in public, nor divorce her husband. In other words, in all three cultures, the wife was a possession without rights.

When a woman became a Christian, she discovered that she was an equal recipient of God's love and grace. She experienced the reception of the Holy Spirit and spiritual gifts for ministry. She was taught that, in Christ, there was no longer "male and female."

The problems that arose from the misapplication of these new principles were predictable. Many of the women rejected the domineering authority of their husbands. If the husband in such a case were unsaved, then he would likely reject the Christian faith because of the attitude of his rebelling wife. Even if the husband were a Christian, the wife's behavior would bring him into cultural disrepute. So Peter gives some words of exhortation to the Christian wives and to the husbands as well.

Instructions to Wives (1-6)

Peter begins by dealing with the attitudes and behavior of wives toward their husbands. He says the wives are to be "submissive" (1 Peter 3:1). Even though we know that there is no difference between male and female "in Christ," there is a difference in culture. There is a difference in physical form and ability. There is, in most cases, a difference in emotional outlook. Brute strength, for instance, is a factor of dominance in the fallen world where there is physical danger all around. A woman feels more secure when there is a man with her who loves her and will protect her. So, since the "fall of man" in the Garden of Eden, woman has been subject to man in the family system, largely because of the fallenness of our environment, both of people and nature. Peter calls women the "weaker partner"—she has less strength of body (1 Peter 3:7). This does not mean that men are more intelligent than women, nor are they more favored by God. It means that someone must be "in charge," must have final authority, must finally be responsible for the well-being of the marriage and family system. Even in our time, very few societies are matriarchal, with women dominating. To make his point, Peter refers to the "holy women of the past," especially Sarah, and how they showed respect for their husbands (1 Peter 3:5, 6).

Peter characterizes the attitudes and behavior that women should have in their relationships with the words *purity* and *reverence* (1 Peter 3:2). A Christian wife should be morally pure at all times. This has to do with sexual faithfulness and with all other aspects of morality, such as honesty and trustworthiness in all relationships. The word *reverence,* from the Greek word φόβος *(phobos),* is a strong word for respect or honor. This "reverence" is to be more than an outward show; it must be a real attitude of the heart.

We see, then, that wives are to be submissive, pure, and respectful in their attitudes and behavior. We see, also, that their appearance is also a matter of concern, as Peter turns his attention to the subject of "beauty" (1 Peter 3:3-6).

To get the full impact of what Peter is saying here, we need to understand the importance of these beauty symbols in the first century. Since women were allowed to do little else, they went to great lengths to enhance their beauty. Their husbands often encouraged this, for their wives were status symbols for themselves, and beauty was considered very important.

Women very seldom cut their hair. Often, then, they would braid their hair so it could be worn on top of their heads, braiding jewels into their hair as they did. They often dyed their hair or wore wigs. Auburn hair and blond wigs were considered very important for improving their status. They wore fancy dresses, with purple being the highest in status, with many jewels sewn into their garments. Some had jewels worth hundreds of thousands of dollars in their hair or on their dresses.

In this setting, Peter tells Christian wives to shun the extremes of their culture and rather bring pride to their husbands through the beauty of the "inner self" (1 Peter 3:4). Both in public and in private, they were to develop "a gentle and quiet spirit." They were to be sensitive to their husbands and to others, and not ever to be overbearing. Christian women were not told to dress poorly, nor were they forbidden to braid their hair. Rather, they were exhorted to concentrate on the inner personality and the development of a Christlike spirit as the source of real beauty. What Peter does not mention, but very well could have, is that such extravagance in dress and jewels also violates the principle of properly using our possessions to meet our own responsibilities and to meet the needs of others who cannot meet their own needs.

Instructions to Husbands (7)

When Peter turns to instructions to husbands, he introduces some culturally revolutionary concepts. Paul does the same in his writings. While both apostles exhort women not to rock the boat culturally, they both give special exhortations to the men as well. This is what Peter does in verse 7.

First of all, he tells the husbands to be "considerate." To understand one's wife, a man must know what she thinks and feels. This demands listening, watching, and interpreting. Christian men are to seek and listen to the thoughts of their wives in all areas of their lives together. Men are to consider their wives' needs and try to meet them. Men are to understand their wives' ideas and thoughts and respect them. All of this is necessary to being "considerate."

Then he reminds men to remember that wives are "weaker partners." They are physically weaker and need the security of their husbands' presence, love, and protection. Just as husbands need "respect," wives need "security." Even though women are more intelligent, on the average, and outlive men by a number of years, they need the security of a husband's love and care.

Next is the real revolutionary statement! Peter tells the husbands to respect their wives "as heirs with you of the gracious gift of life."

Christian husbands are exhorted to look to their wives as equals before God and in life. God has given to both male and female alike physical life and new life through Christ. In God's love and forgiveness, there is no difference! In worth, there is no difference! The ideal is what is called for here—equality before God. The "real" in the fallen world is authority and order, and the "ideal" is equality. The Christian couple must find the balance of the "ideal" and "real" in their relationship.

Peter closes with a word of warning to the husbands. If they do not accept these responsibilities to understand, protect, and honor their wives before God, it will affect their relationship to God—their prayers will be "hindered." In our continuing relationship with God, we must learn to forgive in order to be forgiven; we must learn to love in order to be loved.

In our own time, the watching world observes the marriages of Christians. Our witness is negated or aided by the way we deal with this most vital relationship. If we do God's will in our marriages, others will be won to Christ without our saying a word (1 Peter 3:1). They will see the difference Christ is making in our lives and they will want to share what we have found in Him.

CHAPTER TWELVE

Submission in Suffering

1 Peter 3:8-22

At this point in the epistle, we find a transition in progress. Peter is still talking about our relationships, but the emphasis is shifting from what we might consider the normal experience to one that is hostile. The Christian was finding more and more that his society was becoming hostile toward him. A discussion of social relationships (principle 11), then, becomes a discussion of suffering. Suffering will continue to be Peter's theme even after he leaves the theme of relationships behind.

Principle 11: Submit in Society (1 Peter 3:8-17)

Jesus had taught the apostles that the world would identify His disciples by the fact that they loved one another and that He loved them. Paul exhorted the Philippian Christians (Philippians 2:1-4) to live in one mind and one spirit, and to do nothing out of selfishness or empty conceit. Throughout the New Testament, there are words of exhortation for Christians to live in harmony before the watching world! Peter now adds his own exhortation in this segment of his letter by instructing his readers to live in harmony with one another and with the surrounding world, even while being abused by the world. He thus passes on, to his first readers and to us, the instructions of the Lord about facing stress. We shall see in this section the basis for, the behaviors of, and the blessings from living in harmony and submission.

The Basis for Living in Harmony and Submission

"Live in harmony with one another," Peter says (1 Peter 3:8). In the midst of stress and suffering, Christians are to live in harmony with one another and—as much as possible—with the opposing culture. From this segment, we see two bases for this submission. The first basis is the lordship of Jesus Christ: "In your hearts set apart

Christ as Lord" (1 Peter 3:15). Peter is saying that we should let Christ rule our thoughts and emotions. The "heart" he speaks of here is not the literal physical muscle/organ that pumps our blood. It is the combination of our intellect and emotions; our thoughts, feelings, and motives. If we let Christ rule our thoughts and motives, we will follow His teachings and His example! Peter is referring to our response to the enemies of our faith, and he instructs us to defend our faith as Christ would, by giving "an answer" for our hope with "gentleness and respect." The question is, "How would Christ respond; what would He say and do?" Peter had put it this way in 1 Peter 2:21, ". . . Christ suffered for you, leaving you an example, that you should follow in his steps."

The second basis for our harmony and submission in society is brotherly love. "Love as brothers," Peter writes (1 Peter 3:8), using here the Greek word φιλέω *(phileo)*. We are to live in harmony and submission with our fellow Christians because we are "brothers"; we are family. We have a declared relationship that is to result in love for one another. Brothers don't always agree, but they always love one another.

The Behavior of Harmony and Submission

Peter gives a number of ways we are to behave in a harmonious and submissive manner. Some of his instructions have to do with attitudes of submission; others have to do with actions of submission. Let's look at the attitudes first.

Verse 8 stresses the attitudes with several descriptive words. "Be sympathetic, . . . be compassionate and humble." To be "sympathetic" is to "feel with" another by listening and watching. We listen and watch so that we might understand and respond. To be "compassionate" is, more literally, to be "kindhearted" (NASB). It is our inner motivation to respond to sensed need. We respond with ourselves and with our resources in a helpful, constructive manner because of our "kindhearted" attitude.

Being "humble" has to do with not being self-seeking in a given situation. It means that we don't look upon ourselves as being better than others. Thus, we are more able to seek the well-being of others without our self interest getting in the way.

Peter also has some instructions that have to do with the actions of submission and harmony. He exhorts, "Do not repay evil with evil" (1 Peter 3:9). We are not to participate in the endless cycle of personal revenge so common in Peter's day as well as our own. In the Old Testament, the law regarding "an eye for an eye" allowed punishing only in like kind, and not in greater kind. Jesus goes beyond that, and Peter agrees, that we should not even respond in like kind, but return good for evil. That breaks the cycle!

Speech patterns are a part of what Peter has in mind in this verse, as he specifies when he says, ". . . or insult with insult." We are not to insult someone back who insults us. It takes two to argue and cause division between brothers. Instead of counterattacking, we should ask, "What is causing this person to attack me; what is really troubling this brother?" Then we can turn our response into a blessing! Peter quotes from Psalm 34:12-16 (1 Peter 3:10-12) to reinforce this idea, but the idea goes beyond speech responses: "He must turn from evil and do good" (1 Peter 3:11); he must be "eager to do good" (1 Peter 3:13); he must display "good behavior in Christ" (1 Peter 3:16) and be "doing good" (1 Peter 3:17). These all have to do with negating aggressive physical responses and with breaking God's laws or the laws of the government. We are to live in submission to the law and live in harmony by not seeking revenge, both within the church and in the surrounding hostile world.

The Blessings of Living in Harmony and Submission

Peter points out some positive results of living in harmony and submission both with the hostile world that is watching, and with God. As to the blessings in our relationship with our surrounding world, he points out that even the world will not "harm you if you are eager to do good" (1 Peter 3:13). In Romans 13, Paul alludes to this fact, telling the Romans that God ordained that governments would have the function of commending the lawkeepers and punishing the evildoers. If Christians live in harmony and submission with one another and with their surrounding world, it will cut back on the negative response of the world to us and to the gospel.

Peter is not naive. He knows that, even if we keep the law, some might bring us suffering anyway. Even then, he says, "you are blessed" (1 Peter 3:14). Part of this blessing actually comes from the world itself, the source of the suffering, because "those who speak maliciously against your good behavior in Christ may be ashamed of their slander" (1 Peter 3:16). Eventually, their lie will be found out; if not in the courts, then in the minds of the people around us.

Not only do we receive some blessing from the surrounding world when we live in harmony and submission, we receive blessing from God! This was the promise of Jesus (Matthew 5:10-12), and Peter points out that "you were called so that you may inherit a blessing" (1 Peter 3:9). In Peter's quotation of the Psalms, he says,

> The eyes of the Lord are on the righteous,
> and his ears are attentive to their prayer,
> but the face of the Lord is against those who do evil
> —1 Peter 3:12.

There are present blessings to those who live in harmony and submission in times of stress. They have the attention of the Lord's eyes and ear! Peter assures his readers that, if they suffer for the right, "you are blessed" (1 Peter 3:14). Our blessings are now to sustain us, and in the judgment to reward us.

Principle 12: Submit Like Christ (3:17-22)

As he does throughout this letter, Peter here refers the suffering Christians to the model of the suffering Christ. We are to submit and suffer as citizens, servants, and spouses before the watching world, just as Christ did, in order to accomplish "God's will" (1 Peter 3:17). God's will is not that we suffer as an end in itself. It is not His will that we suffer just to suffer. It is God's will, however, that we accomplish His goals and plans even if it requires suffering for Him! God accomplished His goals of salvation for mankind and creation via the suffering of Christ, His unique Son. God's goal was not that Christ should suffer, but rather that man be brought back to Him. It took Christ's suffering to accomplish that goal. It may also take our suffering to accomplish that goal. Our suffering may be emotional, social, or physical. It may even be unto death.

Joseph made a poignant statement to his brothers about the ordeal he had endured after they sold him into Egyptian slavery. He pointed out to them that "you intended to harm me, but God intended it for good" (Genesis 50:20). They sold him into slavery to get rid of him, but God used it to provide for their future salvation from starvation and to accomplish His purposes for the flow of the history of Israel. So it was with Christ's suffering, and the suffering of those to whom Peter was writing, as well as for us today. God will use suffering for His ultimate purposes!

The Reasons for Suffering Submissively

Peter points out two kinds of suffering experienced by Christians. "It is better, if it is God's will, to suffer for doing good than for

158

doing evil" (1 Peter 3:17). First, there is suffering that comes from doing evil. In exhorting submission of servants, Peter had pointed out (1 Peter 2:20) that there was no credit for justly suffering for evildoing. It is not simply suffering that accomplishes God's purposes, but suffering for the right, and for doing good. If society punishes a Christian for a crime, the Christian deserves the punishment, and society holds him and his faith in disrepute. Christ's cause is set back by such suffering.

The second kind of suffering is for doing the "good," doing what is right. If a Christian suffered for doing God's will, God would reward him, and society would finally respond to him and to his message. Christ suffered "for sins" (1 Peter 3:18), the sins of the "unjust," the sins of others. He did not sin, yet He suffered. The goal of His suffering was to "bring you to God." Here we see God's purpose, to bring mankind to himself. God's justice was satisfied by Christ's death in our place. Christ's suffering and death draw us to God by clearly showing forth His real love for us. Love, expressed by His willingness to suffer and die for us, is God's lure to bring mankind to himself. Christ said, "But I, when I am lifted up from the earth [on the cross], will draw all men to myself" (John 12:32).

The Results of Submissive Suffering (18-21)

We have seen that Christ's suffering made possible our coming to the Father by satisfying God's justice, and also by stating God's love for us in terms that we could understand. Peter is clearly trying to show us that God can use our suffering to accomplish His purposes—that significant good can be accomplished by us even while we are suffering. So he points out that, even though Christ "was put to death in the body" (1 Peter 3:18), He was "made alive by the Spirit"—He was accomplishing something. In the depths of His suffering, even while physically dead, He accomplished God's will and the good of mankind.

"He went and preached," Peter says (1 Peter 3:19). Even while He was dead, Christ's ministry of proclamation continued. The inference is that we, too, can have a real proclamation to others while we are suffering. The "preaching" that Christ accomplished while dead is one of the most difficult passages in the New Testament to understand. It says He "preached to the spirits in prison who disobeyed long ago when God waited patiently in the days of Noah" (1 Peter 3:19, 20). The controversial question is, "Who are these 'spirits'?" Some refer to Genesis 6:1-13 and say these spirits are the "sons of

159

God," or fallen angels, who lusted after "daughters of men," or human women, and married them and had offspring, resulting in severe evil in the world and culminating in the punishment of God in the flood. This reasoning usually results in saying that Christ preached their impending doom to them while He was dead, or in the grave. Others say that the "disobedient spirits" are those who sinned in such a terrible manner in Noah's day—not just the angels—and that Christ preached their doom to them for rejecting Noah's preaching. Yet others say that these specific "spirits" represent all of the dead, and that Christ preached to all of those who were dead before Noah, and after Noah, until His coming as Savior. They contend that Christ gave them a chance to repent and accept His offer of forgiveness. They point to Peter's statement in 1 Peter 4:6 that the gospel had been preached to the dead who were judged in the flesh as men, but who were given a chance to live in the spirit according to the will of God. This would mean that all who have lived before Christ have now had a chance to accept Him as Savior, in spite of their sin, just like those of us who have lived since Christ.

I am not sure which, if any, of these is meant by Peter, but the last concept seems to fit the thrust of the text. Peter is showing that, even while His suffering was at its worst, and even while He was dead, Christ was proclaiming the gospel and some were being saved. He is pointing out that, while we are suffering the worst, we are proclaiming the gospel for the salvation of some.

Salvation is a second result of submissive suffering, for it naturally follows proclamation. Peter points out that the result of Noah's proclamation was that eight persons were brought safely through the water and were thus saved from God's judgment. The result of Christ's preaching was salvation, and the result of our proclamation is salvation of others. Peter then alludes to the baptismal aspect of salvation in the New Covenant by pointing out the similarity to Noah's time when they were saved "through water" (1 Peter 3:20). Peter says that this event corresponds to water baptism and our salvation now (1 Peter 3:21).

In Noah's time, when the rains came and the foundations of the deep were opened up, the ark came through the water and those within were saved. They were saved by their faith in what Noah was saying, and by their posture of obedience in getting into the ark. They were not saved by the water, but rather from it, or through it. Baptism is like that. We submit to it out of faith in Christ and His death for our sins, followed by His resurrection. In baptism, we, like

160

those in Noah's day, are buried believers who are brought back to new life through the water.

When our bodies are put into and under the water, it looks like a physical cleansing for salvation, but Peter points out it is an inner, spiritual cleansing, resulting in a good conscience. The "pledge" in 1 Peter 3:21 refers to a legal agreement. We are accepting God's legal offer of salvation, we are agreeing to His terms, and the result is a good conscience. Just as in Noah's time, we were raised from burial to new life, as Christ was raised from burial to new life. Through the resurrection of Jesus Christ and our identification with it in baptism, we experience salvation and a good conscience. So, as proclamation resulted in salvation in Noah's time, and as Christ's death and preaching resulted in salvation, even so our present proclamation in suffering can result in salvation.

The Rewards of Submissive Suffering

After Christ submitted to unjust suffering, resulting in proclamation opportunities, which in turn resulted in the salvation of others, He was raised from the dead, went into Heaven, and was seated at God's right hand (1 Peter 3:22). This is not only true of Jesus, it is true of all of us who suffer for God's purposes. We, too, will experience "resurrection" from the dead at Christ's return (1 Thessalonians 4:13ff; 1 Corinthians 15). We will be with Him in Heavenly places and reign with Him in all of eternity. The conclusion to be drawn is that Christians must be submissive, even to the point of suffering and death. Christ is our role model. The result will be proclamation and salvation, with the rewards of resurrection, Heaven, and reigning with Christ.

CHAPTER THIRTEEN

Looking Toward the Goal

1 Peter 4:1-19

Peter's reference to the rewards of suffering (resurrection and Heaven) leads him to focus on the goal of the Christian life. His words in the fourth chapter, then, are a strong appeal for living in the present by keeping an eye on the future. "The end of all things is near," he says (1 Peter 4:7), but he does not say it with the doom and gloom normally associated with such messages. Rather, it is a message of hope and an appeal to godly living. From this, we draw three principles of perseverance: overcome the flesh (1 Peter 4:1-6), live in hope (1 Peter 4:7-11), and rejoice in the midst of suffering (1 Peter 4:12-19).

Principle 13: Overcome the Flesh (4:1-6)

As the first readers of this letter well knew, Christians are not immune from suffering. Peter begins this segment of the letter by reminding them again that Christ also suffered. Satan attacked Christ with temptation during forty days of suffering in the wilderness. During a period of suffering or persecution, a believer is vulnerable to Satan's onslaught. Christ suffered spiritually as He anticipated the cross while He was in the Garden of Gethsemane. He suffered emotionally when the multitudes who had praised Him turned against Him during His trial. He suffered physically as He was crucified—the most painful death possible. As Christ suffered physically, emotionally, and spiritually, so also do His followers suffer in all ways during this life.

In the American culture, as well as in the other cultures of the Western world, Christians still suffer for their faith. Persecution is more blatant elsewhere, perhaps, but Western Christians do suffer. Theirs is a subtle persecution, not so violent as that of first-century Rome, but problematic just the same. For example, we might note the generally negative portrayal of conservative Christians by the news and entertainment media. Again, the world is watching us as to how we will live and react in the midst of our suffering. Will our faith prove genuine? Can it withstand the pressure? Or will we give in? This segment of Peter's letter contains a word of exhortation to the suffering Christians—both in Peter's day and in our own—to live morally in the midst of suffering.

Suffering

Peter exhorts his readers to "arm yourselves also with the same attitude" as Christ had during His suffering (1 Peter 4:1). Then he says something very interesting, and just what he means by it is a source of considerable debate: He says the reason we should take this attitude is that "he who has suffered in his body is done with sin."

There are three possible understandings of this phrase. First, Christ resisted the temptation to sin in the midst of His suffering. Second, surviving suffering makes us strong. By this I mean that suffering is a test of strength and a source of strength, and, therefore, we grow stronger each time we resist the temptation to sin in the midst of suffering. As a result, we gradually cease from sinful patterns of behavior. Third, and this is the most likely meaning, Peter was referring back to a concept in the previous chapter (1 Peter 3:18) when he wrote that Christ suffered and "was put to death in the body but made alive by the Spirit." Suffering, then, is a form of death, death to the flesh and to its dominating instinctive drives that we are so prone to misuse. (See Romans 6.) The more the Christian suffers in the flesh, the more "death" of the flesh he is experiencing. But God gives "life in the Spirit" to the Christian who resists temptation in the midst of suffering.

So, when we suffer, we die in and to the flesh and come alive in the Spirit, thus overcoming the desires of the flesh. Peter clearly states that one of the results of one's suffering in the flesh is that "he does not live the rest of his earthly life for evil human desires, but rather for the will of God" (1 Peter 4:2). Suffering is gradually killing the flesh and its desires so we can live totally within the will of God.

This is the same idea Peter had introduced earlier (1 Peter 1:6-9) when he compared suffering and trials to fire, which tests and purifies. James also presents the values of suffering as a tool for growth in James 1:2-4 when he calls his readers to "consider it pure joy" when they suffer because of the strengthening factor of suffering. Paradoxically, suffering is used by God for the Christian's growth and strengthening. But this is so only if the believer allows it to result in this manner. As Paul put it, we are to consider ourselves "dead to sin but alive to God" (Romans 6:11).

Sanctification

Suffering can either result in our growth toward sanctification, or it can result in our disillusionment and cause us to return to the world and its life-style. Peter exhorts his readers to choose the sanctification route in their suffering. He refers to the life-style of the world as "what pagans choose to do" (1 Peter 4:3).

Each of us has instinctive drives, given to us by God to use in a good and healthy way. God's will for our use of these drives is clearly stated in Scripture. However, man is prone to misuse these instinctive drives, and Peter says this is what the "pagans" do. The wrong use of these drives is called sin, and the right use is called righteousness. The inclination to misuse these drives is called "the flesh." Peter goes on to describe the common misuses of the flesh with words like *debauchery* (which is our proneness to be more aware of our "wants" than of our "needs"), *lust* and *drunkenness* (or our proneness to use our drives obsessively), *orgies* and *carousing* (which represent our proneness to sin with others), and *detestable idolatry* (the practices of the pagans to use sex and drugs as worship forms). Our surviving of suffering can make us stronger in combatting these patterns of behavior in our life-style.

The choice is ours, though we are empowered by God with the strength to make right choices. When we make the right choice, we no longer "plunge with them into the same flood of dissipation" (1 Peter 4:4). As our lives change, the differences are perceivable by others. It changes what we do, where we go, and with whom we have social contact. We no longer run with the same gang because of their behavior patterns.

Of course, it is predictable, as Peter says, that the old crowd will "heap abuse" on us (1 Peter 4:4). We suffer this same malignment today. In the church that I serve, we have a young single Christian who slipped back into the world for a time, though he never lost his faith. He was known as a backslidden believer by some and as a blatant sinner by others. He made a serious decision to come back to the Lord. The factors were his obvious dissipation and what it was doing to his life, and the influence of his Christian friends who never gave up on him. However, the friends with whom he ran in the world have maligned him and ridiculed him since his decision. He has had to realign his friendships while trying to witness to his worldly friends. He still hopes to win some of them, but he cannot run with them any longer.

The story is told about Augustine, who had been an adulterous man before accepting Christ as his Savior and Lord. After his conversion, he was confronted by one of his former prostitute friends, but he showed no recognition. She said to him, "Augustine, don't you recognize me? It is I." He replied, "Yes, I know you, but it is no longer I." In other words, he was no longer the same man whom she had known before. His conversion had affected with whom he ran as well as how he behaved.

Salvation

Those who malign the steadfast believer and who continue in the desire of the pagans will not get away with it. Someday, they "will have to give account to him who is ready to judge the living and the dead" (1 Peter 4:5). God will judge all people, both those who are alive at Christ's coming and those who have already died. Paul indicates in 1 Corinthians 15 and in 1 Thessalonians 4 that some will be alive at the coming of the Lord. The Revelation of John also deals with this event (Revelation 20:11-15), stating that judgment follows a general resurrection of all those who have died in order that all of the living and the dead might be judged.

Peter indicates that the preaching of the gospel was for the purpose that "those who are now dead . . . might be judged according to men in regard to the body, but live according to God in regard to the spirit" (1 Peter 4:6). "Those who are now dead" may be those to whom Peter refers in 1 Peter 3:19 and 20 to whom he says Jesus preached, who were "spirits in prison." (See my comments on that section in the previous chapter of this work.) More than likely, he is referring to that incident as a basis for introducing the broader principle that all sinners are "dead" and need the preaching of the gospel. Paul often uses the phrase "dead in sin" to describe lost people. It appears that Peter is here saying that the purpose of preaching the gospel is to bring people from a state of being dead in sin to a state of being alive in the Spirit.

This is what salvation is all about, a change of our status here to an ultimate change of state. We are now alive in the Spirit, but there is more to our salvation than this. Though alive in the Spirit, we remain in dying bodies, but we shall be altogether alive in the Spirit after the resurrection. Salvation, then, is both now and also in the future. It is the "will of God" that we be alive in the Spirit here and now, and that we ultimately be fully alive in His presence in the Heavenly places.

We have seen in this chapter that the overcoming of the flesh is a blessing that results from enduring suffering. Suffering purifies us and strengthens us. As we grow, we see our behavior changing unto sanctification. All of this leads to the ultimate purpose of the gospel, our salvation now and in the final day.

Principle 14: Live in Hope (4:7-11)

In the previous segment, Peter has pointed to the judgment of God that is coming against the flesh and those who submit to the flesh. The incentive presented for staying faithful in the midst of suffering was that suffering could be used of God to help us overcome the flesh. Now Peter moves on to another incentive, the impending "end of all things." Not only is judgment coming, he says, but it is coming soon.

Premise

The premise for faithfulness and service in this segment is the imminent coming of the "end" (1 Peter 4:7). The apostolic writer takes the position that the return of the Lord in glory and the judgment that will follow is to be expected soon. The Lord had made it clear that no man was to know the date of the second coming (Matthew 24:36). However, the apostle Paul uses inspired logic when he states in Romans 13:11, "Our salvation is nearer now than when we first believed." The simple passing of time brings us closer and closer to that great day. Since that time is getting closer, Paul goes on to say, "the hour has come for you to wake up from your slumber." The call is to constant expectation of Christ's return and to a constant alertness of life.

John also calls for constant alertness based on the assumption of the imminency of Christ's return. "This is the last hour," he says (1 John 2:18). He says they can know it is the last hour because "many antichrists have come," referring to the rising Gnostic heresy. In 1 Thessalonians 4 and 5 and in 2 Thessalonians 2, Paul uses the "thief in the night" simile to describe the coming of the day of the Lord. He also talks about the great "falling away" or apostasy that will precede it.

In the latter apostolic period, there was the "falling away" of the Judaizers—an attempt by Jewish Christians to return to law-keeping for salvation and to force it on the rest of the church as well. Then came the Gnostic heresy, which denied the divinity of Christ in the flesh and the moral implications of the Christian life. (See 2 Peter and 1 John.) These were forms of apostasy, and the apostles linked such apostasy to the imminent return of Christ. There are still many forms of apostasy today, so we also should assume that the day of the Lord is at hand. We can see that Peter's premise was shared by Paul and John, and it should be shared by us today.

Practices in Light of the Premise

Based upon the premise of the imminent "end of all things," Peter exhorts his readers to practices that will keep them ready for divine intervention. He begins with two attitudes. First, he calls them to be "clear minded" (1 Peter 4:7). When one is in the midst of crisis and persecution, he often loses his sense of rational judgment. Peter calls the Christians to rational patterns of thought. Second, he calls them to an attitude of "self-control" or serious-mindedness. Patterns of thought are to be rational and serious, with all consequences considered. The primary consideration is to seek the Lord's will, for this is both rational and serious. Verse 7 closes with a call to "prayer," in recognition of the source of wisdom to make decisions in the midst of crisis (cf. James's call to ask God for wisdom—James 1:5). Peter is here calling Christians to prayer mixed with sound judgment and a sober spirit. Third, he calls upon them to "love each other deeply" (1 Peter 4:8). The attitude of love is essential in dealing with stress, persecution, and temptation. He says "love covers over a multitude of sins." This is true from many angles. God's love covers over our sins; Christ's love covers over our sins; our love for others keeps us from sinning against them; and love makes us forgiving when we are wronged. Paul taught that love fulfills the law (Romans 13:8-10). *Agape* love seeks the well-being of the one loved and greatly enhances relationships with others (1 Corinthians 13) and with God (John 14:15).

With a clear mind, self-control, prayer, and love, we are to meet the needs of others. Peter chooses the word *hospitality* to describe our meeting others' needs. We are to welcome fellow sufferers to our homes; we are to feed and clothe them, if needed. Out of love, we meet needs, and thus all can survive the stress times that befall all believers.

Beyond "hospitality," Peter looks at the special "gifts" Christians receive. When he says that "each one should use whatever *gift* he has received" (1 Peter 4:10), he is referring to the gifts of the Spirit, the *charismata,* that Paul discusses in 1 Corinthians 12, 13, and 14. In the twelfth chapter, he sets forth the fact that every Christian receives some gift and is expected to minister with that gift as a functioning part of the body of Christ. Here, Peter declares that "each one" receives a "gift," an enabling from the Holy Spirit, to minister to others in the church—we are to "serve others" (1 Peter 4:10). Our use of our spiritual gifts is a "stewardship," a responsibility for which we will be held accountable (as seen in the parable of the talents; Matthew 25:14-30).

May I note here that some of the gifts were uniquely apostolic; that is, they were given to the apostles only. If they were passed on to others, they were passed on directly by an apostle by "the laying on of hands." (See Acts 8:18-20; 2 Corinthians 12:12; 2 Timothy 1:6.) The revelation and inspiration gifts and the miraculous, confirming gifts (Mark 16:20) were gifts of the apostles, while the general ministering gifts were distributed by the Spirit to all believers, and still are. Peter here divides these ministering gifts into two categories: speaking and serving (1 Peter 4:11). The enhanced enabling of a believer by the Spirit to speak included "prophesying" (proclamation), "teaching" (explanation), "encouraging" (counseling), and being "evangelists" (convincing concerning Christ). The serving gifts were "serving," "leadership" (organizing and overseeing), "contributing to the needs of others" (making and giving money to kingdom needs), and "showing mercy" (meeting the needs of those in severe circumstances). These gifts, listed in Romans 12:3-8 and Ephesians 4:11 are still in existence. Some of these are also included in the listings in 1 Corinthians 12:8-10, 28-30. Also included in these latter listings are some gifts in the domain of the apostles that had been passed on by their "laying on of hands."

Peter exhorts the gifted believers to use their speaking gifts to communicate the truth of God, and their serving gifts to meet needs, realizing that the strength comes from God. By using the manifold gifts of God, all of the needs of the believers could be met, even in the midst of the persecution.

The Purpose of Practicing the Gifts

Obviously, the purpose of ministering to others is to meet the needs of others and to make it easier for them to stay in the faith. But, even more importantly, the stated purpose is "that in all things God may be praised through Jesus Christ. To him be the glory and the power for ever and ever" (1 Peter 4:11). Our purpose in life is to glorify God, and we glorify God most fully when we do His will. We do His will most fully when we, in love, meet the needs of others and bring them to faith or keep them in the faith. God is also glorified by those to whom we minister with our resources and spiritual gifts. This is especially true if God is credited for the ministry, for the gift that enabled the ministry, and for the strength to serve. Another group that might glorify God as a result of our ministering to others is those who observe the service and mutual love of the believers. When loving ministering is taking place, God is glorified and people are helped.

The end is near, Peter reasons, because persecution is increasing. In light of this, believers should be serious, sober and in prayer, and should fervently love one another by hospitality and by using their spiritual gifts to meet needs and thus to glorify God.

Principle 15: Rejoice in Suffering (4:12-19)

The committed Christian should expect to suffer. Contemporary TV preachers often promise health and wealth to all who are faithful to Christ and, of course, to their TV ministries. They proclaim that if you really believe, you will not suffer ill health and God will bless you with wealth. They are saying what their listening audiences want to hear instead of what Christ warned would really happen to the committed Christian. In this segment, Peter calls upon his fellow believers to rejoice in the midst of the inevitable suffering that will be a part of their lives.

Expectation

"Dear friends, do not be surprised at the painful trial you are suffering, as though something strange were happening to you" (1 Peter 4:12). Peter strongly infers here that his readers had been warned that it would be hard, at times, to be a follower of Christ. It should come as no surprise if they face suffering. It should not be seen as something unusual. Instead, they should consider that they are sharing the "sufferings of Christ."

In this letter, Peter has already appealed to the suffering of Christ as an example that they were to follow (1 Peter 2:21; 4:1). Christ suffered every kind of pain possible. He suffered social rejection, hunger, thirst, and exhaustion. He was financially poor; He was physically beaten; He was unjustly tried; He was imprisoned and killed in a most painful death.

Jesus himself gave clear indication of the suffering aspect of discipleship. He warned potential disciples to "count the cost" before following Him. After Peter tried to intercede with Jesus about His announcement regarding His impending suffering in Jerusalem, Jesus warned Peter and the others, "If anyone would come after me, he must deny himself and take up his cross and follow me" (Matthew 16:24). He warned His disciples that they would be imprisoned, martyred, and even betrayed by their families. These teachings of Jesus were obviously passed on by the Twelve to the early Christians. Paul wrote to the young preacher, Timothy, that "everyone who wants to live a godly life in Christ Jesus will be persecuted" (2 Timothy 3:10-12). Peter has also warned his readers previously regarding this principle.

Christians should not expect the "health and wealth" syndrome of life. They should expect to be persecuted and to suffer.

Examination

Not only should suffering be an expectation of the believer, he should view it as an examination. How do we interpret the suffering we experience as followers of Christ? Some assume that it is punishment from God for severe wrongdoing. They reason that God punishes the most severe sinners now with pain, sickness, and persecution. Peter does not agree. He says the suffering is used of God as a test or an examination. His use of the phrase "painful trial" reminds us of his discussion of the purpose for the ordeal of the Roman persecution and cultural rejection the believers were experiencing (1 Peter 1:7). This "painful trial" purifies and proves. It purifies by getting us down to basic values, and it proves by seeing our faith survive it all. We know our faith is strong if we can stand under the pressure, and certainly God already knew. Additionally, the world knows how strong we are in our commitment to the Lord, for we stand firm in the face of adversity.

Peter further indicates that the suffering of the believer is the beginning of judgment, which begins with the "family of God" (1 Peter 4:17). God is using the present suffering of the Christians as an analogy of the future suffering of those who oppose God and do not obey the gospel of God. In other words, if they are causing God's people to suffer now, how much more will God cause them to suffer at judgment! Suffering and judgment, then, are equated. Our suffering is the world's judgment of us, and their suffering will be God's judgment of them. God is using our present suffering as a judgment, or testing, of our faith. It is, therefore, the early stage of the final judgment to come.

Emulation

In this segment, Peter urges Christians to view their own suffering as a participation in the suffering of Christ (1 Peter 4:13). When a Christian suffers for his faith, he is suffering like and for Christ. Paul said that he wanted to "know . . . the fellowship of sharing in his sufferings" (Philippians 3:10). In Colossians 1:24, Paul indicates that he viewed suffering as a continuation of the suffering of Christ: "I fill up in my flesh what is still lacking in regard to Christ's afflictions." Christ suffered for the salvation of man, and we are to emulate that suffering, to imitate it, to continue it.

In Romans 8:17, Paul indicates that suffering precedes glory in the life of a follower of Christ, just as it did in the experience of Christ. Christ suffered and then was glorified; so it is with Christians. "Everyone who wants to live a godly life in Christ Jesus will be persecuted" (2 Timothy 3:12).

In our segment here, Peter points out that, "If you are insulted because of the name of Christ, you are blessed, for the Spirit of glory and of God rests on you." Glory and suffering are put together, one with the other. The Christian who suffers is identifying with Christ and is sharing the glory of God that Christ had. We are emulating Christ; we are identifying with Him in suffering. Thus, to the early Christian mind-set, it was a privilege to suffer for Christ. It was the ultimate identification with Him.

Exultation

When a follower of Christ realizes that suffering in his life is a continuation of and an identification with the suffering of the Master, he is no longer humiliated; he is rather honored. Humiliation turns to exaltation. As a result, we are "overjoyed" (2 Peter 4:13). Our exaltation leads to exultation! We experience a bit of it now as the awareness of our emulation grows, but we shall experience it altogether and completely when we see Christ's glory and we are "glorified with Him."

In Romans 8:17, Paul refers to the principle that suffering is followed by glory for the Christian. "Now if we are children, then we are heirs—heirs of God and co-heirs with Christ, if indeed we share in His sufferings in order that we may also share in his glory." Suffering is worth it now as we realize we are emulating Christ and identifying with Him. Suffering will be fully worth it when we see Him in His glory and share fully in His glory. We shall be overjoyed. We shall exult.

Of course, we should expect no glory if we suffer "as a murderer or thief or any other kind of criminal, or even as meddler" (2 Peter 4:15). Peter inserts a warning here that not just any kind of suffering leads to glory. Justifiable suffering—that is, suffering for wrongdoing—should cause us to feel "ashamed." But if we suffer for the gospel, we should feel no shame, but should rather exult. We should "praise God that [we] bear that name" (2 Peter 4:16). God is being glorified by our suffering; we have passed the "judgment" of God. We can count on Him to do us right as we have done the right!

CHAPTER FOURTEEN

Closing Exhortations

1 Peter 5:1-14

Effective leadership is always crucial in the church, but it is most crucial in times of stress. Christ was a leader—a servant leader, a leader by example. In His relationship with the apostles, He was developing leaders for His church—servant leaders, role-model leaders. They, in turn, were to develop servant leaders from among the disciples that would come after them. Jesus told the Twelve to teach later disciples all that He had taught them (Matthew 28:20). Among those principles is the servant-leader concept.

Principle 16: Follow Your Leaders (5:1-5)

During the last half of their first missionary journey, Paul and his team returned to the churches they had previously established, "strengthening the disciples and encouraging them to remain true to the faith." Then they "appointed elders" to continue the work after the missionaries had left (Acts 14:21-24). These elders were mature men in the local fellowships whose task it was to oversee the spiritual development of their fellow disciples as they grew in Christ.

In Acts 15, we see that the apostles and elders met together with Paul and Barnabas to resolve a doctrinal matter among the churches. In Acts 20, we see that Paul met with the elders from Ephesus for a final word of encouragement and exhortation about guarding the flock over which the "Holy Spirit" had made them (gifted them to be) overseers. The apostles were preparing a future leadership for the church, something that was desperately needed if the revolution was to continue.

Peter also gives words of exhortation to the leaders among the churches. He challenges them to be leaders worth following, the kind of leaders of whom the "Chief Shepherd" (1 Peter 5:4) would be proud and whom He would reward. They needed to be the kind of leaders that could be followed in the midst of stress.

Mandate for Leadership

Peter gives this mandate, this "appeal" to the elders, as a "fellow elder" (1 Peter 5:1). He looked upon his role in the church as being that of an "elder"—an overseer of the fellowship of followers. He was both an "apostle" and an "elder." I believe that the elders (pastors, overseers) are the heirs of the oversight task of the apostles. The apostles were initiators of the truth—the message of the New Covenant. They were also confirmers of the truth through their miraculous powers. And they were overseers of the church. The revelation and confirmation aspect of their work was completed by them, but their ministry of oversight needed to be continued. This continuation is in the pastor/elder role today.

Peter mandates the elders to suffer in order to receive glory, as Christ had done and as Peter himself was doing. Then he tells them, "Be shepherds" (1 Peter 5:2). Shepherds guard and protect their sheep. They lead and guide them.

Paul had exhorted the Ephesian elders less than a decade earlier to "be shepherds" (Acts 20:28). He exhorted them to "keep watch" over themselves and the flock, watching out for "savage wolves" who would "not spare the flock." These would be persecutors from outside and false teachers from within. Elders are shepherds—they are to guard the flock.

Peter also tells the elders to serve as "overseers" (1 Peter 5:2)—as guides and directors. In addition to protecting the sheep from the wolves, ancient shepherds led the sheep to grass and water. Leaders are mandated here to be sure the disciples are taught, counseled, and disciplined. Guard and guide is the mandate. If this is to happen, the leaders must lead, but, also, the flock must follow. In the midst of stress and suffering, the church must follow its leaders. The leaders must be willing to suffer, if need be, just as Christ had suffered and as Peter was suffering.

Motives of Leadership

After exhorting the elders to guard and guide, Peter explains to them the proper motives for leadership. Only properly motivated leaders can be Christlike leaders. Only properly motivated leaders can lead in the midst of stress in a church. Only properly motivated leaders are worth following at any time, and especially when the going gets tough.

Peter uses two phrases to describe proper motivation for leadership in the church. The first is, "Not because you must, but because you are willing" (1 Peter 5:2). An unwilling, resentful leader is not a strong leader. He will fail under pressure and stress. If he fails, the church is weakened, and immature Christians will falter. A gifted, mature man will want to lead—to be used of God. He will be leading voluntarily, gladly, "as God wants [him] to be." He will not quit when the going gets tough.

The second motivation for leadership is "not greedy for money, but eager to serve" (1 Peter 5:2). A leader who is only in it for the money or for the power and esteem will be a poor leader. There will come a time or situation when he will conclude that the money isn't worth it. If he leads in order to obey Christ and to meet needs out of love, he will be there in all situations. He leads because he is "eager to serve," to meet needs. That's the reason Christ came—because He loved us and wanted to meet our needs. He sought what was best for us, even to the point of death. He sacrificed His Heavenly glory and suffered for us out of love. Leaders in the early church, including elders, were sometimes paid to meet their physical needs while they served the church (1 Corinthians 9:7-12; 1 Timothy 5:17). But this is not the reason they led—to receive a salary. They led because it was God's will and they wanted to serve.

Method of Leadership

Peter uses an interesting phrase to indicate the method of leadership expected of the elders in the church. He says they are to serve, "not lording it over those entrusted to you, but being examples to the flock" (1 Peter 5:3). The negative part of this exhortation, "not lording it over," means the elders are not to lead by issuing orders and edicts. They are not to lead by "bossing" from an ivory tower of non-involvement. They are not to lead by telling others what to do while they stand by idly watching or, even worse, criticizing. Leadership is not a "master-slave" relationship in the church.

Peter says the elders are to get involved; they are to lead by being "examples to the flock." A leader should be able to say, "Do as I do," not simply, "Do as I say." The kind of leadership taught here is role-model leadership, like that of Christ. Leadership by example is far more effective than leadership by edict.

In the midst of suffering, if the early Christians saw an elder enduring and yet remaining faithful, they could also remain faithful. Seeing is a better way to learn than simply hearing in every case. Statistics have been kept in educational circles that show that if one both hears and sees something, he will retain it much better than if he merely hears. Christians need to hear and see from the leaders of the church what it means to be a Christian.

Manifestation Coming to Leaders

Peter reminds the elders that Christ is the "Chief Shepherd," and that He will "appear": He will return into the flow of human history (1 Peter 5:4). He will be "manifested" to Christians when we "see him as he is" (1 John 3:2). At the coming of Christ, the elders will receive special attention. They will be held more accountable (Hebrews 13:17), but they shall also receive "the crown of glory that will never fade away" (1 Peter 5:4).

The "crown" is a victor's wreath awarded in the ancient Olympic games and other sporting events. These wreaths were placed on the winners' heads after the race was completed. The Olympic wreath in ancient days was made of vegetation and eventually withered. Peter assures the elders that, if they remain true to their faith and to their oversight, they will receive a winner's crown that will last forever—it "will never fade away" or wither. The reward of Christ to faithful leaders in His church will be an eternal wreath! At Christ's return, there will be resurrection and reward.

Principle 17: Humble Yourselves (5:5-14)

In reminding the "young men" to be "submissive to those who are older" (1 Peter 5:5), Peter is applying the principle of humility for all Christians. He quotes Proverbs 3:34, "God opposes the proud but gives grace to the humble" (1 Peter 5:5). Submission has been a major theme in Peter's letter—submission to whatever the world throws at us, to whatever the Lord allows to happen to us. It takes humility to submit. Younger people are to submit to the more mature in life, especially to the elders of the church. But the broader concept of submission is now brought out by Peter, even submission to suffering for a time.

Humiliation

Peter begins verse 6 with an exhortation, "Humble yourselves." This means we are to submit to God and to His will for us. We do that, in this case, when we are patient with our situation of suffering. When we are patient, we demonstrate that we trust God to care for us and to strengthen us through the trials we face. Peter points out that we are submitting "under God's mighty hand." This is a reminder that Christians are in His care, even when the going gets tough. God allows Christians to suffer for a time, though never beyond our ability to bear it (1 Corinthians 10:13). If God, whose hand is mighty enough to deliver us immediately, chooses not to deliver immediately, then we are to accept—to submit to—God's choice. In order to do this, we must be "humble." We must view God as wiser than we, as well as stronger, in all areas of life—even in the area of our suffering.

This humiliation of submission to God's will takes on the form of trust. We trust in His "mighty hand," in His power to intervene when He decides to intervene. We are to "cast all [our] anxiety on him" (1 Peter 5:7). Suffering and stress cause anxiety—a sense of uncertainty about our future and our safety. We are to have constant awareness of His mighty hand—His power—in the midst of anxiety. We must remember that His mighty hand created us and our world. His power is without limit.

Not only are we reminded that we are "under God's mighty hand," we are also reminded that He "cares" for us (1 Peter 5:7). Not only is God mighty, He is loving and concerned. The knowledge that the almighty God loves us and is aware of our needs is reason enough to humble ourselves and submit to His care.

God's care for us is clear to the Christians, for we know God gave His unique Son to die in our place. He planned for our salvation even before He made us with a free will and in His image. He cared for us before we sinned, and He still cared for us after we sinned. He cared for us in His planned sacrifice of His precious Son. His care is also seen in His daily ministry to us and to all of His creation—the provisions He gives. He is still caring for us! So it seems it should be easy for us to submit totally to Him—to humble ourselves. Of course, we all have had experiences when it didn't seem so easy. We all need Peter's reminder.

Confrontation

The source of the suffering and stress to which God allows us to be subjected is our "enemy the devil" (1 Peter 5:8). Satan has been our enemy since the Garden of Eden. He is the enemy of God and the enemy of man. He seeks to destroy us as he "prowls around like a roaring lion looking for someone to devour." We are his prey. When he wins in our lives, it satisfies him as a meal of prey satisfies a ravenous lion. We confront Satan each day in our temptation to sin. We confront him in our setbacks and suffering. He wins, not when we are tempted and suffer, but when we lose faith in God in

179

the midst of our temptation and suffering. He wins when we submit to him instead of to God.

True, we are to trust God in these circumstances because of His strength and His love. But, in addition, we are to use our God-given strengths to prevail in the confrontations that we face in His name. Peter suggests that we be "self-controlled"—that we take these confrontations very seriously. Another word used to translate this Greek word is *sober*. We should be "self-controlled" in that we are not overconfident in the midst of our confrontations with Satan.

Peter says we are to be "alert," or watchful. We can never let down our guard and assume that Satan has left us for a while. Peter exhorts us to "resist him" in the confrontation (1 Peter 5:9). In doing this, we exercise our choice, our free will to say "no" to Satan and "yes" to God. John writes (1 John 4:4) that we can "overcome" the enemies because "the one who is in you is greater than the one who is in the world." We can resist because of the Holy Spirit's presence in our lives, working with our own free will.

Peter says we resist Satan by "standing firm in the faith" (1 Peter 5:9), continuing to believe in a God who loves and a Christ who died for us in the midst of life's stress. He closes this segment by reminding us that our "brothers throughout the world are undergoing the same kind of sufferings." We are not alone. Our fellow Christians all suffer with us. It is always encouraging if we know others are struggling and winning the victory.

Exaltation

Peter again calls our attention to the "God of all grace" (1 Peter 5:10). God is a God who gives gifts—forgiving gifts and empowering gifts. The present gifts He gives to the suffering saint include restoration—renewing our strength to the level it was before the stress of suffering and then going beyond. He will "make you strong," Peter promises, "firm and steadfast." While we are being "self-controlled" and "alert," while we are "resisting and standing firm" with all our might, He will "restore [us] and make [us] strong, firm and steadfast" (2 Peter 5:10). We do what we can do to resist, and He does the rest! The power He gives us comes through the Holy Spirit's presence in our minds and wills. It comes through the principles and promises of His given Word. It comes through the modeling and encouragement of other believers—through the church. It comes through His intervention in our life situations. It comes in many ways, but it all comes from Him.

It will all finally culminate for the steadfast believer when we are, in His time, called "to his eternal glory" (1 Peter 5:10). He has not called us to suffer forever—the suffering will end. Just as He has not called us to suffer without the strength He provides, even so He has not called us to suffer without the reward He has promised. After suffering will come exaltation. Out of our present suffering, we experience the exaltation of victory through His empowerments. And, one day, we shall experience the final exaltation following a life of stress when we receive His "eternal glory."

Getting Acquainted With 2 Peter

The author of this epistle is the author of 1 Peter, Simon Peter, the apostle of Christ. As was the first epistle, this letter was written to scattered Christians, many of whom lived in Asia Minor. First Peter dealt with the persecutions these Christians were facing from Rome and from the pagan culture. It dealt with the resulting stress upon the believers and upon their faith. This letter deals with the false teachings of that pagan culture, namely the Gnostic heresy as it was beginning to coalesce into what would become the major worldview of the Greeks and Romans of that time. Some deny Petrine authorship of this letter because the Gnostic heresy had not fully developed until the second century A.D. However, even though it was not yet fully developed, all the basic tenets of Gnosticism were present even in Peter's day.

As with virtually all heresies, Gnosticism did not spring up out of nowhere and appear on the scene of theological thought without warning. Late in Peter's lifetime, the seeds of this Graeco-Roman philosophy were already emerging. Thus, the chronology of Gnosticism presents no real objection to the Petrine authorship of this epistle, but rather confirms it.

Still in Rome, and nearing the end of his life, Peter wrote this letter to Jewish and Gentile Christians in Asia Minor as a follow-up to his first letter. He was no doubt concerned that this heresy would infiltrate the church and lead many astray, so he wrote this letter as a warning and as an encouragement to remain faithful. He knew that, when a Jew or a Gentile became a Christian, he did not leave behind all of his previous education, philosophy, and worldview. One's mind-set is not erased at conversion. Thus, when a Jew accepted Jesus as Messiah, he often retained his concepts from the Old Covenant with its rites and rituals. He might hold the view that a person must become a Jew to be a child of God. Therefore, by this view, a Gentile would need to become a Jewish proselyte by the accepted ritual, and then he could accept the Jewish Messiah as his personal Savior.

When a Gentile became a Christian, he also would often retain his pagan philosophies and worldview. The pagans had become quite adept at merging various philosophies into a single system. This practice, called syncretism, often combined ideas that were contradictory into a supposed unity of thought. What seem to us to be irreconcilable differences were accepted without question by the pagan mind. When the church came on the scene, proclaiming redemption in Jesus Christ, the pagan seized on that idea and attempted to blend it with traditional pagan ideas. The result was more pagan than Christian, and would develop into what came to be called "Gnosticism." This philosophy taught that the material world was created by a distant offspring of a perfect god. The more distant the offspring, the less perfect. It was this distant, less perfect, evil offspring of the perfect god that created our material world. This is how they explained evil in the world. All "matter" was evil intrinsically, and our bodies are matter. Therefore our bodies are evil by nature, and we are rendered incapable of being, or doing, good.

This pre-Gnostic view affected their view of Christ. They had a hard time accepting that Jesus could have been "God incarnate"— God in the flesh, for flesh was matter, and matter was evil. There were two heresies that emerged. The first group taught that Jesus was not really in the flesh; He only appeared to be so. He was a "flesh appearing ghost." John deals with this heresy in his epistles. The second group said that Jesus, the man, was adopted by God at His baptism, and deserted by God prior to His death. The Spirit of God entered the man Jesus for a time but did not become man, or flesh. The problems with these views are evident. If Jesus was not flesh, He did not take the sins of the world upon himself and actually "die for our sins." Without the real death of Jesus, the penalty for sin has not been paid. If Jesus was just a man who had the Spirit of God from His baptism until just prior to His death, then the man who died was not the sinless Son of God, taking upon himself the sins of the world. He was but a mortal, sinful man, dying as a martyr. We are still in our sins.

This philosophy also affected morals. If matter is evil and incapable of good, and our bodies are matter, that means man is incapable of ever doing good while he is in the flesh. Man cannot obey God. Man cannot give his body as a living sacrifice to God, as Paul commanded in Romans 12. Man cannot, even with the help of the indwelling Spirit, overcome the flesh.

Two groups emerged from this heresy. The first group taught that everything our flesh desires to do is evil, so we must not give in to these desires. If it feels good, you must not do it. If it tastes good, you must not eat it. If it makes you feel fulfilled, you must not experience it. It is essentially the same problem Paul resisted when he wrote that the false teachers taught, "Do not handle! Do not taste! Do not touch!" (Colossians 2:21). The second group was more "liberal." They taught that, since our bodies are evil and not capable of moral good, it is useless to try to restrain them. With our minds, we believe in Jesus as Savior, but we allow our bodies to do what they will. To them, it made no difference what one did as long as he believed. Saving faith had no resultant commitment to the holy life-style, for the holy life-style was impossible for man in his evil flesh.

The primary focus of much of the Epistle of 2 Peter is upon this aspect of the emerging Gnostic heresy. Peter stresses that God has given the Christian the power for godliness and holiness. He warns against the false teachers who teach immorality in the midst of faith. He warns that deep immorality can cause a loss of one's faith and, thus, of his salvation.

There are several aspects of Gnosticism that are not addressed in this epistle. The most logical explanation for this is that such issues would not emerge until the second century. This, then, supports the idea that Peter did, indeed, write this letter in the first century, probably very shortly before his death in A.D. 68.

It should be noted that 2 Peter and Jude deal with much the same subject matter—this emerging Gnostic heresy. Some believe that Jude may have collaborated with Peter in dealing with the problem these false teachers.

CHAPTER FIFTEEN

Resources for Perseverance

2 Peter 1:1-23

The emerging Gnostic heresy taught that man, being flesh, was completely incapable of doing good. Such an idea could easily discourage struggling Christians. In the face of strong opposition, they might say, "What's the use? I cannot do good anyway. Why should I even try to resist?" Immediately, Peter gives two principles to discredit this false view and to explain that the Christian does have resources for perseverance. First, Christians have power for godliness (2 Peter 1:1-11). Second, they have a certain word from God (2 Peter 1:12-23).

Principle 1: You Have Power for Godliness (1:1-11)

Peter sensed the lordship of Christ very deeply. He saw Jesus as Lord not only because of who He is, but because of what He has done for us and what we owe Him. We owe Him a debt we can never repay. He has given us life—eternal life with the Father! So he calls himself a "servant" (2 Peter 1:1), a bond servant or debtor servant. We are all bond servants; we all owe the same debt that can never be repaid. (See the author's comments on 1 Peter 2:18 in chapter 11, above.)

As an "apostle," Peter claims authority. Though a servant, he is a servant with apostolic authority and power. His authority comes from Christ, not himself, for he is the Lord's "servant and apostle." His readers, also servants of Christ, will do well to heed what he says to them.

He addresses this letter to those who have received the faith, the truth about Jesus as Messiah and God, and the truth from Jesus about salvation and life-style. This faith and salvation come by the "righteousness" of our God and Savior, Jesus Christ. He was righteousness. We are declared to be righteous by faith in Jesus as Savior and as Lord.

Peter gets right down to business here as he begins dealing with the faulty assumption regarding the Christian's inability to live the holy life before God. He reminds the readers of their "call." He presses home the idea of their power for holiness, given by divine power. He says that Christ "called us by his own glory and goodness" (2 Peter 1:3). We are "called" by Christ's glory in that we believe because of His divine power manifested by His miracles and His resurrection from the dead. He showed power over disease, nature, and even death. He was seen again after being dead. John wrote in his Gospel, "We have seen his glory, the glory of the One and Only, who came from the Father, full of grace and truth" (John 1:14). We believe that His claims are true because He proved them by His manifestations of power!

We also are called by His "goodness"—His moral nature. Lifestyle has something to do with our faith. If Jesus had worked miracles, but had lived an immoral life outside of God's revealed will, we could not believe He was divine. God is holy—He is perfectly moral. Jesus was morally perfect, yet He was in flesh! We are called by His moral excellence! This concept ran directly counter to the growing Gnostic teaching, which taught that "the flesh is incapable of any good." Countering this Gnostic threat, of course, was exactly Peter's intent.

Not only is a part of our "call" the morality of Jesus, but Peter also points out that one of the benefits of being called is the reception of "everything we need for life and godliness." Get that? His grace is sufficient to save, and His power is sufficient to change our lives—our life-style. He has given us, by His divine power, all of the resources we need for godliness!

An extensive list could be compiled to comprise what "His divine power has given us," but space limits us to just a few. Since Peter focuses on "our knowledge of him who called us," we start with the source of that knowledge, the inspiration of the Holy Spirit. He inspired the testimony of the apostles and prophets who preached in the first century, and He inspired the writing of the New Testament to continue to declare God's propositional truth for the New Covenant even to our own time (2 Peter 1:20, 21). The concepts and principles of the Word are from Jesus, through the minds of the inspired apostles and prophets. Some of these writings were available even before Peter wrote. (See 2 Peter 3:15, 16.) This Word is a vital part of what He has provided for "life and godliness."

All of us, then, have this "knowledge of him who called us." Therefore, we have the power to understand and apply the inspired truth to our minds and lives. The Gnostics would teach that only a few receive this power, and they were the special "knowers." Peter says we have received "everything." Paul also speaks of this power to understand things of God in 1 Corinthians 2. In the early portion of the chapter, Paul deals with the inspiration given to the apostles, but later in the chapter he deals with the believers' ability to understand the principles inspired by the Spirit (1 Corinthians 2:14, 15).

We have "everything we need for life and godliness." Peter is talking about more than just knowing the truth. And he is talking about more than just understanding it. He is talking about integrating it into our choices of will. We have these gifts so that we can live a life of "godliness," so that we can "participate in the divine nature and escape the corruption in the world caused by evil desires" (2 Peter 1:4). Again, this runs counter to the Gnostic philosophy that flesh and divinity are incompatible. Not only could Jesus be God in flesh, but fleshy humans can share in the "divine nature." This participation comes from the indwelling Spirit of God. Romans 8:1-14 clearly states that all Christians have the Holy Spirit and, thus, the power to overcome the flesh as a process of maturing (Romans 8:13). The "flesh" in Romans 8 is the same as the "corruption . . . caused by evil desires" Peter says we can escape when we answer "him who called us" (2 Peter 1:3).

The Process of Our Participation (5-9)

God has given us "everything we need for life and godliness" (2 Peter 1:3), the tools we need to be victorious. He has given us His Spirit, whom we did not have before! Now Peter points out what we must supply—our response to the "call," if you will—in the process of attaining behavioral godliness.

Note the phrase, "Make every effort" (2 Peter 1:5). We must do our part with determination and consistency. We must be constant and committed. The power is from God, the participation is from us, with diligence!

Peter lists several steps that we must take in the process that leads to godliness (2 Peter 1:5-7). The basic step is "faith." This is our belief resulting from His "glory and goodness." This is our conviction that Jesus is the Messiah (Christ), and that He is God and Lord. If Jesus is the unique Son of God, and we have accepted Him as Lord of our lives, we should trust what He did as being right and what He

189

said as being true. This faith is our reference point for godliness. If Jesus did it, we do it. If He said it, we obey it.

The second step is "goodness," and we are to supply it, adding it to our faith (2 Peter 1:5). This is our commitment to the Lordship of Christ. This is our determination to do His will, to become like Him in how we think, feel, and behave. In fact, it is the same term Peter used to describe Jesus, "who called us by his own glory and *goodness*" (2 Peter 1:3). The "goodness" we seek, then, is our commitment to making His values and His system of relationships our own.

The third step is "knowledge." Once we accept Jesus as Lord, and supply the desire to be like Him in "goodness," we must attain to knowledge—the knowledge of Him and His will for our lives. This knowledge is of Him personally. We come to know, through the Word, what He was like. We see how He behaved and how He responded to various situations: to temptation, to human need and suffering around Him, and to the will of the Father. Knowledge also is contained in our discovery of the teachings of Jesus. We must come to know what He said about life, relationships, values, priorities, purpose, meaning, the future—all of life. We must "know Him and His will" personally, and experientially.

The fourth step is "self-control" (2 Peter 1:6). Faith in Jesus and the desire to do His will, even followed by knowing His will, are not yet enough. We must participate in the process of making moment-by-moment choices to do His will. We are at war with the flesh, even though we have the Holy Spirit. Paul confessed this in Romans 7:14-25. He confessed that he still had a battle with the flesh—his old self. He still struggled to subject it to the will of God! The Holy Spirit empowers, but we still must make the choice of "self-control." Our will plays a part in the process.

The fifth step is "perseverance," constantly, consistently choosing the way of the Spirit. When we make the right choice that first time, then it's easier to do the second time. Then it is easier to make the right choice the third time, and the fourth, and on and on—until making right choices becomes an integral part of our life-style, of our character. Repetition is a vital part of integrating the new life into our actual life-style.

The sixth step is "godliness," a relationship to God that results in our being more like Him. Out of faith, our desire, our knowledge, and our perseverance, we are coming into a deeper relationship with God. We want to worship Him more and praise Him. We want to celebrate before Him because of the new life He has given us in

Christ, and the new life we are actually discovering in our daily walk. We are closer to Him in faith and now in behavior!

The seventh step is "brotherly kindness." This new character expresses itself in our relationships to others. The more "godly" we become, the more we will look to the needs of others. We will become others-centered instead of self-centered. We will begin to look upon others as our brothers and treat them with sensitivity and kindness.

The final step indicated by Peter is "love"—the sacrificial meeting of the needs of others. John writes that "God is love" (1 John 4:8). If we are to be godly, we must be controlled by sacrificial love, love that meets needs. Jesus called this love the identifying mark of His disciples (John 13:35). Love is said by Paul to be the basis of all that the law taught—if we love, we will instinctively not steal, lie, commit adultery, commit murder, or covet the possessions of others (Romans 13:8-10). This love is the summation of godliness, of maturity in Christ.

The Promises of Our Participation (8-11)

Peter points out that, if we are in this process, we will find our efforts at becoming like Christ not to be useless or unfruitful (2 Peter 1:8). But, he warns, if we are not in this process, we are "nearsighted and blind," and likely to be forgetting our purification from our former sins (2 Peter 1:9). In other words, it is dangerous to fail to make use of the power God has made available to us for godliness.

By participating in the use of God's resources for godliness, we can be "sure" about our "calling and election," and we will not stumble (2 Peter 1:10). Certainty is a vital ingredient to the salvation life. We can be certain of our "calling and election" of God if we still believe, if we want to do His will, if we are growing in the knowledge of His will, if we are in a posture of obedience to His will, and if we are growing in love. The apostle John gives these same signs of assurance in his first epistle. The three basic tests, though there are others mentioned, are the belief test, "Do I still believe?" (1 John 2:21-24; 4:13-15; 5:1), the righteousness test, "Do I still want to do His will?" (1 John 2:3-6), and the love test, "Am I growing in my desire to seek the well-being of others?" (1 John 3:14-19; 4:7, 8).

The result of being in this process of using God's provisions is that we will "never fall" and that we "will receive a rich welcome into the eternal kingdom of our Lord and Savior Jesus Christ" (2 Peter 1:10, 11). God saves through Christ, empowers by His Spirit, and calls upon us to participate. Thus, we can be assured of our ultimate salvation!

Principle 2: We Have a Certain Word From God (1:12-23)

Besides the problems with Christology and morals, Gnosticism brought with it the problem of false revelations. The Greek word *gnosis* (the root for *Gnostic* and *Gnosticism*) means knowledge or knower. The Gnostic teachers would claim special knowledge from the gods. This idea was already showing up in the church of Peter's day; the false teachers claimed to have extra truth—that is, truth not taught by Christ or the apostles. Only a few were "special knowers," according to this line of reasoning.

Peter has already begun to deal with this issue. In the previous section, 2 Peter 1:1-11, he has used the word *knowledge* five times (2 Peter 1:2, 3, 5, 6, 8).[11] Each time, it has been something available to all Christians, not an enlightened few. Now he expands his argument, dealing with the problem of authority and truth. He claims to have a "certain word" (2 Peter 1:19) from God to which his readers must pay attention! In the midst of the many claims and heretical doctrines of the false teachers, Peter proclaims again the "certain word" and calls his readers to continue in it—and in it alone! In the midst of many teachers of "continuing and special revelation" in our time, we, too, need this sure word.

The Source of the Certain Word

Peter makes clear what the certain word was not. First, it was not "cleverly invented stories" (2 Peter 1:16). The Graeco-Roman philosophers were constantly in quest of a new idea (cf. Acts 17:21). Paul wrote to Timothy that they had "itching ears" (2 Timothy 4:3). Peter is making it clear that this "certain word" is not like the many philosophies circulating in his day; it is not simply a new manmade idea appearing on the horizon of philosophical thought; it is a sure word from God.

Second, Peter says the source of his "certain word" is not a misinterpretation of some true revelation from God. He says that Scripture

---

[11]The words for *knowledge* in this text are *gnosis* (verses 5 and 6) and a form of *gnosis* that means "full knowledge": *epignosis* (verses 2, 3, and 8). Peter would allow no claim to special or more complete knowledge for an elite few; every Christian, he says, has "full knowledge."

did not come by personal "interpretation" from a human mind, but is inspired of the Spirit (2 Peter 1:20). Thus, it must be understood in the Spirit and understood by all that the Spirit has said in other Scripture. Certainly the human, natural mind is able to misinterpret Scripture and thus come up with wrong ideas and false doctrines. But the Scripture itself is true; it is from God.

Both problems still exist. The two main sources of false doctrine today are alleged continuing special revelations and faulty interpretation. The Mormons have a structured set of "latter" revelations, which they have codified in their *Book of Mormon*. Charismatic groups are less structured, purporting subjective continuing revelations. As for misinterpretation, there could not be the three hundred and more denominational differentiations if each group followed the Bible alone and understood it the same way. Since we understand it differently, there must be some degree of human misinterpretation in some, or every, fellowship.

In this segment, Peter also identifies the source of this certain word. If it is not simply a new philosophy or a misinterpretation of true revelation, what is it? Peter says it is a direct revelation from God through Jesus (2 Peter 1:14). Remember, the false teachers with whom Peter is dealing claim to be Christians, followers of Jesus. They believe in divine revelation. Some claim it. So Peter sets out to contrast the certain word he has to their pseudo-revelations.

First, Peter says his certain word was out of what he had *seen*. He says, "We were eyewitnesses of his majesty" (2 Peter 1:16), that is, the majesty and power of Jesus as He proved He was God. Peter had seen this one who claimed to be one with God prove His claims by mighty deeds of healing, raising the dead, multiplying food, calming stormy seas, walking on water, and living after He was dead. There was something else he had seen, and that was the life-style of Jesus. He had seen His morality—which stood out in bold contrast to growing Gnostic-type immorality. A part of the "majesty" was the holiness of Jesus.

The second source of the certain word was what Peter had *heard*. He had heard the teaching ministry of Jesus as He taught about himself and His claims of being God. He had heard Christ's teachings about morals, relationships, values, marriage, and forgiveness. Beyond that, He had heard the very voice of God testifying, "This is my Son, whom I love; with him I am well pleased" (Matthew 17:5). The incident had left a deep and convicting impression on Peter. The Father himself had spoken to Peter—and to James and John—and then added, "Listen to him!" The Father was saying that Jesus was His revelation. He was to be heard!

This sounds so much like John as he also dealt with the seeds of Gnosticism in his epistle. John claimed revelation as his source of knowledge, testifying to that "which we have heard, which we have seen with our eyes, which we have looked at and our hands have touched" (1 John 1:1). It was empirical revelation—all the human senses capable of perceiving and understanding were brought into play in the giving of the certain revelation.

The third source of the certain word was the moving of the "Holy Spirit" (2 Peter 1:20, 21). Jesus had promised the apostles He would send them the "Counselor," the "Spirit of truth" (John 16:5-16), to remind them of what He had taught (John 14:26), bear witness of Him and interpret His teachings and ministry (John 14:26, 27), and teach them the new truths they were not ready to receive during His ministry—truth from and about Jesus given by the Spirit (John 16:7-17). Paul discusses this concept of Spirit revelation in 1 Corinthians 2:1-13 and clearly differentiates between worldly philosophies and divine revelation. Peter here claims Spirit leadership for his certain word, and for all Scripture. Peter would agree with Paul's view of Scripture (cf. 2 Timothy 3:15-17), as well as with the other Scriptural warnings of certain teachers who would claim revelations that were not from Jesus (cf. Hebrews 1:1, 2; Galatians 1:6-12; Colossians 2:18).

The Substance of the Certain Word

The substance, or content, of the certain word was, first of all, a word *about* Jesus. It was about Christ's "power" and "majesty." It was about His "coming" (2 Peter 1:16), both His first coming as a suffering servant to die and to reveal the New Covenant, and the second coming in glory. Even as a suffering servant, Jesus claimed authority and reinforced those claims with mighty deeds. God the Father had claimed Jesus as His Son and called on His followers, then and now, to "listen to Him!" Jesus was the authoritative teacher, not those who claimed some special new knowledge! Jesus was divine, the Son of God, with "majesty and power"—the final word from God in all things. He is the one who could say, "All authority in heaven and on earth has been given to me" (Matthew 28:18).

Second, the substance of the certain word was *from* Jesus. Peter's teaching about life and morals were not really his; they were from Jesus. Peter had already introduced this concept in the first half of this chapter. In Christ, God has given us all we need pertaining to life and godliness. We see, then, that Peter is pointing his readers to Jesus as the authoritative teacher about life!

The Stability That Comes From the Certain Word

In this segment, Peter tells them—and us—why he is reminding them of the certain word: so they will remain strong in the Lord and stable in their commitment. Amidst the barrage of false teachers and their strange doctrines that opposed the authoritative word from Jesus, these Christians needed a stable faith. Peter's statements in this segment indicate a progression toward stability. Although Peter mentions them in reverse order, as if starting at the readers' current position and working back to the beginning, we will consider them here from beginning to the level of maturity.

The first step toward stability of faith is found in 2 Peter 1:19, "You will do well to pay attention," to hear and learn the truth. We begin the godly life by learning what the godly life is about from God himself. We must pay attention to the certain word.

The second step is, "Remember these things" (2 Peter 1:15). Having learned and understood them, we must come to integrate these truths into our pattern of thought. We must allow these truths to control our thinking. The way to do that is to keep them continually in our memory.

The third step is, "Refresh your memory" (2 Peter 1:13), or, as the New American Standard Bible translates, "Stir you up." We must not only learn and remember the Word, we must be "stirred up by it." It must affect our thinking and our feelings. It must affirm good behavior in us and cause us to feel guilt for bad behavior through our conscience. It must make us angry—stir us up—when we hear false teachings.

The final step toward stability in the certain word is found in 2 Peter 1:12, "established in the truth." Once we have learned truth, can remember truth, and are stirred with conviction by truth, we can be established and stabilized in truth.

CHAPTER SIXTEEN

Reasons to Persevere

2 Peter 2:1—3:18

When you read 2 Peter, you are left with the deep impression that Peter was convinced about the evil of the growing Gnostic heresy and the very real danger that it posed to his readers. Could he see prophetically into the future and see just how seriously this heresy and its teachers would wound the church in the centuries to come? And what of us today? Is there not still a danger from false teachers and false doctrine?

Peter has laid the foundation. He has made it clear that we have divine resources for perseverance in the midst of difficult situations (2 Peter 1). No Christian can say he was not equipped for dealing with the problems imposed on him by the hostile culture in which he finds himself. Now Peter will provide us with some good reasons for tapping these resources. In this segment (2 Peter 2:1-19), he paints a portrait of a false prophet, describing his character, his corrupt concepts, and his condemnation.

Principle 3: There Are False Teachers (2:1-19)

The Character of a False Teacher

We want to lift from these verses Peter's description of the personal character of the false teachers of his time. No doubt, as we do so, we will recognize many of the false treachers active in our own time as well.

First, he says several things about the *motives* of the false teachers. They "despise authority" (2 Peter 2:10). They refuse the confinements of the certain word (2 Peter 1:12-21) of the apostles. As a theological point of reference, they used their own ideas and personal revelations. They were "boastful" (2 Peter 2:18). A boastful man is unteachable; he thinks he knows everything. The false teachers of Peter's day claimed there were only a few who were the real "knowers." These special "knowers"—themselves—were the final word, even to the point of rejecting the teachings of Christ and of the apostles.

Twice Peter uses the word *greed* to describe the false teacher's motives of character (2 Peter 2:3, 14). This is no surprise. We know a greedy person is self-seeking. He may seek power or he may seek money. False teachers usually seek both. They constantly build themselves up and seek money for their "special projects," many of which have nothing to do with kingdom growth or expressing Christ's love to the world.

Peter also paints a picture of the morals of the false teachers. They are "shameful" or sensual (2 Peter 2:2). They are "creatures of instinct" (2 Peter 2:12). Here Peter is describing people who are driven by their wants, their instinctive drives. As we have already noted, these drives are given to us by God and are not evil when they are used properly and with self-control. But the sensual, instinct-driven person is controlled by his desires. He does not follow his conscience or the moral precepts given by God. The laws of God inform man how He intends for us to react to our drives and instincts. We develop a system of "oughts" in our conscience to control our "wants."

Peter goes on to say that the false teachers have "eyes full of adultery" (2 Peter 2:14). They are not only controlled by their wants, they are constantly looking and lusting for ways to satisfy their desires. Peter points out that this activity is unceasing sin; it is a matter of life-style.

The subject of the *methods* of the false teachers is the third aspect of character with which Peter deals. Here we see a progression: the false teachers start out seeming to be quite innocent and harmless, but they become extremely dangerous. In 2 Peter 2:1, Peter says they are "among the people." They appear to be part of us and may really consider themselves to be a part of the church of our Lord. They identify themselves as Christian, as followers of Christ. But then, Peter says, they "secretly introduce destructive heresies." As a part of the group, they gradually, secretly, carefully introduce false teachings. In this case, it was the idea of the impossibility of God (who is good) to become flesh—thus "even denying the sovereign Lord" (2 Peter 2:1)—or of man (who is flesh) to do good. "Why struggle with the impossible?" they reasoned. "God understands and forgives, so go ahead and sin." The Biblical principle of salvation by grace was a golden door through which they entered with this heresy. Since we are saved by grace and not by moral perfection, they alleged that morality was impossible and irrelevant. There is a great difference, however, between being saying no one can be morally *perfect* and saying no one can behave with any morality *at all.* As Peter has already explained, "His divine power has given us everything we need for life and godliness" (2 Peter 1:3). These false teachers were twisting the Scripture and citing their own alleged revelations as authority, using, in Peter's words, "stories they have made up" (2 Peter 2:3).

After being secretive at first, they gradually become more "bold and arrogant" (2 Peter 2:10). Once the false teachers gain power, they become more blatantly heretical and more public and open in their proclamation of false ideas. They understand what people want to hear, and they know how to play on their wants. They keep "appealing to . . . lustful desires" so they can "entice people" (2 Peter 2:18).

Finally (and reassuringly), Peter says they are temporary. They fail to show any real substance. They are "springs without water" and "mists driven by a storm" (2 Peter 2:17). They are here today, get their "converts" and their money, and are gone tomorrow. But they are not gone from God's attention!

The Corrupt Concepts of the False Teachers

As we have seen repeatedly, the first aspect of the heretical teachings of these false prophets has to do with *morals.* This is Peter's chief concern in this epistle. This is where it usually begins, with moral freedom resulting in immoral behavior as a pattern in the Christian's life-style. Seldom does the false teacher begin with an attack on Christ. He begins by saying what our instincts want to hear—a concept of freedom to do, experience, and attain anything we desire. We also want to hear that while having this freedom we can "stay in God's grace." Peter uses several words and phrases in this segment to describe his view of this false notion that the Christian is free to be immoral: "shameful ways" (2 Peter 2:2), "corrupt desire of the sinful nature" (2 Peter 2:10), "carouse in broad daylight" (2 Peter 2:13), "appealing to the lustful desires" (2 Peter 2:18), and "promise . . . freedom, while they themselves are slaves of depravity" (2 Peter 2:19). They sold people on the notion that they were free to do whatever felt good, looked good, gave them power, or made them appear good in the eyes of others, as long as they still "believed."

The opposite view, not directly dealt with here, held that all bodily instincts are intrinsically evil, so we must deny all desire! This is false doctrine as well, and Paul deals with this aspect in his Colossian letter. Our drives are not evil in and of themselves. It is their misuse that is sin. Their proper use before God is "righteousness." This element of the developing Gnostic heresy was evidently not strong in the churches to which Peter was writing, so he does not mention it. It is a problem today, however, with certain sects that teach a rigid system of self-denial as a means of attaining righteousness and salvation.

The second aspect of the corrupt concepts of the false teachers had to do with their *Christology*. Peter points out that the false teachers were guilty of "even denying the sovereign Lord who bought them." As we have already pointed out, this heresy had two basic problems in the area of Christology. First, since flesh was evil and God was perfectly good, the one group said God could not become flesh. The other group taught that Jesus was just a man in whom God's Spirit dwelt for a time from His baptism by John until just before His death. In contrast, the apostle John taught "every spirit that acknowledges that Jesus Christ has come in the flesh is from God, but every spirit that does not acknowledge Jesus is not from God" but is "the spirit of the antichrist" (1 John 4:2, 3). The Bible affirms again and again that faith in Jesus as Messiah and Son of God is essential to salvation.

These false teachers, then, began by teaching freedom for immoral behavior, and they ended with denying that Jesus was really the "sovereign Lord." And any who followed them down the path of immorality was sure to follow down the road of denying the Lord, as well. The natural end of a believer's going back into submission to his instincts and back into the world system of immorality is to deny the lordship of Christ in his life. He cannot say, "Jesus is Lord," or "Jesus is Master," while blatantly, continuously, willfully living a life that is outside His will. This person no longer even wants to please the Lord in life-style. This is not the typical Christian in struggle. This is the believer who makes an intellectual choice not to submit to Christ's will because he does not want to submit.

We have seen from this segment that the false teachers were to be recognized by their character and their corrupt concepts. As if that were not enough to show how undesirable they are, Peter now points out that they are under condemnation.

The Condemnation of the False Teachers

Peter makes it quite clear in these verses that God will judge the false teachers with a sure condemnation. He declares that they are "bringing swift destruction on themselves" (2 Peter 2:1). This indicates that their judgment by God will not take long. In fact, they are condemned already, for they love the darkness rather than the light (John 3:18-21). Peter puts it this way: "Their condemnation has long been hanging over them" (2 Peter 2:3).

To demonstrate the assurance that false teachers and those who practice gross immorality and deny the Word of God will be condemned, Peter uses some previous judgments of God as illustrations. He points out the judgment of the angels who sinned and were sent to "hell . . . into gloomy dungeons to be held for judgment" (2 Peter 2:4; cf. Jude 6). Peter does not specify what sin these angels committed. Perhaps he refers to those angels who rebelled with Lucifer in the Heavenly places, or—if the "sons of God" in Genesis 6:2 refers to angels—to those who intermarried with the daughters of men before the days of Noah. Whatever the case, angels were judged to condemnation by God.

The second illustration is in verse 5, where Peter reminds his readers of God's judgment in the days of Noah when He destroyed the "world of the ungodly," saving only righteous Noah and his family. The third reminder was of God's judgment of Sodom and Gomorrah in Abraham's day, preserving only Lot (2 Peter 2:6-8). All of these judgments came to those who totally flaunted the known authority and laws of God.

Peter is clear in pointing out the serious danger posed by the false teachers. He identifies their character and their corrupt concepts. He clearly states their sure condemnation. He makes it crystal clear that the false teachers of his time, and of ours, will also be put into the "blackest darkness" (2 Peter 2:17) to be held (2 Peter 2:4) until the final punishment that comes on the "day of judgment" (2 Peter 2:9).

We certainly have similar false teachers today! We still have those who teach that it does not matter how deeply one returns to the world, as long as one continues intellectual assent to the divinity of Christ. There are, alternately, those who teach that any joy in life is sin. There are also those who deny the divinity and the lordship of Christ. These are clearly false teachers.

There are some doctrines upon which we can disagree and allow misunderstanding and still not be considered condemned false teachers. But, when it comes to basic Christology and the doctrine of moral submission to the lordship of Christ, there can be no disagreement. This is not to say we must attain moral perfection. But we must take the attitude that says, "Jesus is Lord; therefore, my desire is to do His will in all areas of my life." We must, by the Spirit, be putting to death the deeds of the flesh (Romans 8:13).

Principle 4: We Can Be Enslaved Again (2:18-22)

Peter now points out the terrifying possibility of being enticed and enslaved again, being influenced by these false teachers. He is especially concerned about the new Christian, the immature follower of Christ. Peter is convinced that believers face a real danger from the work of the false teachers, then and now.

The Escape From the World

Peter uses the phrase *just escaping* (2 Peter 2:18), referring to the new or immature convert. Later, he describes all who accept Christ as Savior and Lord, new and mature Christians, as those who have "escaped the corruption of the world" (2 Peter 2:20). They have escaped the philosophies of the world, the wrong ideas, the wrong values, the wrong moral concepts, the wrong views of God, Christ, truth, and right. They have escaped the wrong behaviors of the world.

The world is full of those who live in contradiction to God's will in every area of life. We lie and steal in business; they are adulterous and unfaithful sexually; they are self-centered in all their dealings; they are rebellious against authority; they are committed to money and things as a value system. These wrong thoughts about God, Christ, and morals, and these wrong patterns of behavior are that from which we—as Christians—have "escaped."

We have seen *that from which* we have escaped; now Peter points out *how* we have escaped the world. We have escaped "by knowing our Lord and Savior Jesus Christ" (2 Peter 2:20). "Knowing our Lord" is, first of all, knowing *who He is*. We know Him to be divine, to be God in the flesh. We know who He is as a result of knowing of His miracles, His unique teachings, His lifestyle, His resurrection from the dead, His fulfillment of prophecy, and how He has affected the flow of human history.

Second, we have escaped by knowing *what He did for us,* and by coming to know Him as Savior. We are lured to Christ as Savior by His love as manifested on the cross. We are also saved by the sacrifice on the cross. By faith and commitment to Him, we experience the forgiveness of the cross. We come to know Him as Savior and are thus declared forgiven and cleansed from the "corruption of the world."

Third, we have escaped by knowing *what He taught* about life and morals. We put into practice the things He taught about lifestyle. Jesus dealt with everyday life-style decisions and behavior as a part of His teaching ministry. He taught about marriage, sex, money, selfishness, forgiveness, honesty, submission to authority, and priorities. Not only are His teachings reflected in the Gospels, but also in the epistles through the teaching ministries of the apostolic and prophetic writers who were taught by Christ, and/or instructed by the ministry of the Holy Spirit. We have escaped by knowing Christ's teaching about life-style, and by submitting to His principles.

The Enticements Back to the World

Satan is the great enticer, as seen from the beginning by his rebellious, deceiving enticement of Eve in the Garden. Satan audaciously sought to entice Christ immediately after His baptism by John in the Jordan. Satan also seeks to entice Christians after they are baptized. Before accepting Christ as Savior, we were under Satan's control; we were yet "in the world." He had us then. But once we have accepted Christ, Satan no longer has us. We are "in Christ." Satan still wants us, however, and he will try to get us!

John 10:27-30 makes it clear that he is not stronger than God, and 1 John 4:4 reassures us: "The one who is in you is greater than the one who is in the world." Even though Satan cannot steal us on his own, however, he can still lure us and entice us. Satan knows we can walk away from God by our own choice, so he works to entice us through the false teachers.

Peter says the false teachers use "boastful words" (2 Peter 2:18). They claim special authority, special revelations, special knowledge. The false teachers were arrogant and "boastful" in that they claimed to know more than Jesus and the apostles. They claimed superior truth and insight into reality. They arrogantly taught a false Christology, saying Christ had not really come "in the flesh." Of course, the dangerous implications of that heresy we have already explained.

These arrogant enticers also taught, as enticers today still teach, immorality as a way of life. They appeal to the "lustful desires of sinful human nature" (2 Peter 2:18). They appeal to our instinctive "wants" and promise "freedom" (2 Peter 2:19) in their use. Every person, both saved and unsaved, still lives in the flesh and is affected by instinctive drives that cry out to be satisfied. Our conscience is developed to control our use of these drives. Our conscience limits our "freedom" to use the drives in any way we choose. Our conscience is trained by parents, teachers, and peers. The Christian's conscience is retrained by the Holy Spirit through the concepts of the Word of Christ, the moral principles of Jesus. These arrogant false teachers seek to "untrain," or "retrain" again, the Christian conscience to give "freedom" to do whatever the bodily instincts want to do. But Peter points out that this is a false "freedom" that they offer, for the one who gives in totally to his instincts becomes "a slave" to them (2 Peter 2:19). These false teachers, and their followers, were not really free at all. They were simply slaves of the world again!

So we see that Satan works through the false teachers who tell us what our instincts want to hear about freedom to sin, and that results in our being enslaved again to the world. This is the way that we are enticed.

The Entanglement in the World

As a result of the enticements of the false teachers, the new and immature Christian can begin to be affected in how he thinks. Peter uses the word *entangled* to describe going back into the world a bit at a time (2 Peter 2:20). This word describes intellectual dabbling in false ideas. The false ideas about Christology and the false ideas about morality begin to enter our thoughts. Most often this process begins with false ideas about morality. Grace is used as a license to sin. The power of the flesh is considered to be unconquerable, even with the aid of the Holy Spirit. The principles of freedom in Christ are misunderstood. The false teachers—and those who accept their teaching—reason that, since nothing is unclean in and of itself, we are free to use and do all things. Gnostic reasoning said that everything was unclean and that we are helpless to do anything else but submit.

However you reach your immoral conclusion, Satan is winning you back to the world.

This wrong thinking leads to dabbling in wrong behavior. Just dabbling, mind you. We usually rationalize that we are not sinning as much as others; therefore we are behaving righteously, at least relatively. A little sin here, another there. "We can't be expected to be perfect," we reason. Subtly, this dabbling becomes a part of our life-style, a pattern of our behavior. Our thinking gradually becomes dominated by the world, and that results in our behavior's becoming dominated.

The Enslavement Back Into the World

The trouble with dabbling in the world is that one becomes entangled to the point of being "overcome" (2 Peter 2:20); he becomes "a slave" (2 Peter 2:19). It is hard to determine the dividing line between enticement, then entanglement, and finally enslavement. All of us are enticed, and most of us become a bit entangled from time to time. Some are finally enslaved again by the world.

Peter points out that such people have "known the way of righteousness" but have "[turned] their backs on the sacred command that was passed on to them" (2 Peter 2:21). This is crucial to understanding the difference between enticement, entanglement, and enslavement. What is this "sacred command" from which the enslaved have turned? In 1 Timothy 6:11-16, Paul speaks of "fleeing" the lures of money and immorality and pursuing righteousness. He speaks of fighting the good fight of faith in order to take hold of eternal life.

Paul points out that the basis of this struggle is the "good confession," that which Jesus testified before Pontius Pilate. He refers to the question, "Are you the Christ?" to which Jesus answered that He was. Paul continues his charge and the flow of thought concerning the "good confession" by telling Timothy to "keep this command without spot or blame" (1 Timothy 6:14). The command that is basic to being a Christian is to believe in Jesus as the Christ, the Son of God. In other words, through the route of gross immorality, the danger to the new and immature Christian is that he will finally come to deny Jesus as Christ and Lord.

In 2 Peter 2:1, Peter points out that the heretical teachers would "secretly introduce destructive heresies, even denying the sovereign Lord who bought them." The same heresy, what would come to be known as "Gnosticism," faced Jude and the Christians to whom he wrote. He summarized the false teaching with two characteristics of these "godless men": (1) they "change the grace of our God into a license for immorality" and (2) they "deny Jesus Christ, our only Sovereign and Lord" (Jude 3, 4). It usually happens in that order—the enticement to immorality, then the denial of the lordship of Jesus Christ. One cannot, for long, live in gross immorality without denying the authority and lordship of Christ, whose teachings the grossly immoral person is refusing to follow.

Peter points out that "they are worse off at the end than they were at the beginning. It would have been better for them not to have known the way of righteousness" (2 Peter 2:20, 21). With knowledge and blessing comes responsibility. Ignorance cannot be claimed. They have heard and accepted the truth, but then they rejected it. Thus, they have denied the only source of their salvation. The one who has not heard still has the possibility of believing and being saved yet before him. But these false teachers and their followers have now rejected their only chance at life—they have rejected Christ.

In addition, they have a negative effect on other believers and on the world, which discounts the reality of such a one's conversion. God will hold accountable those who once believed but have then openly denied Christ to live an apostate life-style. In a rather straightforward and picturesque analogy, Peter compares such a decision and life change to a dog returning to his vomit and a pig returning to the mire.

God never quits loving us. The Father is stronger than Satan, who cannot steal us from the Father's hand. The Holy Spirit, who is in us, is greater than Satan. God will never change His mind about salvation by grace, and no one can accuse the saved person at judgment. All of this is Scriptural truth and gives us assurance. However, it is also true, according to this text, that the believer can decide, by his own choice, to return to gross immorality and to become so hardened by sin that he no longer cares for the things of the Spirit. Continuing in such a life-style, the former believer ultimately reaches, as it were, a point of no return, where repentance is no longer an option. He comes to deny Jesus as Master and Christ, and thus loses his salvation! (See also Hebrews 6:1-8; 10:19-31.)

Principle 5: The Day of the Lord Is Coming! (3:1-18)

The false teachers and the fallen believers seem to be getting away with their heresy. God does not seem to be doing anything about it. There does not seem to be any accountability for the gross immorality practiced and taught by the heretics; no God-given consequences. Peter reminds his readers that the day of the Lord is coming with certainty. The false teachers have been saying that judgment was not coming. Peter refutes this false teaching by pointing out the weakness of their arguments and reminding them again of what he has previously taught them regarding the second coming and the judgment. He even mentions that he has written them before, and is now writing to them again in order to "stimulate you to wholesome thinking" (2 Peter 3:1) about the teachings he has given them, that the Lord himself had spoken, and that the prophets of old had predicted.

The Promise of His Coming

First, Peter reminds them of the promise of Christ's coming again. Jesus had told them He would come again (see, for example, John 14), and that His return would be accompanied by judgment (cf. the parable of the talents, among others). The angels had announced His return at the event of the ascension, that He would return again in the same manner the apostles had seen Him go (Acts 1:10, 11). The apostolic teachers and writers, including Peter, had clearly taught what Jesus had taught them regarding the return of Christ in glory and the judgment.

That the second coming of Christ will be accompanied by judgment is certain (2 Peter 3:10-13). This judgment will be against all of creation, which fell at Adam's sin. In verse 10, Peter points out that the earth and its works will be burned up in intense heat. He says, "The present heavens and earth are reserved for fire" that is, they are "kept for the day of judgment and destruction of ungodly men" (2 Peter 3:7). From this, we see the judgment will be by fire, and that the ungodly people will be a part of the fire judgment. These include the false teachers who have denied Christ and the moral precepts of Christ and the Father. We see that fallen man, his works, and his environment will be judged by fire and the intense heat of judgment. Verse 10 also states that these events of the day of the Lord will come like a "thief," or unexpectedly. We are aware of the danger of a thief, but we do not know for sure when he will come. Thus it is with judgment. We know it is coming, but when?

Not only did the promise include the second coming of Christ and judgment of the fallen creation, but it also included the new heavens and earth (2 Peter 3:13; cf. Revelation 21). A whole new environment will be brought into being by God after judgment to replace the destroyed fallen environment. Note also the phrase, "the home of righteousness." This indicates that sin, Satan, and sinners will not be there. Only forgiven sinners will dwell there.

The Gnostic heretics will not dwell there, nor will those who follow their false teachings.

Peter has said that his readers already know these truths, and he is simply reminding them of them. They needed to hear these truths again in face of the false teachings. So do we!

The Problem With the False Teachers

The sources of information regarding the promised coming were threefold (cf. 2 Peter 3:2): (1) The "holy prophets": the proven, accepted Old Testament prophets who predicted the first coming of the Christ—to suffer and die—and the second coming of the Christ to judge, rule, and reign; (2) the Lord: in His own teachings regarding His second coming; (3) the apostles: those whom Christ had personally taught and who proved their message was from God by the confirming miracles. Those who now oppose these truths about judgment and accountability are called "scoffers" by Peter (2 Peter 3:3). In order to get their ideas into the thinking of the new and immature Christians, they not only introduce their strange teachings about Christ and morality, but they are also "scoffing"—making fun of—the teachings that Peter and the other apostolic teachers have presented to them regarding Christ, morality, and judgment and accountability.

Peter summarizes some of their false reasoning in verse 4: "Where is this 'coming' he promised? Ever since our fathers died, everything goes on as it has since the beginning of creation." In other words, matter is still intrinsically evil; God did not really intervene in the flesh in Christ; and He will not intervene in the future. In verses 5 through 7, Peter answers this false idea by reminding the readers that the creation brought change, for it was out of water, "the surface of the deep" (Genesis 1:2), that the physical creation emerged by God's creative will—from water to land and water. From water came living creatures in the water, on the land, and in the air. All of the creation process was change. God intervened after the "beginning" by changing that which was into that which it became. Then Peter argues that another intervention came from God that also involved water. This time it was a form of judgment that brought change: the flood. The flood judgment changed history, destroyed much of mankind, and brought physical change to the earth's surface and the environment. So it was not true that things have always been the same, for God has intervened during the creation process and at the flood.

Peter goes on to point out that the next divine intervention will be by fire, which is "kept for the day of judgment." God will intervene again in the final judgment, which will do more than cosmetically change the environment; it will destroy it. Then God will remake all things anew. Thus Peter answers the arguments of the heretics, counteracting their evil influence on the minds of the new and immature Christians.

The Patience We Must Have as We Wait for His Coming

Peter now finishes up his counterattack upon the pre-Gnostic arguments by pointing out that God figures time differently from the way man figures it. Man determines time by his short life span and by his limitations of time and space. "With the Lord a day is like a thousand years, and a thousand years are like a day" (2 Peter 3:8). We should not judge God as being "slack" or "slow"—He will intervene in His time.

Rather than being "slow," Peter says, God is "patient" in putting off of His intervention and judgment (2 Peter 3:9). God is not judging and intervening now so that more might have an opportunity to repent. It is interesting to note that God does not wish for any to perish, but for "everyone to come to repentance" (2 Peter 3:9). Those who take the position of total divine determinism and "double election" have to deal with this stated desire on God's part—He wants *all* to repent. If He "causes" repentance, and He wants all to repent, all would then repent. No, He "allows" repentance and calls upon man to repent—He gives opportunity to repent and avoid judgment. It is man's choice to repent, and repent we must in order to be saved. God "grants" repentance in that He gives opportunity to repent and be forgiven of sins. But He also allows rejection.

Peter instructs us to regard God's "patience" to be "salvation" (2 Peter 3:15), pointing to Paul's teachings regarding the return of the Lord, which we find in his Corinthian and Thessalonian letters. Not only is God being patient and not slow, we should be patient with His patience, understanding that He delays to allow more to repent and be saved. We should pray for His soon return while at the same time being patient, for He knows best as to the time.

The Preparation for His Coming

Besides patience, the believer should have other attitudes and behavioral responses in his life as he anticipates Christ's coming and judgment. We should "look forward to the day of God and speed its coming" (2 Peter 3:12). We should live in constant anticipation and preparation for God's intervention, and we should hasten it by our prayers and our witnessing to call all to repentance. As we seek His coming and judgment, and as we call those to repentance that can be saved, we move His return forward. God knows who will come to repentance, even though He does not cause it. Perhaps when all have come that He knows will come, He will then intervene. Of this we cannot be certain, but this is one way of looking at how we "speed" the day of God.

Another way in which we stand prepared for that day is found in verse 14: "Make every effort to be found spotless, blameless and at peace." In the midst of the enticements of Satan through the false teachers, Peter challenges his readers to remain as believers and thus in a peace relationship with God—to remain in a moral life-style and be found "spotless" and "blameless" (2 Peter 3:14). We are spotless and blameless by God's declaration of the forgiveness of our sins through our acceptance of His offer of grace. We are also spotless and blameless in life-style as we seek to do His will in all of our moral decisions. If we still believe, and the continuing and overwhelming desire of our hearts and minds is to live within His will, then we are, indeed, spotless and blameless. We have not gone back into a pattern of sinfulness in faith and life-style. Peter is not talking about an occasional sin, but of a pattern of sin—a life-style of willful, rebellious, and flagrant sin.

A third challenge to the believer who is preparing for the day of God is to "be on your guard so that you may not be carried away by the error of lawless men and fall from your secure position" (2 Peter 3:17). This is another way of saying that Christians must remain believers in order to maintain their position of salvation. We must be on guard and continue to believe in spite of the onslaught of the false teachers and worldly philosophers. There is a member of my own family who was a Christian—who even gave thought to the ministry—who is now an agnostic. He bought into the philosophy of those who mocked the Christian faith while he was in college and later. The barrage of modern "Gnostics" enticed him, and he chose entanglement and slavery—much to my despair and heartbreak. I know this can happen to a believer.

Finally, Peter suggests that our preparation involves growth "in the grace and knowledge of our Lord and Savior Jesus Christ" (2 Peter 3:18). If we concentrate on His grace and gifts, and if we are growing in our knowledge of Him, then we will not be "blown here and there by every wind of teaching and by the cunning and craftiness of men," as Paul warns (Ephesians 4:14). Knowing the truth is the best defense against being lured by what is not truth. We grow in strength and assurance as we know about Christ, know His teachings, and come to know Him intimately through prayer, worship, and obedience.

When we are growing like that, then we can join in Peter's song of praise with which he closes the letter: "To him be glory both now and forever! Amen."

So be it—in your life and in mine.

INTRODUCTION

Getting Acquainted With Jude

This brief and very focused letter was written by Jude, the brother of James and a half brother of Jesus. (This relationship is clarified in Mark 6:3 and Matthew 13:55.) In Jude 1, the author clearly states his earthly relationship as a "brother to James." He could likewise have declared himself to be a "brother of Jesus," but chooses, instead, to call himself a "servant of Jesus Christ." In his mind, he prioritized the divinity and the messiahship of Jesus over the fact that he and Jesus were sons of the same earthly mother, Mary. Jesus was, first and foremost, the "Christ"—the Messiah of God!

Jude was not an "apostle," either. He separated himself from that office by a statement in verse 17, referring to the prediction of the falling away in the last days made by the apostles. More than likely, Jude, like James, had come to accept Jesus as the Messiah very late during Jesus' ministry, perhaps following the resurrection. Like James, Jude obviously had emerged to a known leadership role in the early church, or why else would he have presumed to write this letter to the church at large regarding the emerging dangers of the Gnostic heresy?

This is a general letter written to Christians, to whom he refers as "called," "loved," and "kept" (Jude 1). The recipients may have been Jewish Christians living in the Graeco-Roman culture in Asia minor or in Greece itself. At any rate, they were being affected by the same heresy as were those to whom Peter wrote. This heresy had as its source the principles of Greek philosophy, so it was in the non-Jewish cultures that it had its most significant impact. Jude would have his greatest influence among the Jewish Christians, as did his brother James, who emerged as a pastor-leader in the church in Jerusalem (see Acts 15). Also, Peter was a great influence on Jude, as seen in the great similarity between portions of 2 Peter and Jude in describing the false teachers. Peter's primary ministry focus was

Jews in Palestine in his early ministry, and Jews in the Graeco-Roman world later.

The emerging Gnostic heresy, which is the focus of Jude, contained two serious errors. The first had to do with Christology: the person and nature of Jesus. The second had to do with morality: the necessity and ability of the Christian to live a holy life. These were serious deviations in that what we believe about Jesus Christ and what we believe to be possible in the area of holiness greatly affect our walk in the Christian life-style. The letter of 2 Peter, the letters of John, and Colossians deal with this heresy at length, and other letters of the New Testament allude to it—even though it was not to emerge as a fully developed concept until the second century. Obviously, the seeds of heresy were sown early. The likely date of the writing of Jude is A.D. 68, about the same period of time Peter wrote 2 Peter to deal with this heresy. In fact, Peter and Jude may well have collaborated and conferred together as seen in the similarity of the letters.

Editor's Note

There are two compelling reasons for placing the comments on the book of Jude here rather than after the Epistles of John, as it appears in our New Testaments. This little book contains an amazing number of parallels with the book of 2 Peter—due, as the author suggests, to the fact that Peter and Jude faced much the same challenge and wrote at about the same time.

The other reason is more pragmatic. In the division of the writing assignment, we have asked one author to write on the writings of James and John and another to write on Peter and Jude. While separating James and John seems practical, isolating the little book of Jude does not. Thus, we include it here, and pray it, as the rest of this book, is a blessing to your study and your life.

CHAPTER SEVENTEEN

Caution and Courage

Jude 1-25

Like Peter, Jude also wrote to provide "principles of perseverance." The challenge was much the same for both writers, so the solution is also very similar. Jude offers two basic principles, which we have labeled "caution and courage." Use caution in your Christian life; there are dangers to avoid. And have courage in your stand against the false teachers. This was Jude's message in the first century, and it is his message to twentieth-century readers like you and me.

Principle 1: Caution: Dangerous Heresy Ahead (1-19)

Jude addresses his letter to "those who have been called" (Jude 1). God has issued the call to reconciliation with Him through Jesus Christ. A Christian is one who has heard the call, believed the content of the call (as to the claims of Christ and His atoning death on the cross and His resurrection with power from the grave), and has acted on that faith to respond to the call and submit to the lordship of Christ. Jude points out that the called ones are "loved by God the Father." This love is *agape,* which sees worth and potential even in the midst of sinful behavior. It was out of this love that God sent His Son into history to die for our sins. He also says that the called ones are "kept by Jesus Christ." Christians are watched over by Christ, protected as sheep by a shepherd. In fact, this very letter of Jude is a "keeping" letter—a watchcare letter—to protect them against the onslaught of the growing Gnostic heresy.

The Sinful Message

Jude points out that he would have preferred to have written to them about their common "salvation"—a positive affirmation of their common faith and relationship to God through Christ. But, instead, he "had to write and urge you to contend for the faith that was once for all entrusted to the saints" (Jude 3). Jude could do no other than to point out the real dangers of the heresy that was beginning to affect his readers. He challenges them to "contend for the faith"—the saving truth about Jesus. When one contends, he vigorously seeks to win—he is in the thick of a contest or a battle. In this case, it was a battle against heretical teachings and teachers.

Jude points out that the "faith" for which they were to contend was "once for all entrusted to the saints." This is a past entrustment—given through Jesus Christ. Jude is taking a stand here against the "special knowers" who claimed continuing special revelations that no one else was receiving. There is no "continuing revelation"—it was given "once for all" time. "In these last days," says the writer of Hebrews, "[God] has spoken to us by his Son" (Hebrews 1:2). Jesus gave the message to the apostles through the ministry of His personal teaching and the work of the Holy Spirit, who would remind them of what He had taught them (John 14:26) and give new insights for which they were not ready during His teaching ministry (John 16:12, 13). Paul spoke in terms of finality like this when he opposed the Judaizers (Galatians 1:6-9) and the pre-Gnostic special revelationists (Colossians 2:18), stating that such special revelations come from their own fleshly minds. Jude says the true message was "once for all entrusted to the saints"; therefore, all "continuing revelation" cults are to be shunned, including many contemporary neocharismatics and such cults as Mormonism and its latter-day revelations. We are to contend with agony for the true faith!

The two basic errors of the current heresy have already been explained, and both of them are noted here in Jude's opening remarks: immoral behavior—they "change the grace of our God into a license for immorality"—and false Christology—they "deny Jesus Christ our only Sovereign and Lord" (Jude 4). Both of these errors wreaked havoc with the "faith . . . entrusted to the saints." Our faith is in Jesus Christ, the Son of the living God (Matthew 16:16), who is "Immanuel . . . God with us" (Matthew 1:23). He is the "Word," and the "Word was with God, and the Word was God" (John 1:1). This faith is expressed in life-style, for "faith without deeds is dead" (James 2:26). Those who believe in Jesus cannot continue in sin (Romans 6:1ff). Instead, they offer their "bodies as living sacrifices, holy and pleasing to God" (Romans 12:1). It is this faith—faith in Jesus the Son of God and faith that produces a holy life-style through the power of the Spirit living within us—for which Jude urges his readers to contend. When one accepts Christ and receives the Holy Spirit, he has the power to understand and obey the will of God. It is possible to obey God in our moral choices and life-style.

The Sinful Messengers

Having clearly defined the battle between the "faith . . . once for all entrusted" and the still-evolving heresy being propagated against that faith, Jude now begins to describe the nature of the false teachers in no uncertain terms. His description is very similar to Peter's diatribe against these false teachers. (See 2 Peter 2 as well as the author's comments on that passage, above.)

Jude points out that these false teachers are secretive and deceptive; they "secretly slipped in among you," he says (Jude 4). They pretend to be Christians, but they are heretics, "godless men." John wrote about some who pretended to be sent by the apostles (1 John 2:18, 19) but were really false teachers of the same sort as these about whom Jude warns.

Those who claim to be Christians but deny Christ still find ways of secretly slipping into many churches and Christian institutions. Some are even in positions of denominational leadership! Their denial is often couched in the guise of "scholarship," but it must be seen for what it is. When the deity of Christ is denied, then the result is not Christian.

Don't misunderstand. There is nothing wrong with learning and the quest for truth. But not all so-called scholars find truth, nor do they all draw true conclusions from evidence.

Another of their methods is division. Jude says they "divide you" (Jude 19); they pretend to be Christians and then divide Christians from one another through their false teachings. The method of "dividing to conquer" has always worked where strength is gained from numbers. In the church, Christians give strength to one another through teaching, exhortation, discipline, and encouragement. Where there is disharmony, doubts begin to arise about the truth being taught and the sincere love of the fellowship.

The moral character of the false teachers is described in such phrases as, "Pollute their own bodies" (Jude 8), "by instinct" and "like unreasoning animals" (Jude 10), "follow their own evil desires" (Jude 16), and "follow mere natural instincts" (Jude 19). These statements clarify the truth that these men were dominated by the flesh, by the natural drives and instincts of mankind. The problem with our instincts is not the instinct itself, but rather with our use of, or satisfaction of, the instinct outside of the purpose of God for its use. Man, as opposed to animals, is capable of moral notions and motions. We develop "oughts" to control our "wants." Empowered by the Holy Spirit, and following the truth revealed by the Holy Spirit, the Christian rises above "mere natural instincts." These false teachers rejected this idea; they viewed man as incapable of bringing his instincts under God's control. The result was total immorality on their part behaviorally and in their system of thought and teachings.

Jude also uses some phrases to describe how these sinful messengers viewed authority. He calls them "godless men, who change the grace of our God . . ." (Jude 4). They don't respect the authority of God or His Word. The same idea is expressed when he says they "reject authority and slander celestial beings" (Jude 8). Jude points out that even the archangel Michael refused to bring a "slanderous accusation" against the devil in a dispute over the body of Moses, but rather left any accusations and judgment to God by saying, "The Lord rebuke you!" (Jude 9). Even the highest angels do not presume to judge God, His messengers, His angels, nor His word. But these audacious, sinful teachers took upon themselves such authority; they rejected what they did not understand (Jude 10). They did not understand the truth of the actual enfleshment of the divine Christ, nor did they understand the power for holiness that is given the true believer in the person of the Holy Spirit. As a matter of fact, it is all summed up in verse 19: "These . . . do not have the Spirit." That means they had no power to understand the "wisdom of God," which is understood only by "spiritual men" (1 Corinthians 2), nor did they have the empowering of the Spirit to overcome the flesh (Romans 8). In short, they were not Christians, for "if anyone does not have the Spirit of Christ, he does not belong to Christ" (Romans 8:9).

The author compares the false teachers to Cain, who thought he had a better sacrifice than what God commanded; to Balaam, who put personal gain above obeying God; and to Korah, who contradicted God's spokesman (Jude 11). They totally rejected the authority of God and His true spokesmen!

Jude also calls the false teachers "blemishes at your love feasts" (Jude 12). They only pretend to have love and concern; they really are concerned only for themselves. They are "clouds without rain," all show and talk with no real blessings to offer. They are "trees without fruit," that is, the fruit of righteousness, destined only to be culled and cut down. They are "wild waves of the sea" in their shameful behavior; "wandering stars," out of their constellation, destined to darkness (Jude 13).

Sentenced Messengers

Jude not only deals with the sinfulness of the false teachers and their message, he also makes clear their sentence and judgment. Again, the author makes very clear the lostness and final condemnation of those false teachers.

He says that their "condemnation was written about long ago" (Jude 4). He reminds the readers of the history of Israel, how God "long ago" judged His people when they rebelled against Him after He had delivered them from Egypt (Jude 5). Only a few in that generation reached the land—the rest died in the wilderness.

Jude refers next to the "angels who did not keep their positions" who are now kept in darkness and chains until judgment (Jude 6; cf. 2 Peter 2:4). Finally, He reminds the readers of God's judgment against the immorality of Sodom and Gomorrah (Jude 7). All of these had rejected God's authority and committed gross immoralities, just like the false teachers of Jude's day. The sentence of the false teachers would clearly be the same!

In verses 14 and 15, Jude refers to Enoch's prediction of God's judgment when He returns through Christ with "thousands upon thousands of His holy ones" to "convict all the ungodly." This is recorded in the apocryphal book of Enoch, not found in our present Old Testament. This agrees with many other statements in the New Testament about the certain judgment to come. These false teachers were destined for judgment and condemnation for their false Christology and gross immorality!

Principle 2: Take Courage; You Can Persevere (20-25)

The message, methods, and character traits of the false teachers have been made clear, along with their certain condemnation. Now Jude deals with the Christian's methods and means of persevering against the onslaught of heresy. He assures them that they can persevere, and this assurance is encouraging.

Methods of Perseverance

Jude has two concerns regarding perseverance. He first suggests methods of personal perseverance, addressing himself to what his readers must do to be sure of their own perseverance. Then he gives suggestions on how his readers can help others persevere. He says,

"Build yourselves up in your most holy faith" (Jude 20). When one is built up, he becomes stronger. Jude suggests that the Christian should do all he can to become strong in his faith—a command to act with a goal in mind. Paul says, "Faith comes from hearing, and hearing by the word of Christ" (Romans 10:17, NASB). Paul writes to Timothy, "All Scripture is God-breathed and is useful for teaching, rebuking, correcting and training in righteousness, so that the man of God may be thoroughly equipped for every good work" (2 Timothy 3:16). We see that faith comes by hearing the Word that corrects wrong ideas and rebukes wrong behavior while equipping (building up) the man of God for His use. Bible study is the method by which we train our minds in the teachings of Jesus and of those whom He personally taught. A Christian who is well versed in Scripture is becoming built up in the most holy faith. One becomes even more built up as he puts the teachings of Jesus into practice, as Paul writes in Romans 12:2, "Do not conform any longer to the pattern of this world, but be transformed by the renewing of your mind." Build yourself up in the faith!

The second suggestion for our own perseverance is to "pray in the Holy Spirit" (Jude 20). The kind of prayer that strengthens us to persevere is not simply form prayer or recitation prayer. It is to be "in the Spirit." Romans 8:26 and 27 makes clear that a part of the Holy Spirit's ministry to the believer is to assist in his prayer life. It says that the Holy Spirit "helps us in our weakness" by "interceding" for us with "groans that words cannot express." Short of that, the Spirit guides our thinking and insights into truth—He is called the "Spirit of truth." He alerts us to the dangers of the "roaring lion," Satan, as he attacks our minds through false doctrine. We thus know how we should be praying to the Father. Prayer "in the Spirit" is guided by, supplemented by, motivated by, and empowered by the Holy Spirit! So we build up our faith by listening to the truth that is from God, and by communicating with the Spirit's help to the Father—total communication by listening and responding.

The third phrase, "Keep yourselves in God's love" (Jude 21), is the outgrowth of building ourselves up and praying in the Spirit. By doing these things, we stay in the realm of God's love—we stay believers in the midst of false teachings. God's love is always there for us, but we must "keep ourselves" in it. We must continue to believe the truth and be submissive to His will. We must not, as the false teachers, deny the sovereign Lord and regress into immorality. The decision to stay is ours—God will never change His mind!

Next Jude deals with how we are to help others persevere against the false teachers. He uses the word *mercy* in several forms with regard to our attitude toward those who are struggling with the onslaught of Satan through the false teachers. He states that the mercy is to be "mixed with fear" (Jude 23). When you show mercy toward someone, it is an attitude and an action. The attitude of mercy is one of sincere concern for the well-being of another. When we see a fellow believer struggling with false teachings concerning Christ, we should have immediate and deep concern, for it is a serious matter. Mercy takes action out of this concern. We are to "snatch [them] from the fire and save them" (Jude 23). If one denies Christ, once having believed, he is in danger of the "fire"; his salvation is in doubt. We are saved only if we continue in the faith until the end—even in the midst of the false teachers.

In helping others in their struggle, we do for them what we are already doing for ourselves—we build them up in the most holy faith and pray for them in the Spirit (Jude 20). We use the Scripture to correct and rebuke and equip them. We do this out of love for them, even though all the while we are "hating even the clothing stained by corrupted flesh." Any sign of denial and a return to the immorality of the pagan world should be hated—any outward sign of "stained clothing" or behavior. This must all be done in "fear"—in all seriousness.

Means for Perseverance

The closing doxology ("glory, majesty, power and authority"—Jude 25) is especially pertinent in that it includes "authority"—the very aspect of God that was denied by the false teachers. Note that the doxology of authority and power is given "through Jesus Christ our Lord," the very one whose sovereignty the false teachers were denying in their teaching.

This powerful, glorious, majestic, and authoritative God is "able," through Jesus Christ, to do several things for the challenged believer. First, He is "able to keep you from falling" (Jude 24). A believer falls when he loses his faith—denies Jesus as Lord. In 1 Corinthians 10:13, Paul wrote,

> No temptation has seized you except what is common to man. And God is faithful; he will not let you be tempted beyond what you can bear. But when you are tempted, he will also provide a way out so that you can stand up under it.

Jesus had said about His "sheep" that "no one can snatch them out of my hand," and "no one can snatch them out of my Father's hand" (John 10:28, 29). God is indeed able. He gives us believers all that we need to stay in Him, to stay saved. He gives us continuing forgiveness. He gives us the power of the Holy Spirit and the clear instruction of His Word. He gives us the encouraging fellowship of believers in the church. He gives us His unending love. We have all we need to be faithful to the end. We must, however, use it. God's ability and our availing ourselves of His ability must come together in order to claim the victory!

Jude also says that God is able to "present you before his glorious presence without fault and with great joy" (Jude 24). This is the final dimension of our salvation—the fullness of it all. This is judgment, when we will be declared to be without fault. The blood of Jesus cleanses us from all sin and unrighteousness. We avail ourselves of this cleansing by faith, and express it in confession of faith and baptism—the picture of the total cleansing. As long as we stay believers, we are "without fault." If we stay believers until the Day of Judgment, we shall be there "with great joy." God gives us initial salvation by faith, and He gives us all we need to stay in the faith so that we can finally experience the joy! To Him be all praise forever!

Part Three

The Epistles of John

Commentary by William R. Baker

INTRODUCTION

Getting Acquainted With John

Just as we mentioned regarding the Epistle of James, the Epistles of John are worth getting to know. But these epistles differ from James in many ways. Before you plunge into them, perhaps you will let me help you break the ice.

First, these writings of John are epistles. In fact, 2 John and 3 John showcase the first-century form of Greek letter-writing. They both open by naming the sender and the addressees before giving a greeting (absent in 3 John). This is followed by a thanksgiving, the body of the letter, a closing, and a concluding word of greeting and farewell. Like most Greek letters of their time, they were written on a single sheet of papyrus about eight inches by ten inches in size. They are personal: 2 John was written to a church spoken of as "the chosen lady" and 3 John to an individual named Gaius. Despite this, they both appeal to a wide Christian audience.

In contrast, 1 John is the least letter-like of any New Testament writing outside the Gospels. The formal aspects of a letter found in 2 and 3 John are entirely absent. There aren't any names mentioned, not even the author's. It seems more like an essay than a letter. Yet, unlike an essay, which addresses the world at large, the author of 1 John tackles a specific problem and directs his remarks to a distinct locale. We can tell this from reading it. It was not published in a newspaper as an open letter, nor was it sent to a theological journal. Rather, it was sent to the church in a particular area. This makes it an epistle, despite its lack of proper form.

Second, these three epistles respond to the same problem threatening different locations perhaps at different stages. First John attacks the problem in a region where Christianity is strong and congregations numerous. Second John forewarns a single congregation in a more remote area into which the problem is spreading. Third John bolsters a relationship with a loyal ally from a congregation in which the problem now dominates local leadership.

The dimensions of the problem are seen most easily in 1 John. According to 1 John 2:19 and 4:5, a sizable group of people disagreed with the church enough to break away and begin meeting separately. They continued to recruit people from the church into their exclusive and, from their view, more enlightened fellowship. They seem to have claimed to have special fellowship with God (1 John 1:6), to be sinless (1 John 1:8, 10), and to have exclusive knowledge of God (1 John 2:4). They denied that Jesus is the Christ or the Son of God (1 John 2:22; 5:1, 5), that Christ came in the flesh (1 John 4:2; 5:6; 2 John 7), that He died in the flesh (1 John 5:6) or even needed to, and that they needed to observe His commands anymore (1 John 2:4). Furthermore, they considered their views advanced understandings of Christianity (1 John 2:20, 27; 2 John 9).

The problem seems related to a second-century heresy called Gnosticism. Although there were many forms of Gnosticism, all forms denied the reality of Christ's humanity in one way or another. One particular brand of Gnosticism, called Docetic, said that Jesus' appearance to be a normal human in the flesh was an illusion from beginning to end. Another, called Cerinthian, moderated this position some and taught that the divine Messiah came down and inhabited the man Jesus, but only temporarily. The Messiah came at Jesus' baptism but left just before His crucifixion.

It is most common to identify the problem revealed in the epistles of John with Cerinthian Gnosticism. The claims of sinlessness and special fellowship with God do not seem to continue in Cerinthian Gnosticism, but the views about Jesus do seem compatible. Also, church tradition maintains that the apostle John and Cerinthus were competitors in Ephesus late in the first century.

Third, 1 John clarifies theological themes in the Gospel of John. Church history tells us that Gnostics used the Gospel of John as the basis for many of their views. This, in fact, hampered the acceptance of the Gospel of John by orthodox Christians as part of the New Testament. It is possible that, in 1 John, the author attempts to set the record straight by denying that certain early Gnostic ideas are valid interpretations of the Gospel of John.

For instance, Jesus' constant deflection of attention from himself to God in the Gospel of John (John 7:18; 8:50; 11:40; 14:9; 17:5, 21) could be interpreted by some to mean that Jesus' human life was insignificant. If so, 1 John 4:3 corrects this. Again, John 1:33 and 34 could be interpreted to mean that Jesus' divinity did not begin until the descent of the Holy Spirit upon Him at His baptism, and John 10:17 and 18 could mean that the crucifixion is relatively unimportant. If so, 1 John 4:2 and 5:6 disallow such views. Some could have understood John 8:46 and 20:22 and 23 to mean that Christians no longer sin, but 1 John 1:8 and 10 undercut this idea. Finally, John 13:35 and 15:12 could be taken to mean that Christian disciples should love one another exclusively. In this case, 1 John 3:23 and 4:8, 16, and 20 deny this limitation.

Fourth, these epistles were written by John the apostle. This may seem self-evident from their titles in our New Testaments. However, we must remember that titles did not accompany these letters when they first were written. When we look at the texts of the letters themselves, we will notice that the author nowhere identifies himself by name. More puzzling yet is that, in 2 and 3 John, the author calls himself "the elder," but this does not appear in 1 John. The first question we must face, then, is whether or not the same person wrote 1, 2, and 3 John. In doing so, we must explain why he does not call himself "the elder" in 1 John.

The fact that 1, 2, and 3 John share the same author is established by the similarities in content between 2 John and 1 John. Second John 5, "I am not writing you a new command but one we have had from the beginning," and 1 John 2:7, "I am not writing you a new command but an old one, which you have had since the beginning," are nearly identical. Second John 6, "This is love: that we walk in obedience to his commands," and 1 John 5:3, "This is love for God: to obey his commands," are just as close.[12]

If 1 John were written to an area where the author himself resided and was a well-known leader of the church, he would not have needed to explain his status. If 2 and 3 John were sent to areas where people had not had as much personal contact with the author, he would need to spell out his authority in some way in order to differentiate himself from others. The fact that 2 John and 3 John have only one original destination, a single congregation and an individual, whereas 1 John was sent to a number of churches in a region, also may have influenced how the author referred to himself.

---

[12]Compare further: 2 John 6 with 1 John 3:11; 2 John 7 with 1 John 2:18, 22, 26 and 4:1, 3, 6; and 2 John 7 with 1 John 4:2.

The conclusion that John the apostle wrote 1, 2, and 3 John arises chiefly from the theological and historical connection we have already seen between 1 John and the Gospel of John. To this may be added two stylistic features of 1 John and the Gospel of John that are similar: both begin with prologues (1 John 1:1-4; John 1:1-5) and both declare their purposes for writing near the end (1 John 5:13; John 20:31). Also, the two volumes use many of the same words, even more than Luke and Acts. Finally, the author of both claims to be an eyewitness of Jesus (1 John 1:1-4; John 21:24, 25).

Thus, we conclude that the same person wrote the Gospel of John and 1, 2, and 3 John. But who wrote the Gospel of John? When we discount the title and read the text, we run into the same problem we did in the epistles: the author does not mention himself by name. Is this a wild goose chase, you ask? No, it isn't because the Gospel author does leave some clues. On a couple of critical occasions, he refers to himself as "the disciple whom Jesus loved." From John 21:20, we learn not only that the author was with Peter in his last conversation with Jesus, but was also sitting to Jesus' right during the Last Supper. He was probably in the high priest's courtyard when Peter denied Jesus (John 18:16, 17). Finally, he is the one to whom Jesus entrusted his mother during the crucifixion (John 19:26, 27). Of Jesus' close associates, only the apostle John, son of Zebedee, fits these situations. Thus, John is the author of the Gospel and, more importantly for us, of these three epistles.

Fifth, John wrote 1, 2, and 3 John from Ephesus in the 90s. John's Gospel presumes the existence of Matthew, Mark, and Luke. Therefore, we must allow a number of years between them. If Matthew, Mark, and Luke were written in the 60s and 70s, we can assume John was written at least in the 80s. If 1 John is an attempt to correct misinterpretations of John's Gospel, a number of years must have elapsed between it and John's letters. That puts them in the 90s. Their current order is probably the order in which they were originally written. Church tradition places John in Ephesus in the 90s. If so, 1 John was written to congregations in Ephesus and in the surrounding region. Second John was written to a distant congregation in Asia Minor. Third John was written to an individual, Gaius, who was a leader in yet another congregation in an area far from Ephesus.

Sixth, the purpose for writing 1 John can be summarized from two different perspectives—one positive, one negative. On the positive side, John wants to fortify the faith of those who remain in the true church in the face of aggressive recruiting by the heretics who have left. On the negative side, he wants to cripple the success of the heretics by undercutting the theological and ethical errors the heretics are teaching, especially their misinterpretations of the Gospel of John. Second, John anticipates the spreading of this heresy outside Ephesus. John writes a drastically condensed letter to warn a distant congregation against the heresy. The purpose of 3 John may or may not be related to the heresy. In it, John seeks to cultivate a base of support for mission travels in an outlying region because one major congregation in the area has cut off such support to John and his representatives.

Finally, 1 John is notoriously difficult to outline. Similar thoughts are repeated variously throughout the letter and many equally important thoughts are stated in the same context. In this sense, it is like James, but the reader has more difficulty determining when one main thought stops and another starts in 1 John. Attempts to outline it, then, vary widely. In each attempt, significant ideas inevitably fail to make the outline.

Early in this century, Robert Law tried to capture the structure of 1 John in the form of a spiral with three cycles. He saw righteousness, love, and belief as "tests" for true fellowship with God (1 John 1:5—2:28), divine sonship (1 John 2:29—4:6), and as related to one another (1 John 4:7—5:21). Many outlines of 1 John today are no more than modifications of Law and are based on Law's threefold division of 1 John.

More recently, a twofold division of 1 John has been suggested. Raymond Brown (*Anchor Bible*) fixes his gaze on two major thesis statements that start: "This is the message. . . ." The first (1 John 1:5) is completed by, "God is light. . . ." The second (1 John 3:11), roughly halfway through the letter, is completed by, "We should love one another." The present work does not follow the threefold division of Law, but is compatible with the twofold division of Brown.

Before you read my specific comments about 1, 2, and 3 John, I encourage you to get better acquainted with the epistles firsthand, as I suggested with James, by reading them through in one sitting.

CHAPTER EIGHTEEN

Prologue: The Word of Life

1 John 1:1-4

In his opening four verses, John prepares us for themes he will examine in depth later: Christ's nature, eternal life, and fellowship with God. However, the significance of what he presses here lies far beyond 1 John itself. He loudly proclaims Christianity's testimony for all the world to hear: "I am real; I can be examined in the person of Jesus Christ; what my followers bear witness to remains open to public scrutiny."

To John's credit, he has fashioned these timeless thoughts to magnify their effect on us. His artistry, almost poetic, is extremely difficult to convey in English. Thus, translations of 1 John 1:1-4 vary greatly. Technically, the subject of verse 1 is not named. Also, the first three verses are one sentence, with verse 2 interrupting in order to elaborate on "the Word of life." Verse 4 is fairly straightforward, announcing one of the reasons for writing the letter.

The Author Has Examined the Word of Life (1:1)

Before my wife and I moved to Aberdeen, Scotland, we had to make a decision on a home to rent without seeing it. We received a notice from the university saying, "A one-bedroom maisonette is available at 143 Crown Street for 150 pounds a month. Inform us as soon as possible if you want it." Being Americans, we didn't even know what a maisonette was, let alone whether we wanted one. We did have a contact in Aberdeen, so we decided to call him and ask him to view the home for us. When we called back a few days later, he told us that it was a quaint cottage-like home on two floors just a few blocks from Main Street and that we would be smart to take it. So we did and were extremely pleased with our decision when we arrived in Aberdeen a few months later.

We prefer to inspect things ourselves, but sometimes we must take the advice of someone who has firsthand contact or simply knows more about the matter. Our Christian faith is grounded in both types of inspection. We examine the evidence available to us now. But because Christ walked on earth for only thirty-three years and had a public ministry for only three years, we must also have confidence in the judgment of eyewitnesses. The New Testament may be viewed as a collection of this eyewitness testimony.

In this opening verse, when John says, "We have heard . . . we have seen . . . we have looked at and our hands have touched," he declares himself to be among those personal original witnesses of Jesus Christ and the gospel He proclaimed. "The Word of life" is the phrase John uses to bring together Jesus Christ as both subject and object of Christian faith. He is both proclaimer and what is proclaimed. As a person, He was seen, looked at, and touched. As a message, Christ is heard and proclaimed (1 John 1:2).

The verb *looked at* is different from *seen* and may be a subtle reference to John 1:14, where it is used in the sense of discerning the supernatural glory of Christ. The verb *touched* is the same word used in Luke 24:39 when the resurrected Jesus invites the disciples to prove for themselves that His body is real. Since the word *seen* is also used there, John may have this very incident in mind as he pens these words. In that case, he proclaims himself here as a witness not only of Jesus' ministry and message, but also of His resurrection. Jesus' resurrection, after all, is what validates His message as God's and that He himself is from God.

The word *beginning* also is found in John 1:1, which declares that Jesus existed before creation, before Genesis 1:1. John reuses the word here in 1 John 1:1 to plant this thought in our minds. John asserts that he is a witness of Jesus from the very beginning of His ministry. Further, he insists that what he has observed in Jesus' life points to His divinity. Jesus' existence in history demands His existence before history (preexistence). Again, Jesus' resurrection may be uppermost in John's mind.

The phrase *this we proclaim* does not actually occur in the Greek text until the third verse, where John tries to recapture the thoughts of verse 1 after the interruption of the second verse. This verse suggests two thoughts for us to ponder. First, our faith is not strictly personal, between us and God, or between us and Christ. Crucial testimony from the apostles bridges the historical gap. That testimony is contained in the New Testament. Second, our faith can and should be scrutinized to be sure it stands up to reason and history. Again, the basis for doing this is the New Testament.

The Word of Life Leads to Eternal Life (1:2)

When we buy a home, we like to inspect it thoroughly. We check for leaky roofs, cracked foundations, rotting wood, peeling paint, and faulty furnaces. We want to assure ourselves that this will be a good place to live, a place where we can be happy for a long time. Similarly, in 1 John 1:2, John declares that after examining every nook and cranny of the Word of life, he is prepared to certify that it is not only a perfect place to move into now, but that, once moved in, the inhabitant may live there happily forever.

John fixes his gaze on the "Word of life" as a person standing before him. In this sense, it is the historical Jesus, who "appeared" and whom John and others "have seen." Many people saw Jesus, but John is part of that select company of apostles who are prepared to give expert testimony about who Jesus really is.

John "testifies" and "proclaims" that Jesus, "the Word of life" is "the eternal life." This is not so much a statement about the eternal life Jesus gives us who believe in Him as it is an assertion of Jesus' divinity. Jesus has been the source of life along with God "from the beginning." When Jesus saves us, He gives this life to us. John goes on to say that Jesus is the eternal life "which was with the Father." In doing so, he uses the same phrase he used in John 1:2, when he said, "He was with God in the beginning."

Finally, John declares boldly that this life "has appeared to us." This repeats what he said at the beginning of this verse and, thus, emphasizes a point he does not want to escape us. The source of life came to earth as a man—Jesus—whom John and the other apostles saw and thoroughly examined.

We tend to think of eternal life in terms of longevity. We talk of living forever. Really, though, longevity is a result, almost a side effect, of eternal life. Eternal life is a quality of life, the nature of life, perhaps even the essence of life. Jesus imparts it to us from God's vast pool to help us live godly, fulfilling lives in the here and now. It gives us "spirituality." It provides longevity because of its nature; it can't be destroyed by death. Ultimately, it means being "with" God eternally, just as Jesus came "from" God. Let us sip this life now that Jesus imparts to us through His Word.

The Word of Life Facilitates Fellowship with God (1:3)

Recently, my wife was looking for a job in corporate public relations in St. Louis, to which we were moving. Generally, jobs of this nature do not appear in the want ads, and one must make contact with people who eventually lead to contacts with people in the companies that have openings. As it happened, a chance contact I made at an academic meeting in Kansas City led to her meeting with the senior vice president of a major public relations agency in St. Louis. In turn, he pointed her to a corporation that was looking for someone with her abilities. Today, she is happily working as manager of corporate relations for that company.

Those two contacts facilitated her getting that job. She would not likely even have known about the position otherwise. Similarly, Jesus facilitates our relationship with God. As we search for God in our lives, it is ultimately Jesus who brings us into God's fellowship. Prior to that, however, someone else leads us to Jesus based upon the witness of Scripture. John says that he and the apostles dependably facilitate our relationship with Jesus Christ, who in turn facilitates our relationship with God. In saying this, John counters the argument of those heretics in the church who say they can lead people into fellowship with God by a route that bypasses the apostles and even Jesus.

Literally, "what we have seen and heard" comes first in 1 John 1:3 and is followed by "we proclaim." John is getting us back into the flow of the first verse after the sidetrack of elaborating on the Word of life (1 John 1:2). *Seen* and *heard* are the same verbs as begin verse 1. *We proclaim* is the principle statement of the first three verses. John accentuates its impact on us by holding it back this long.

John's proclamation of the message of Jesus' divinity is bold and confident. It is also clearly motivated: "so that you also may have fellowship with us." He broadcasts the message of the Word of life to which he has had firsthand access in order to draw people into association with him. Once one is in fellowship with John and the apostles, he will find he is also having fellowship "with the Father and with his Son, Jesus Christ" (1 John 1:3).

Notice that "Jesus Christ" is now mentioned for the first time, climactically concluding the three-verse sentence. Jesus Christ is the "Word of life," the "eternal life," the message proclaimed, the ultimate facilitator of fellowship with God the Father. John does not want his readers to be outside the fellowship with God, which they will be if they are outside fellowship with him and the apostolic witness he represents. The purpose of this letter, then, is to keep them within the true fellowship of God's genuine family based upon the verified apostolic testimony about Jesus, the Word of life.

We need to be aware of whose testimony about Christ we are following as we grow in our faith. Authoritative apostolic testimony resides in the New Testament. Studying it will lead us into deeper and deeper fellowship with God and Jesus Christ. We must take care to distinguish true teaching from false, anti-Biblical teaching, or we may be led outside of God's true fellowship. Also, we need to be facilitators. We need to bring people into contact with the apostolic witness of Jesus in the New Testament, which will lead them into contact with the real Jesus Christ, who in turn will lead them into true fellowship with God.

Proclaiming the Word of Life Fulfills the Author (1:4)

Sometimes, the need to speak can become an emotional burden. The longer we put it off, the more weighty the burden gets. We just can't stop thinking about it. It can get to the point that we realize it is more important to get whatever it is out of our system than to worry about how it might be taken by the other person or persons involved. What is sought is relief from the burden. Proposing marriage, confessing sin, confronting sin, even saying good-bye can be like this.

John is burdened emotionally and spiritually about writing this letter. He expresses this in 1 John 1:4. He cannot rest until he makes this written attempt to bring as many people back into proper fellowship with God as he can. He must expose the errors of the false teachers broadly and publicly. He hopes that his efforts will reap positive results not only in the present church but in the future presence of God. Regardless, it makes him feel that he has done what God wants him to do, and that makes him feel better.

So when he says, "We write this" (1 John 1:4), the *we* refers to John himself more strictly than it does when he uses it in verses 1-3. He expresses his personal, emotional condition and not that of the apostles collectively. The *this* refers primarily to the body of the letter, which begins immediately after this final sentence of the prologue. However, it is still grounded in the general apostolic burden of testifying to Jesus as the Word of life, which dominates the prologue itself.

The phrase *to make our joy complete* states a second purpose for the letter in addition to the desire stated in 1 John 1:3 that his readers "may have fellowship with us." This second purpose has a personal dimension, as already stated above, but that is not all. It also has an eschatological, or future-life, dimension. We know this because John also writes about completing joy in John 15:11 and

16:21-24. There it comes from the lips of Jesus. Jesus asks His disciples to remain in His love and obey His commandments "that your joy may be complete," and He promises that a time is coming when "no one will take away your joy." John's echo of this phrase here does not seem accidental. He wants his readers to know he believes his letter will enable them to be eternally with him in fellowship with God the Father and Jesus the Son in Heaven.

Like John, we need to feel a pastoral burden for those in our Christian fellowship who are being tempted by unhealthy ideas that are leading them away from orthodox Christianity. Maybe it is Hinduism, Mormonism, the New Age, or just plain old secularism. Regardless, we should not be content to allow them to be taken away from Christianity without a struggle. We need to perceive when God calls us to speak and not to be comfortable with ourselves until we do. On the other side, like some of John's readers, perhaps you are currently listening to the siren songs of those who discount the central doctrines of Christianity. I plead with you to give John's message your undivided attention.

CHAPTER NINETEEN

Living in the Light

1 John 1:5—2:11

This new section carries over some of the same themes as appeared 1 John 1:1-4. Key words are repeated: *life/live* (1 John 1:1, 2; 1:6), *word* (1 John 1:1; 1:10), *fellowship* (1 John 1:3; 1:6,7), and *heard* (1 John 1:1, 3; 1:5). A synonym, *declare* (1 John 1:5), replaces *proclaim* (1 John 1:2, 3), and a related noun, *message* (1 John 1:5), appears.

Despite this overlap from the prologue, in 1 John 1:5—2:11, John launches his public response to the false claims of the separatists who have left the genuine church fellowship. He initiates this with a series of six conditional sentences (sentences that begin with *if*). The first (1 John 1:6), third (1 John 1:8), and fifth (1 John 1:10) conditionals represent positions of the separatists and are denounced by John. The second (1 John 1:7), fourth (1 John 1:9), and sixth (1 John 2:1) are John's viewpoints, which also represent the view of the apostles and the orthodox church.

The conditionals may also be recognized as pairs addressing the same theme from opposite points of view. The first and second conditionals address the question of whether or not our sin affects our relationship with God. The third and fourth address whether or not we retain our sinful nature after we become Christians. The fifth and sixth address whether or not we actually commit sins after we become Christians. To each of these questions, the separatists say no, but the apostle says yes.

In 1 John 2:3-11, John continues his response to his opponents in a different but clearly marked format. In these verses, the heretics are characterized as "the man who says" (1 John 2:4), "whoever claims" (1 John 2:6), and "anyone who claims" (1 John 2:9). All these phrases translate the same Greek word. What follows these phrases in each case is a different way of expressing that one knows God: "know him," "live in him," and "be in the light." It is possible that these are actual statements John's opponents were employing to entice prospects into their camp.

Thesis: God Is Light (1:5)

One of my proudest moments as a junior higher came when I got to portray God. The central activity of my youth group involved putting on puppet plays. Our usual procedure was to lip sync our puppets to professional recordings. One time, we presented the story of Job. A central character in this play, of course, is God himself. Portraying God as some kind of puppet seemed inappropriate. So we came up with the idea of using a light bulb, out of view, that was made to go on and off by wiggling an electrical plug around in the socket of an extension cord as God spoke. That was my job.

It's not all that surprising that my youth group decided to portray God as light. In the Old Testament, Psalm 104:2 says that "He wraps himself in light"; Psalm 36:9 says that in God's light "we see light"; and, in Exodus 3, God appears as fire in the burning bush. Light is also a common way to represent God in the Greek, Egyptian, and Iranian literature. So it is not surprising that John says, "God is light." What is surprising is that the phrase does not appear anywhere else in the entire New Testament. This surprise is magnified when we realize that John says "this message" that he has heard is "from Him" (the antecedent for "Him" being "Jesus Christ" at the end of 1 John 1:3).

What does appear in the New Testament, especially in the Gospel of John, is the idea that Jesus is light. John calls him light in the prologue (John 1:4, 5, 9) and records Jesus himself declaring, "I am the light of the world" (John 8:12; 9:5). In fact, John uses "light" to refer to Jesus nineteen times in his Gospel. We can draw from this that 1 John 1:5 is saying that God is light based on the fact that John knows Jesus, who is light, has come from God and shows us what God is like. He has also come to dispel the darkness of the world (John 1:5; 12:35).

Speaking of God as light could refer to the glory of His person, His absolute knowledge or truth as opposed to falsehood, or to His holiness as opposed to wickedness. The fact that John underlines his point by saying "in him there is no darkness at all" indicates that he has the ethical implications uppermost in mind.

By laying down a thesis like "God is light," John begins on common ground with his opponents. What he will attempt to show in the following six conditional sentences is that they have drawn the wrong conclusions from this axiom. Also, they wrongly cut Jesus out of His mediating role between us and God.

The fact that God can be described as pure light without darkness means that, when His light shines, no shadow is even created (James 1:17). His light is all encompassing. Jesus came to the world to take the darkness, even the shadows, out of the world. He wants us, as His servants, to let the light He gives us shine before the world (Matthew 5:16).

We Must Walk in the Light (1:6-7)

I don't know about you, but, when I am walking down a street at night, I will choose to stay on the side with the best lighting. It is safer in the light. Similarly, if God is light and I am God's servant, I will choose to walk in the light. I will strive to live righteously because I want to be compatible with Him. I will shy away from unrighteousness as much as possible, even though I know I cannot outrun it entirely, because unrighteousness distances me from Him.

In 1 John 1:6 and 7, John utters his first argument against the separatists based on the mutually agreed principle that God is light. The first "if" sentence represents the separatist view, which he spurns. The second "if" sentence, being the flip side of the first, John offers as valid.

The *we*, repeated throughout these verses, is not apostolic or personal as it was previously. Now it is intended to separate those who agree with John from his opponents. It includes those loyal to the orthodox position he represents and excludes those who have left the church with the false teachers.

Given John's premise that God is light and contains no darkness, his logic is sound. How can someone who still chooses to "walk in the darkness" really be God's associate, or "have fellowship with him" (1 John 1:6)? If we are chasing after sin, we are moving away from God, not toward Him. We are stumbling in darkness, not skipping in the light.

The word *walk* helps us visualize the ethical direction we are taking in our lives. One can walk along paths that lead to destruction or follow the course God has set. God challenged Abraham to the latter (Genesis 17:1), as He did David and his descendants (1 Kings 2:4). Here, John exposes the inconsistency of his opponents who are saying Christians can straddle the paths and it makes no difference in our relationship with God. Once God has accepted us, we can do what we want. Sin becomes irrelevant.

John insists that any so-called Christian who believes this fallacy commits double jeopardy. In the very proclamation of such a view, he demonstrates that he is outside God's fellowship. John accuses, "We lie and do not live by the truth." Remember, light can relate to God as the origin of absolute truth. The lie of those who are being led away from the truth by false teachers may not be overt, but it doesn't matter. What they are doing in their conduct torpedoes God's truth in the galactic battle between falsehood and truth, darkness and light.

When John formulates the orthodox response in the second conditional (1 John 1:7), he throws us a curve. The proper contrast to the first conditional would result in: "If we walk in the light, as he is in the light, we have fellowship with him." But that is not what John says. Rather, he says, "We have fellowship with one another." He assumes the unstated and dramatizes something more profound: fellowship with God is not gained apart from fellowship with fellow believers. Unmistakably, John is specifying that a saving relationship with God is not attainable outside the church. Leaving the church as the separatists have done is inherently wrong. Such actions spotlight the error of their whole position.

Consistently living the way God wants us to not only should result in a bond with others traveling the same way; it also validates the work of Christ who died for our sin. In speaking about "the blood of Jesus," which "purifies us from all sin" (1 John 1:7), John strikes the core of Christian teaching. Blood, the physical essence of human life, was drained from God's "Son" as the eternal and sufficient price of our redemption.[13] Christ died for our sins. His sacrifice enables us to get close to God. However, as opposed to John's opponents, Christ's work does not allow us to be indifferent about our sin, but all the more conscious of it and, indeed, sorry for it. We don't forget that our relationship with God cost Jesus His life. Nor should we.

The mention of "blood" and the use of "Jesus" as opposed to "Christ" are significant because they underline the reality of Jesus' physical nature. As mentioned in the "Getting Acquainted With John" section, John's opponents denied that the Messiah (Christ) was truly human.

---

[13]See Romans 3:25; Hebrews 9:12-14; and 10:19-22. Important Old Testament background includes Exodus 30:10; Leviticus 16:15-19; 17:11.

According to 1 John 1:6 and 7, then, becoming a Christian is no cause for ethical complacency. We are expected to parallel the holiness of God himself, ever conscious of our unworthiness to walk beside Him in the light except for the sacrifice of Jesus. Let us never become content with where we are in our walk, but let us become more and more honorable servants of God.

We Must Confess Our Sins (1:8, 9)

Sometimes we try to excuse our sin by rationalizing. One might say the abusive language that he hurled at his spouse came because he was tired and had a headache. Another might say he cheated on his income taxes because the government charges too much tax. Someone else might say he lied about something he did because he really didn't intend to do it. We can come up with an excuse that seems reasonable to us for any sin.

John's opponents rationalized sin away in one fell swoop. They simply said that, because Christians are in the light of God, by definition their sin nature is gone. They might do something that appears sinful, but it can't be.

In some sense, 1 John 1:8 and 9 anticipate the opposition's rejoinder to verses 6 and 7, which lash out at their sinfulness. The first "if" sentence condemns the position of John's opponents, who claim to have no sin. The second "if" sentence advocates the orthodox position of admitting our sins.

We wonder what could lead people who were once in the church to promote what seems like such an obvious falsehood as to "claim to be without sin" (1 John 1:8). As I mentioned in the introduction, they may have misread something in John's own Gospel. In John 8:35 and 36, Jesus is recorded as saying that the Son sets a person free from being a slave to sin. John's opponents could have taken that quite literally to arrive at their position that a Christian's sin nature is eradicated by his relationship with God through Christ. John's response disallows this denial of reality. As Francis Schaeffer stresses in *True Spirituality,* the cross frees us from the bonds of sin, but dealing with the results of the bonds of sin in our lives is a lifetime proposition.

If we hold the position that we are sinless, John says, "we deceive ourselves and the truth is not in us" (1 John 1:8). It's more than being liars. We are deluded, mentally unbalanced, because we deny reality. Furthermore, we reveal the wide gulf that exists between ourselves and God, the author of truth.

Rather than denying our sinfulness, John advocates that we "confess our sins" (1 John 1:9). This will do much more toward advancing our relationship with God than ignoring our sin, as the separatists advocate. Sincere confession has a sure result: forgiveness. The reason for this lies in the solid and reliable character of God. God is "faithful." This is the bedrock of Biblical truth (Psalm 89:1-4; Hebrews 10:23). He holds fast to His covenants with Adam and Eve, Noah, Abraham, Israel, and David (Genesis 3:15; 9:9; 15:18; Exodus 19:5, 6; 2 Samuel 7:13). Moreover, Micah says he will "tread our sins underfoot and hurl all our iniquities into the depths of the sea," and He "will be true to Jacob, and show mercy to Abraham" (Micah 7:19, 20).

God's faithfulness leads to forgiving our sins. The fact that God is "just," or, more literally, "righteous," leads to the fact that He will "purify us from all unrighteousness" (1 John 1:9). As in Isaiah 51:5, God's righteousness here refers as much to His action of scrubbing us up through the work of Christ as it does to His moral character. The extensiveness of His action is significant, too. He does not save us from the self-condemnation of our sinful nature in some partial way. He cleanses from head to toe, inside and outside. Just as the "blood of Jesus . . . purifies us from all sin" (1 John 1:7), the righteousness of the Father will "purify us from all unrighteousness" (1 John 1:9).

Baptism signifies this cleansing action of Jesus' blood and God's righteousness. As we are washed by the water, we appropriate the promise of this passage. We are made acceptable to align ourselves with God. Appropriately, our baptism is preceded not only by profession of Christ as Lord and Savior, but also by initial confession of our sinfulness and need for a Savior. John's opponents, and many today, deny the necessity of all this. John declares it to be the truth of God. Let us continue to confess our sins to God daily as we walk closer and closer to Him.

Jesus Is Our Atoning Sacrifice (1:10—2:2)

A four-year-old child is trying to pour himself a glass of strawberry punch from a glass pitcher. He knows he shouldn't be doing this because it is too heavy for him, but he wants to demonstrate his independence. It slips from his hand and crashes to the floor, scattering glass and the staining liquid everywhere, even on the nearby living-room carpet. The child is just about to try to clean up the mess with tissues when his father and mother appear in the doorway. The frightened child runs to his father, crying out that he is sorry. The mother reminds the father that, although the child did wrong, he is quite incapable of cleaning up the glass and washing the stain out of the carpet. The father then asks the mother to wipe up the room on behalf of the child.

According to John's picture in 1 John 1:10—2:2, Jesus is like the mother in this story. He is both our advocate before the Father, who is displeased with our sin, and the one the Father sends to wash away our sin. In these verses, John's deepening discussion of Christ's role in our acceptance before God culminates his third and last attack on his opponents' position. He has condemned their position that the Christian's inclination to sin is expunged by his acceptance by God (1 John 1:8, 9). Now, in these verses, he decries their position that, once one becomes a Christian, he actually ceases to commit sinful acts.

In the first conditional sentence (1 John 1:10), John simply denounces their "claim" that "we have not sinned" by standing it up against what Scripture states. The universal reality of human sin is a staunch Biblical truth. One of many passages that could be quoted, Ecclesiastes 7:20,[14] says: "There is not a righteous man on earth who does what is right and never sins." To deny such a basic principle of Christianity, as far as John is concerned, flaunts falsehood in God's face. It is to call God "a liar" and to reveal disdain for "his word." As in verses 6 and 8, the very expression of such an idea illuminates the separation of John's opponents from God. He hopes the people in the church will now be able to see this.

John turns his face more directly to his readers as he writes the first verse of chapter 2. Notice that his appeal is made more personal by changing from the "we" he has been using to "I," and by affectionately referring to his readers as "my dear children." This is the first of numerous times he calls his readers "dear children" (cf. 1 John 2:12, 28; 3:7, 18; 4:4; 5:21), but this is the only time he uses the possessive *my* along with it.

The change of address causes a new chapter to begin here in our English translations. Really, though, the sentence is simply a personal interlude between the fifth and sixth conditional sentences in John's challenge to the beliefs of his opponents. The appeal he makes to his readers in this interlude, however, is significant. He

---

[14]See also 1 Kings 8:46; Psalm 14:3; Isaiah 53:6; 64:6; Romans 3:22-24.

does not wish his position to be misconstrued. The fact that he espouses the reality of sin and encourages confession of sin does not mean he advocates sin. On the contrary, he writes "so that you will not sin." He pleads with them not to think that what God has done for them in Christ makes them free to sin. He also pleads with them not to sin by taking up with his opponents who rationalize and deny sin and, thereby, insult God.

The sixth conditional begins, "But if anybody does sin" (1 John 2:1). This does not assume that John's opponents might be right. Rather, it assumes that Christians do sin. The second part of the condition explains how God handles this. The key is Jesus. First, John explains, "We have one who speaks to the Father in our defense." Jesus is our defense counsel. This is the same word John uses to refer to the Holy Spirit in John 14:16, 26; 15:26; and 16:7. There, the Spirit is Christ's advocate to us. Here, Christ is our advocate before the Father. His qualifications to serve on our defense are not a matter of academic degrees but of moral character: He is "the Righteous One." The significance of this is revealed in the next sentence, when we are told what He has to do to gain our release. He cannot defend our actions because we are guilty. He can only gain our pardon by volunteering to work out our sentence for us. It is only because of His moral perfection that God allows this.

Thus, we read: "He is the atoning sacrifice for our sins" (1 John 2:2). He offers himself in our place to make right the offense our sin has done to God. Translations divide over whether to follow the King James Version's "propitiation" or the Revised Standard Version's "expiation" here. The Jerusalem Bible, Today's English Version, and New English Bible follow the latter, while the New American Standard and the Living Bibles are with the King James. Neither word conveys much meaning to a modern audience, but the New International Version is probably correct to try to use more modern equivalents and to include the sense of both words: "atoning [propitiation] sacrifice [expiation]." The difference between the two words is a matter of the direction in which John sees Christ rendering His services on behalf of the sinner. If Christ primarily works to placate God's wrath, *atone* (propitiate) conveys this. If Christ primarily works by receiving the punishment for our sin, then *sacrifice* (expiation) conveys this.

Outside the Bible, the Greek word for "atoning sacrifice" is used almost exclusively when people attempt to placate the wrath of capricious gods with offerings. Inside the Bible, however, we see evidence of both concepts. In Zechariah 7:2; 8:22; and Malachi 1:9, God is viewed as the receiver of offerings to gain acceptance. In Psalm 78:38; 85:3; 103:8-10, and Micah 7:18-20, God seems to initiate forgiveness. In the New Testament, Christ is named as the ultimate sacrifice on our behalf (1 Peter 3:18; Hebrews 5:3; 10:6-26; 13:11). Importantly, John recognizes that Jesus' sacrifice averts the wrath of God in John 3:36. Yet he also expresses that God initiates the sending of the offering in John 3:16 and, significantly, in 1 John 4:10, the only other use of *atoning sacrifice* in this epistle. Within the immediate context of 1 John 2:2, we see that Jesus speaks to God on our behalf (1 John 2:1), but that God initiates forgiveness (1 John 1:9).

Therefore, Jesus atones for our sins as the perfect sacrifice. God appoints Him as our counsel and accepts His offer to sacrifice himself in place of the condemnation we deserve for our sins. Further, His work is not exclusive. What He has done with regard to sin, He has done "not only for ours but also for the sins of the whole world" (1 John 2:2). The work has been accomplished on behalf of all mankind, past, present, and future. Our salvation stands ready to be received by any of us who confesses Jesus as Lord and Savior. He is the only remedy for our sin. It is only by His work that we can walk daily in the presence of our Heavenly Father. Will you express your thankfulness to God? If you haven't before, will you claim the salvation God has prepared for you through Jesus Christ?

We Must Obey God's Commands (2:3-6)

"Knowing about" is different from "knowing." A television or radio sportscaster can know all about major-league baseball because he knows the players' batting and fielding statistics, averages against left-handed pitchers versus right-handed pitchers, home runs hit against particular teams, and pitchers' earned-run averages and strikeout percentages against every team. He may even know all the rules. But he doesn't really know major-league baseball because he doesn't play major-league baseball. That's the reason he does so many interviews with players and managers. A ten-year-old boy may idolize and know all about Orel Hershiser, but unless he is Orel's friend, he doesn't really know him.

In the same way, John asserts that intellectual knowledge of God is not the same as truly knowing Him (1 John 2:3-6). Truly knowing God comes from walking in His presence enough to have some of His moral character rub off on us. It is a relationship that shows up in the way we act. John's focus remains trained on his readers because he cares deeply for them and wants them to remain loyal to the truth. However, he still has an eye on his opponents, those heretics who have already left to begin a distinct fellowship and who continue to recruit followers.

In "Getting Acquainted With John,"[15] I drew a simple picture of the "Gnostic" beliefs that may have taken root in John's opponents. We don't know how they initiated new converts into the knowledge of God—whether it was mystical or purely intellectual. Regardless, they seemed to think only they could impart this special knowledge, and it was better, or at least more assuring, than whatever John and the orthodox church offered. Also, they disregarded both the relevance of Jesus' work and the believer's behavior.

The opening clause of verse 3, "We know that we have come to know," mimics Gnostic language, "We know that we know." John, then, is setting out the only certified way to examine the depth of our relationship with God. How do we know the claim we have staked in Christianity is valid? What may surprise us is that what he says has nothing to do with doctrine, our view of the Bible, or whether or not we go to Sunday-evening church, speak in tongues, or have been baptized. What John pinpoints is obedience. He calls for behavior that exhibits God's will, God's character. We must "obey his commands" (1 John 2:3).

We assume that John has God in mind when he says "him" and "his" in this passage, even though the last mentioned name is "Jesus Christ" (1 John 2:1). The reason is that the subject John has been addressing since the fifth verse of chapter 1 has involved knowing God and having fellowship with Him. This continues through the end of chapter 2. He even speaks of God as "light" again in 1 John 2:9. Notice also that, when John expresses in the negative his point about obedience (1 John 2:4), he says the person who "does not do what he commands" is "a liar, and the truth is not in him." This is virtually identical with what he says in 1 John 1:6, 8, and 10, where God is the main point of reference.

John then returns to a positive assertion about obedience (1 John 2:5). This time, he widens the field from obeying God's commands to obeying His "word." Our relationship with God should go beyond

---

[15]See also the co-author's remarks in the introductions ("Getting Acquainted") to 2 Peter and Jude.

merely obeying the letter of the law to understanding His will and doing that. The entire Bible is our field of knowing God and what He wants us to do—not just the imperative sentences. Notably, John draws a contrast between those who obey and those for whom God's "word has no place" (1 John 1:10).

John discloses the positive result of a person's obedience to God: "God's love is truly made complete in him" (1 John 2:5). Both God's love for him and his love for God become manifested in his life. He demonstrates that he knows God because he acts like God in his love for others. His love for others is driven by his love for God. We see, though, that obedience is more than the condition of knowing God and more than a demonstration of knowing God. Obedience is the way one comes to know God. In doing what God desires, we experience God—we learn what He is like.

We see further evidence that John does not have a list of rules in mind when speaks of obedience. He offers us a model. He says, "Whoever claims to live in him must walk as Jesus did" (1 John 2:6). Jesus' exemplary conduct as a real man in history is the official example of how we ought to live. In John 14:7, Jesus himself says, "If you really knew me, you would know my Father as well," and in John 13:15, "I have set you an example that you should do as I have done for you." In projecting Jesus as our ethical role model, John parallels Acts 10:38; Philippians 2:5-11; and 1 Peter 2:21. He also assumes that knowledge of Jesus' life is available to people in the church, probably as it is today in the four Gospels.

It should be noted that *Jesus* does not actually appear in 1 John 2:6. What is present there is a Greek word that means "that one." More literal translations, like the King James and Revised Standard Versions and the New American Standard Bible translate it as "he." Others, like the Today's English Version, the Living, Jerusalem, and New English Bibles, and the New International Version explicitly name "Jesus" or "Christ." John refers to "that one" other than God last mentioned in 1 John 2:1, "Jesus Christ, the Righteous One." Employing "that one" is part of John's style and always refers to Jesus (1 John 3:3, 5, 7, 16; 4:17; John 7:11; 9:12, 28; 19:21).

For most of us, doubt about our religious choice reasserts itself every once in a while. We feel empty and wonder whether we are really plumbing the depths of Christianity. We wonder where God is in our lives. We wonder whether all the meetings and services we are attending are worthwhile in our quest to know God. Momentarily, we may be attracted to the secrets of knowing God that Mormons,

Jehovah's Witnesses, and New Age proponents dangle in front of us. If so, we need to meditate deeply on what John has said here. He has said there are no tricks, no secrets; there is no intellectual or metaphysical hocus-pocus to knowing God. We come to know God and have sweet fellowship with Him in the very act of doing His will, in the very act of asserting love. We come to know His will by studying His Word and by meditating on the character of Jesus revealed in the Gospels. There is no gimmick here. Assurance comes from exercising God's will.

The Command Is Both Old and New (2:7, 8)

Some things can be old and new at the same time. An old house with a new coat of paint, new carpet, and an addition is, in a sense, new. I may say I bought a "new" car when what sits in my driveway is a three-year-old Chevy Citation with 40,000 miles on it. A daughter wearing her mother's wedding gown makes it new. Baseball, America's oldest pastime, has new rules, new teams, new stadiums, new uniforms, new players, and new fans. An old idea becomes new by giving added emphasis or applying it in a new context.

John asserts that the command he is promoting his readers follow is irreversible precisely because it is both old and new (1 John 2:7, 8). Its relevance and applicability will last forever. John does not say what the command is in these two verses, but he reveals later (1 John 2:10) that it involves loving one's brother. This old/new command to love recurs throughout the rest of his letter. It's hard to know whether his opponents are attacking it because it is old and their ideas are new or the reverse. In either case, John's argument challenges their false propaganda.

The command to love is old in the sense that it is written in the Pentateuch in Leviticus 19:18. It is old also in the sense that John's readers learned it from their first days as Christians. This is probably what he means when he says they have had it "since the beginning" (1 John 2:7). When he says it is the "message you have heard," he very likely means that he or other apostles taught it to them. Loving one's neighbor has a fixed place in official Christian teaching. The nine quotations of Leviticus 19:18[16] make it the most quoted Old Testament verse in the New Testament.

---

[16]Matthew 5:43; 19:19; 22:39; Mark 12:31,33; Luke 10:27; Romans 13:9; Galatians 5:14; James 2:8.

Of course, the reason the command to love is so prominent in Christian teaching is that Jesus emphasized it. In Matthew 22:39, He calls it the second-most important commandment, next to loving God, and proclaims that the two of them are the heart of Old Testament teaching. John calls it "a new command" here because, in his Gospel (John 13:34), he records Jesus' saying, "A new command I give you: Love one another." Jesus could call this principle new for a number of reasons. First, He made it more prominent than it had ever been before. Second, He himself embodied God's love for mankind (John 3:16). Third, He made His behavior the standard of love (John 13:34). Fourth, He enlarged the circle of love to include our enemies (Matthew 5:43, 44).

Furthermore, in the passage at hand, John asserts that love is new daily as it is personalized and actualized by you and me. "Its truth," he says, "is seen in him and you" (1 John 2:8). Love is viewable in Jesus but also renewed by His followers as we go from day to day.

Finally, the evidence of Jesus' new command to love one another is found in the fact that "the darkness is passing and the true light is already shining" (1 John 2:8). Christ's love for humanity, demonstrated in His life but supremely on the cross, shattered the rule of evil and hatred in the world. The "darkness" continues to dissipate as we His followers show love for one another and for our fellow man until that future but certain day when evil is totally banished and the love of God will rule.

Let us vow daily to renew God's love in our lives and participate in evil's ultimate doom.

We Must Love Our Brothers (2:9-11)

Sometimes neutrality is desirable. In world politics, Switzerland prides itself in its neutrality. Reporters are supposed to seek to be unbiased as they report the news. Scientists are supposed to assess their research critically. Judges and juries are to weigh evidence without favor toward the prosecution or the defense. However, in our relationship to God, neutrality is just as bad as antagonism.

John describes a cosmic battle between darkness and light (1 John 2:9-11). The arena is not a sky filled with flashing swords. Rather, the arena is people and the way we treat one another. Those who "fight" with love extend the light of God and demonstrate their true and deepening relationship with Him. Those who fight with hate champion the darkness and the forces of evil. Those who are neutral, who say they believe in the light but offer no active love for others in the arena, are standing in the darkness—whether they know it or not.

The symbolism of light and darkness in these verses seems to be inspired by statements of Jesus recorded in John 8:12; 12:35; and 12:46, where He speaks of His being light and overcoming darkness. The ethical emphasis seems more inspired by the connection Jesus made elsewhere, like Matthew 22:34-40; Mark 12:28-34; and Luke 10:25-29, between loving God and loving one's neighbor. That is the reason it is unfair to exaggerate "whoever loves his brother" in verse 10 and elsewhere in this letter. John is not advocating love that excludes non-Christians. It is only that his main squabble is with a competing "Christian" group that is acting unloving toward the orthodox church and, probably, toward the apostle himself. Regardless, their unloving actions and lack of concern with godly behavior altogether, as far as John is concerned, disqualifies their claim to be "in the light," to know God, or to be Christians. He wants those remaining loyal in the church to recognize this.

The phrase *in him* (1 John 2:10) has an important alternate translation in the New International Version footnote, "in it." The translation "in him" signifies that the Christian does not do anything to cause his brother, the second "him," to stumble. There is certainly merit in this understanding, given that every previous instance of this phrase in 1 John (2:5, 6, 8) has been to a person.

The translation "in it" suggests that the light does nothing to cause the Christian to stumble. This understanding is preferable because the subject of concern in these verses is the Christian, or the one "who claims to be in the light." If our hypothetical person is truly "in the light," he will not stumble because there is nothing in the light to make him do so. As James 1:13 indicates, God does not tempt anyone. Also, this understanding makes verse 11 a better reverse of 10: just as darkness is the culprit in 11, light is the protection in 10. Finally, the three references to "in him" noted in support of first option refer to God or Jesus, not to people, and there is no doubt that "light" in 1 John 2:9 refers to God and perhaps secondarily to Jesus.

Then John reverses the imagery, this time fusing hatred with darkness (1 John 2:11). He pictures someone groping "in the darkness," not knowing "where he is going." As his unloving behavior continues to manifest itself, he moves deeper and deeper into the darkness away from the light, away from God. Eventually, he reaches a point where he is numb to evil. It is pitch black, and there is no way he can find the light again unless someone rescues him. As John says, "The darkness has blinded him." From John's perspective, this is an apt picture of his opponents. They delude themselves into thinking they are close to God, but their lack of concern for behavior is contrary to God's agenda. In reality, God is totally out of view. They can't know God and not love others. It's as simple as that for John. Anyone who buys their line is as foolish and deluded as they are.

There is a good way to visualize the difference between John's view of Christianity and that of his opponents. His opponents see themselves as stationary with respect to the light. They are "in" it. It is a position they occupy. Movement, or conduct, is irrelevant. John, on the other hand, holds that Christians should be dynamic within the light. Christians must live out the love for others that God shines upon them, the light that has enabled them to have a relationship with God to begin with. Christians love God and man because God first loved us.

What if there were a gauge that registered between "Stationary" on one end and "Dynamic" on the other. Where would the needle fall if the gauge were fastened to you? Is your Christian life stationary? Do you feel you are "in" because you joined the church once or because you were baptized? If so, you are in league with John's opponents. They considered themselves to be Christians, too. It is my hope that your gauge would be nearer to "Dynamic," meaning that you attempt daily to live out the love God has for you, which He demonstrated in His Son, Jesus Christ. If so, you are attuned to the mind of John.

CHAPTER TWENTY

Remaining Children of God

1 John 2:12—3:10

John fears that the people he is writing are attracted to the teaching of those who have already left the church and that more may be lost to this gross perversion of Christian truth. His anxiety emerges in this large grouping of verses as he pleads with "his children" to remain true children of God and goes so far as to brand these false teachers antichrists. John ceases using the light terminology, but the question of what it means to be in God's true circle, initiated with the thesis statement of 1 John 1:5, continues to cast its shadow over all the verses through 1 John 3:10.

Certainly, the repeated statements regarding John's purpose for writing (1 John 2:12-14) make these verses a fitting conclusion to what he has said in 1 John 2:1. However, their dramatic impact in assuring John's readers of their place with God already—without joining the separatists—also makes it an attention-getting preamble to the verses that follow.

The Author Dramatizes the Faithfulness of His Readers (2:12-14)

One of the best remedies for insecurities about ourselves is positive reinforcement. We just need to hear someone we respect tell us we are doing OK. As I write this manuscript and occasionally feel blah about parts of it, nothing helps me more than to hear my wife or an editor tell me it's good work. Our children come to us with a coloring they say is our house, and we tell them it's wonderful, even though it bears little resemblance to our house. Appreciative congregations encourage their ministers year after year.

John's readers were not perfect, but they needed to hear they were doing all right in their Christian walk. He had just spent the last three verses (1 John 2:9-11) depicting how wrong some people are in their religious choices without even being aware of it. He wants to assure those who have remained true to his apostolic teaching that

253

they are doing the right thing. He does this in tightly defined style with a great deal of repetition. The New International Version exhibits this nicely in its layout, beginning each of the six "I write to you" statements to the far left and indenting each of the six "because" statements two spaces.

John addresses "dear children," "fathers," and "young men." Does he have in mind literally three ages groups? Probably not, since the order is illogical for this. Perhaps he is thinking figuratively in spiritual terms: children (recent converts), fathers (established Christians), and young men (in between the other two). This is unlikely because, again, the order is wrong. Also, there seems to be no obvious difference in characteristics when John describes the "children" as having "known the Father" and the fathers as having "known him who is from the beginning."

More likely, when John addresses "dear children," as with the seven other times he does this in his letter (1 John 2:1, 12, 18, 28; 3:7, 18; 4:4; 5:21), he has in mind everyone in the church to which he is writing. Furthermore, the comments following "dear children" refer to forgiveness of sins and knowing the Father (1 John 2:12, 13). These ideas are appropriate for all Christians.

This general understanding of the "dear children" clauses has caused some to suggest that "fathers" and "young men" are terms John substitutes for elders and deacons. However, such substitutions do not appear elsewhere in Scripture, nor does this readily suggest itself here. So we return to the question of whether "fathers" and "sons" are age or spirituality groupings in the church. My judgment is that spirituality is uppermost in mind, but that age may play a factor. Older Christians, or those who have been Christians for a long time, may very well face the crisis of looking back and wondering whether they have been right to give themselves over to Christianity. To them, John underscores appropriately that they have indeed "known him who is from the beginning" (1 John 2:13). Young Christians, or those who have not been Christians very long, are often in the thick of temptation and dealing with old sin patterns. Confidently, John embraces them with assurance that they indeed "have overcome the evil one" (1 John 2:13) and ratifies that they "are strong" (1 John 2:14), strong enough to deal with temptation because in them "the word of God lives" (1 John 2:14).

A key word, recurring frequently in 1 John 2:12-14, is *because.* No doubt, the positive attributes that follow the six *because*s are intended to contrast the negative comments about those "in darkness"

(1 John 2:9-11). Indeed, John writes not to those who have followed the heresy, but to those who have remained loyal. But does he write because he thinks his readers' confidence level matches the strong words of victory he pens or because they lack confidence and need to hear him reassure them? I think the latter. John's tone, especially through verse 10 of the third chapter but really throughout the letter, evidences that the heresy had really rattled the church. Those remaining were being told by the separatists that they were spiritually inferior and following the wrong course. They needed John to infuse them with confidence and determination.

John does three other things to strengthen his readers. First, notice that all the verbs in the "because" clauses are present perfect tense ("*have* been forgiven . . . *have* known," and so on) rather than simple present or past. The only exception is "are" and "lives" in the sixth "because" clause. Using the present perfect tense six times underscores that, in their present condition, the readers have completely accomplished whatever the verbs describe. They "have been forgiven," "have known," "have overcome."

Second, notice the large amount of repetition between the first three clauses and the last three. This is another way that John stresses the truth of what he is saying about them and their position before God.

Third, the tense of the last three *writes* is past, not present as the New International Version has. The New American Standard, Jerusalem, and New English Bibles translate it "have written." This change of tense is significant partly because it justifies the huge amount of repetition between the first three and the second three clauses. It does more than that, though. It also provides a platform for expressing in poetic fashion John's own intense feeling about affirming the loyal Christians remaining in the church.

Christians are by no means perfect. In fact, all of us at times wonder whether we have hooked our lives to the right star. We wonder whether we really are doing what God wants us to do. We question whether God truly has dealt with our sin. We doubt. Sometimes, what we need to hear is not apologetics but simply affirmation. We need to hear sermons that tell "the old, old story." We need positive reinforcement from someone we respect. Let's keep this in mind for ourselves and also as we minister to others in the church.

We Must Not Love the World (2:15-17)

We live in an age of materialism. The accumulation of goods is the highest priority for most of the people around us, perhaps even of ourselves. Houses, cars, boats, campers, and clothes are a measure of success and, to a limited extent, provide joy in life. When we say we love these things, we usually don't mean that we love them more than our family and friends, but it can get that way. For *Sesame Street*'s Bert, the need to find his favorite green paper clip sometimes causes him to ignore the serious personal needs of Ernie or other friends. When this happens, because of the ludicrousness of loving something like a paper clip, we easily see that Bert has gone beyond harmless idiosyncrasy. Certainly, there are worse things in the world to love than a paper clip, but putting things above people is wrong—no matter what the "things." Loving things above loving people is tragic and does inexplicable damage.

John makes a point very much like this, but he puts it in more spiritual terms. He appeals to his readers not to be enticed by the sins that the materialistic, human society offers. After a command to this effect, he offers a reason: because loving both the world and God are mutually exclusive (1 John 2:15). He then explains why this is so (1 John 2:16) and offers a second reason for not loving the world: because the world is temporary and moving ever closer to extinction (1 John 2:17).

When John says, "Do not love the world" (1 John 2:15), we first need to be sure we understand that he does not mean the earth or its people. Unlike our language, Greek does not treat the two different words, *world* and *earth,* as synonyms. *World,* related to the word from which we get *cosmetics,* sometimes refers to the decoration with which God adorned the earth: creation of plants, animals, and people. We understand John 3:16, "God so loved the *world*," in this general way, although focused on people. Heavily in the New Testament and in John,[17] *world* has an entirely negative meaning referring to the evil distortions man has made of God's good. It includes everything in human society that opposes God and pulls man away from Him. John clarifies that this is what he means when he adds, "or anything in the world."

John, then, challenges his readers to see that love of the world and love of the Father are polar extremes. Attaching oneself to the things of the world means that one is not drawing toward God. John challenges

---

[17] 1 Corinthians 2:12; 3:19; 5:10; 7:31; 11:32; 2 Corinthians 5:19; 7:10; James 1:27; 2 Peter 2:2; and especially John 8:23; 12:25, 31; 13:1; 15:18, 19; 16:11; 17:14, 25; 18:36.

his readers to examine themselves in this way, but especially to look at the life-styles of John's opponents. There his readers will see clear evidence that his opponents' ideas about getting to know God must be wrong. They can't know God if they live in ways that reveal they love the world.

In 1 John 2:16, John amplifies what he means. The "cravings of sinful man" is, more literally, the "desire of the flesh." Our physical body demands food, drink, exercise, and sex; and the demand can become insatiable when our spiritual needs are ignored. The "lust of the eyes," literally, is the "desire of the eyes," repeating the same word from the first phrase. With no spiritual glasses, our eyes become attracted to the superficial. The evil and material of the world enchant us. The "boasting of what he has and does" is, literally, the "pride of life." Without God, we become overconfident in our secular life. We believe in ourselves and our destiny but repress the nagging, spiritual void.

John, then, is not requiring that we hate the world or run away from society. He calls us away from worldliness, away from attachment to things, away from a secular worldview. A healthy spiritual dimension will infuse our lives with the ability to enjoy the world God has created for us without distorting it into evil.

John then supplies his second reason for not loving the world. Quite simply, the world will not survive into the permanent future (1 John 2:17). Even now, "the world and its desires pass away." They move ever closer to destruction. Their death knell was struck on the cross and in the resurrection of Jesus Christ. The spiritual battle against evil is won. Note that Paul says something very similar in 1 Corinthians 7:31. Only the last acts of the universe must be played out. Those of us who live out our lives in "the will of God," exercising spiritual vivacity against the secular will carry over into the realm that lasts "forever."

Secularism can creep into our lives so easily. As Christians, we must post a guard to check its progress. We must be vigilant to keep a spiritual perspective forefront in our lives. We must stop ourselves from becoming overly attached to the things of this world. We must put our stock in eternity. Each of us needs to identify the materialism that has crept into our lives and expel it. New spiritual development will result.

The Separatists Were Never Really Part of the Church (2:18, 19)

The 1919 Chicago Black Sox may have been the best baseball team ever assembled. With .400 hitter Shoeless Joe Jackson in the outfield, a veteran pitching ace with twenty-nine wins named Eddie Cicotte on the mound, and numerous other talented players like Buck Weaver, Hap Felch, Lefty Williams, Swede Risberg, and Chick Gandil, they were so good that everyone considered the best-of-nine World Series with the Cincinnati Red-legs a foregone conclusion. But something went very wrong. Because the team was so underpaid by owner Charles Comiskey, Risberg and Gandil successfully recruited six other players in their plot with mobsters to throw the World Series. The result was the opposite of a team effort, with members of the plot making intentional errors to lose and others striving that much harder to win. As the games progressed, more and more abandoned the plot, until only Risberg and Gandil were left pressuring others to lose. In the end, they were caught, and eight players were permanently suspended from baseball.

Is there any sense in which Risberg and Gandil could be considered part of the team when they intentionally plotted against it and brought catastrophe upon so many great players? I don't think so. John faces a similar question here. He speaks directly about his opponents (1 John 2:18, 19) for the first time in this letter. Since the separatists have turned against the church and against orthodox beliefs about Christ himself and are working to bring other believers with them, how do we assess their motives while they were in the church? Were they ever really part of the church in the first place? John says, "No!" Whether or not they knew they would someday spurn the church is hard to ascertain. Certainly God knew that rebellion was in their hearts and that they would not complete their faith. They may have been members of the visible church, but they were not part of the true church.

Once again, John calls his readers "dear children" as he seeks their attention to what he is about to say. The thrust of his message, that "the antichrist is coming," contrasts purposefully with his message the next time he uses "dear children" (1 John 2:28). There, the message is about the second coming of Christ.

John begins by declaring that "this is the last hour" (1 John 2:18). The *last days* is a phrase frequently used by New Testament writers to depict the period inaugurated by Christ's first coming and concluded by His return and judgment.[18] It picks up on an Old Testament

---

[18]Acts 2:17; 1 Timothy 4:1; 2 Timothy 3:1; Hebrews 1:2; James 5:3; 1 Peter 1:5, 20; Jude 18.

eschatological term, *Day of the Lord* (Joel 2:28; Isaiah 11:1; Malachi 4:1-6). By "last hour," used only here in the New Testament, John must mean the last period of the last days, though he gives no indication that he knows how long this last period will be. He knows that times are urgent. No doubt, he believes Christ's return is very near. Despite the fact that thousands of years have passed since John's time, we remain in the last hour (perhaps the last minutes).

The reason John says "we know it is the last hour" is that forerunners of the coming "antichrist," which he calls "antichrists," have come. Although we employ the word *antichrist* frequently to refer to a powerful end-time deceiver, John is the only New Testament writer to use it, and he only uses it here and in 1 John 2:22; 4:3; and 2 John 7. Paul speaks of "the lawless one" (2 Thessalonians 2:1-12), while Jesus speaks of "the abomination that causes desolation" (Mark 13:14). Revelation (16:13; 19:20; 20:10) speaks of "the false prophet." The coming of these figures is associated with the end times. Jesus also spoke of "false Christs and false prophets." This may very well be where John gets his plural.

John boldly asserts that his opponents are "antichrists." This tag is appropriate not so much because they are masquerading as Christ, but because they question the humanity of Christ and trample on the value of Christ's work for salvation (cf. 1 John 1:7, 9). They are also actively recruiting people away from the orthodox church into their heresy. John is sure they are antichrists because they "went out from us." They have left the church. They have spurned the truth in order to preach falsehood. John figures if they justify doing that, there must have been something wrong with them deep down from their very first association with the church. Thus, he says, "None of them belonged to us" (1 John 1:19). Rather, they belonged to the antichrist. John has in mind not just the teachers of this heresy, but all who have followed or will follow them out of the church.

It might be tempting to call anyone who leaves the church an antichrist. However, we must not do that. John is witnessing a major attack on the central teaching of the church about Christ and on how Christians ought to live out their commitment to God. Unfortunately, one of the reasons he is so outraged is that these heretics are winning substantial numbers of people away from the church. They are splitting the church.

Almost certainly, the spirit of the antichrist is actively at work whenever a dispute divides a congregation, regardless of the issue. Despite this, John charges us to stand as sentinels over the centrality of Christ in the church, to understand what the Bible teaches about our salvation, and to query those who soften the gospel message (1 John 2:18, 19). Falsehood is sometimes taught in the church, knowingly or unknowingly. In either case, we must be prepared to speak the truth in order to demonstrate the deficiency of the false teaching, just as John is doing in this letter.

Antichrists Deny That Jesus Is God's Son (2:20-23)

In 1 John 2:20-23, John exploits the fatal flaw in his opponents' claim to have a saving relationship with God: their belief that Jesus is unnecessary. They reject Jesus as God's legitimate and full-fledged Son and, thereby, the necessity of His role in salvation. In his own Gospel, John records Jesus' saying, "No one comes to the Father except through me" (John 14:6), and, "He who loves me will be loved by my Father" (John 14:21). In their rejection of Jesus, the separatists annul their claim to be able to lead others to a deeper knowledge of God.

One of my best friends in high school was named Richard. Richard did not live all that close, but we would often go to his house after playing tennis at nearby courts. In due course, I got to know his parents and others in his family. When I applied for jobs that required references, I would always write down the name of Richard's father because he was the owner of a well-respected nursing home in town. I didn't know Mr. Katz all that well personally, but I knew him through his son just as he knew me through his son. That was good enough, and he was happy to be a reference for me. Without Richard, though, I would never have known his father or have been able to use him as a reference.

This is the same point John makes about Jesus and His Father. We would never know the Father without knowing the Son. Since the separatists reject the Son, they cannot know the Father, despite their claims to the contrary.

John begins this section by speaking of his readers and the special capacity they have as Christians to recognize truth. Their loyalty to the church, in contrast to the heretics who have left the church, demonstrates this. John's readers "have an anointing from the Holy One," which assures that they "all . . . know the truth" (1 John 2:20).

The word *anointing* here refers to what has been applied, or the "ointment," rather than to the action of anointing or some kind of ceremony. Oil was poured over Aaron's head to consecrate him as high priest (Exodus 29:7; 30:25; 40:15) and over David's head to consecrate him as king (1 Samuel 16:13). In Acts 10:38, Peter says that "God anointed Jesus of Nazareth with the Holy Spirit." In 2 Corinthians 1:21, Paul says that God has "anointed us" by putting "his Spirit in our hearts." And John 16:13 describes the Spirit as "the Spirit of truth," who will guide us "into all truth." Uppermost in John's mind here, then, must be the Holy Spirit, who indwells all Christians.

John probably also intends us to connect the anointing of the Holy Spirit with our reception of the gospel. Ephesians 1:13 does this when it unites receiving the Spirit with having "heard the word of truth, the gospel of your salvation." Here, sandwiched between John's only two references to anointing (1 John 2:20 and 2:24), John implores his readers to retain "what you have heard from the beginning." What assures John that they recognize truth from falsehood is their submission to the gospel and the work of the Holy Spirit in their lives.

When John says that this anointing is "from the Holy One," we may think at first that he means God, since He is so often called "holy" in Scripture.[19] However, only Jesus is actually called "the Holy One."[20] Even more significantly, it is Jesus who sent the Comforter in John 15:26–16:16, the passage that seems to be the foundation for John's remarks here. Thus, the importance of Jesus is stressed once again.

Knowledge of the truth in Christianity is not isolated to a few special people, as John's opponents may have claimed for themselves. Thus, John emphasizes that the truth is known by "all of you." This fact is underlined when John adds his confidence that they also know "no lie comes from the truth" (1 John 2:21). He is certain they can see that people like the separatists, who falsify the gospel, are liars and cannot possibly lead anyone into the truth of God.

John as much as calls the heretics liars in 1 John 2:22. He infers that they deny "that Jesus is the Christ." He explains that such a denial makes the label "antichrist" appropriate. But what did John's opponents actually deny? It is doubtful that they simply denied Jesus was the Messiah. More likely, they denied what was involved in His messiahship, especially when we see that John changes his terminology from "Christ" to "Son" in his next three references to Jesus.

---

[19]See, for example, Psalm 71:22; Isaiah 5:16; John 17:11; 1 Peter 1:16.

[20]Mark 1:24; Luke 4:34; John 6:69; Acts 3:14; Revelation 3:7.

As I pointed out in the introduction, the heretics were probably associated in some way with Cerinthian Gnosticism. This brand of Gnosticism denied that God's Son came as a babe and later died and rose as a man. This would be too undignified. Rather, God's Son took over the life of a righteous man named Jesus at His baptism and left before the crucifixion. John rightly identifies that this negates the true sonship of Jesus. The heart of the gospel is that God became man. He suffered the indignity of confining His perfection, glory, and power in the body of a man, from birth to death, through to the resurrection. That's what the hymn to Christ in Philippians 2:6-11 is all about.

As far as John is concerned, nullifying the sonship of Christ amounts to blasphemy and comes out of the mouths of people speaking on behalf of the chief of liars (cf. John 8:44). Denying "the Son" means they deny "the Father." By denying the true sonship of Jesus, they cut themselves off from God, who testifies to His Son. They disregard the gospel as the truth and gag the Holy Spirit. How can they possibly lead anyone closer to God when they dishonor His Son? In fact, they insult God and work against Him and the church.

All of this does not mean that Christians are not allowed to discuss theology or Christology. To wonder how or why God became man in Jesus Christ is not wrong. But to override what the Word of God says with our own speculation is dangerous. Rather, what we think must be rooted in what God says in Scripture. If we study it with diligence and remain tuned to the voice of His Spirit within, we will not fall into error as John's opponents did. We should refrain from accepting the teaching of those who lessen the work of Christ, whether it comes from a modern-day cult or from someone within the church.

We Must Remain True to God (2:24-27)

A Boy Scout promises to do his duty to God and country and to be brave, clean, and reverent. A Girl Scout promises to help people at all times. A female college student pledges to her sorority and a male to his fraternity. As citizens of the United States, we pledge allegiance to the flag. Many churches display the Christian flag, and Vacation Bible School opening programs always feature a pledge "to the Savior for whose kingdom it stands." Sometimes even a pledge to the Bible is heard: "God's holy Word, a lamp unto my feet, a light unto my path."

Loyalty is important in society and in Christianity, and this is what John solicits and reinforces in this section. Loyalty to God demands loyalty to Christ. Loyalty to Christ is insured by loyalty to apostolic teaching about Him and by remaining true to our anointing of the Holy Spirit. By discounting their heritage of teaching and by listening to themselves rather than to the Holy Spirit, the separatists have lost the promise of eternal life they thought they had. In contrast, those who remain loyal have not.

The *you* in "see that what you have heard from the beginning" (1 John 2:24) is emphatic. The New American Standard Bible's "as for you" is helpful in getting this across. John wants to set his loyal readers over against the separatists and their views. What distinguishes the loyalists from the separatists is their respect for the apostolic teaching they received from their earliest contacts with Christianity. They treasure it rather than trample on it. It "remains" in them. A concern for loyalty to this teaching is expressed in many of the New Testament letters.[21] Here, John goes on to express that loyalty to apostolic teaching, which is safeguarded in the New Testament for us, will result in a secure relationship with "the Son" and, thereby, with "the Father." John's use of *Son* reminds us that foremost in John's concern right now is the heretics' stripping Jesus of His true humanity in their teaching.

John articulates a domino theory that leads from apostolic teaching, to Christ, to God, to eternal life (1 John 2:24, 25). From the perspective of the loyal Christians, it's a matter of setting them up. From the perspective of the disloyal Christians, it's a matter of knocking them down. Opposing apostolic teaching has led John's opponents to forfeit what they say they offer: life with God, life in the light—both now and in the future. Supporting apostolic teaching leads to the permanent relationship with God that Jesus "promised us" (1 John 2:25), related in John 10:10, 28, and 17:2. That relationship begins now and lasts forever.

John publicizes the harmful intent of the separatists in 1 John 2:26. He admits he has been trying to warn his readers from "those who are trying to lead you astray." I don't suppose John would mind so much if these false teachers had remained to themselves. What alarms him is that they continue to spread their poisoned apples in the church and are drawing people away to the doom they face. He writes this letter to halt their success.

John remarks that he believes in his readers' continued loyalty because of "the anointing you received from him" (1 John 2:27),

---

[21]See 1 Timothy 6:3; 2 Timothy 1:13; 4:3; Titus 1:9; 2 Peter 3:2; Jude 17, 20.

referring again to the Holy Spirit Christ gave them to reinforce the gospel they first learned. Because of this, John reasons, they need no teacher, certainly not from the separatists. They don't really even need him.

This is not to say that a Christian is totally self-sufficient, or that teachers are not important in the church. Some are specially gifted to teach (1 Corinthians 12:29; Ephesians 4:11). Also, the *you* throughout this verse is plural and refers to the corporate church body. Within the church, the Spirit and Scripture (apostolic teaching) and its teachers should be sufficient for Christians to teach "about all things."

The separatists may have been baptized and may claim that their teaching comes from the Holy Spirit. However, since they discard apostolic teaching about Christ, their anointing must be "counterfeit," says John. If the Spirit speaks through the apostles (John 20:22; Acts 1:8) and in us, then teaching that conflicts with that of the apostles reflects badly on the Holy Spirit. John's opponents—if they are right—are bringing the Holy Spirit into conflict with himself. But this is not possible, so their teaching must be wrong, and the apostle warns his loyal readers to "remain in him."

I began this section speaking about the value of loyalty. But loyalty to a bad cause is not good. Loyalty to a gang, a crooked boss, or a friend who is lying, is bad. Loyalty to a false religion like Hinduism or to a cult like Mormonism is bad. Loyalty to family can even be bad, if it keeps us from being a Christian (Luke 14:26). So we need to check out our loyalties as we ponder this section. Are we remaining loyal to that confession we made when we were baptized? What if the person who led us to Christ told us now he had been naive then and that New Ageism is better? What if our father, mother, husband, or wife were to forbid us to worship Jesus Christ? What if our country made it illegal to be a Christian? What would you do? Perhaps a test of your loyalty to Christ is now occurring. What are you doing?

As Children of God, We Should Be Like Christ His Son
(2:28—3:3)

Maybe you've done it too. You meet someone for the first time and, as you talk, you keep looking at eyes, nose, and hair thinking surely you've met this person before. The person sees your perplexity and finally says, "Oh, I'm so-and-so's brother" or "sister." And you say, "Of course, you are; I can see the resemblance now that you mention it; but you're a little taller, and your hair's a little darker, isn't it?" If you know the parents, you might add, "Now, you look a little more like your mother than he does."

The theme of 1 John 2:28—3:3 is family resemblance. John says that we are "children of God" (1 John 3:1, 2). For him, this means not so much that we should be like God, but that we should be like Jesus, His Son, through whom He is known. We should emulate His "righteous" and "pure" behavior (1 John 2:29; 3:3). Since the world does not know God, it rejects us just as it rejected His Son (1 John 3:1). When Jesus returns, our resemblance to Him will be made complete (1 John 3:2). Our heritage as God's children will be finalized at Christ's second coming just as it was made possible by His first (1 John 3:2, 4-6). We must "continue in him" to secure our present and future relationship with God (1 John 2:28).

The interpretive dilemmas in this section primarily involve the masculine pronouns that are used. The words *he, him,* or *his* occur twelve times in the New International translation (although it should be recognized that the Greek text itself does not have an actual pronoun each time). Each time one of these occurs, a case can be made for its referring to God or Jesus, or one implying the other. This is a common problem in 1 John because John draws a very fine line between the two in his own mind. His very high view of Christ's divine nature may explain this. Nevertheless, the pronouns must be sorted out to understand John's thrust here. My explanation in the previous paragraph assumes decisions about these pronouns that require some elaboration. The Today's English Version enhances my view by translating "Christ" or "God" for each pronoun in the same way that I understand them.

All the masculine pronouns in 1 John 2:28 refer to Christ. This follows from the decision that "the Holy One" (1 John 2:20) is Christ, which makes "his anointing" and "remain in him" in verse 27 refer to Christ. The phrase "continue in him" in verse 28 picks up from "remain in him" above (actually identical phrases in the Greek text). "When he appears" and "his coming," then, refer to Christ's second coming.

Other New Testament authors, especially Paul, prefer the word *coming* to speak of Christ's return,[22] although this is its only use by John. It is often transliterated into English as "parousia." Outside the New Testament, *parousia* was often used to speak of the "coming"

---

[22]See 1 Corinthians 15:23; 1 Thessalonians 2:19; 3:13; 4:15; 5:23; 2 Thessalonians 2:1, 8, 9; James 5:7; 2 Peter 1:16; 3:4, 12.

of a royal dignitary, perhaps one who was passing through a village on a journey. People would line the road and give honor as he went past. John has this in mind when he speaks of being "confident and unashamed before him" (1 John 2:28). Rather than sneaking off into a corner like a traitor, we rush to see our beloved King Jesus. Knowing that we "continue in him," both morally and spiritually, makes this possible.

In verse 29, we get a good example of how God is never far from John's thoughts. The phrase *he is righteous* refers to Christ, while *born of him* refers to God. Although John has described God as righteous, or just (1 John 1:9), and Christ as "the Righteous One" (1 John 2:1), the text of verse 29 still is under the shadow of verse 28, where *Christ* was the subject. Our moral example in the New Testament is Jesus.[23] Doing "what is right" like Jesus, the Righteous One, shows that we have been "born of" God, as He was.

The idea of being born of God occurs regularly throughout the rest of 1 John (1 John 3:9; 4:7; 5:1, 4, 18) and also in John's Gospel (John 1:12, 13; 3:3-8). Spiritual rebirth is a major New Testament concept,[24] which signifies not only our new relationship with God but also our new ambition to conform our activity to His will. Of course, our rebirth is only possible through Christ and His work for us on the cross.

The next verse, 1 John 3:1, elaborates on the role of "the Father" in our rebirth. There is no room for confusion about who is in mind here, and it clarifies the reference in 2:29. Like a husband's love for his wife bears fruit in children, so also God's love brings about "children of God." These children are not the result of procreation, but of a love in which He "gave his one and only Son" to die for us (John 3:16). Although unusual, our relationship to God is legitimate because the Father has "called" us "children of God," just as a father in New Testament times publicly named his children (cf. Luke 1:63). John underscores this reality with the pronouncement, "And that is what we are!"

The *him* in the third sentence of this verse refers to God, since knowing God has dominated the letter so far. God and the world

---

[23]See John 13:13-17, 34; Romans 15:7; Ephesians 5:2; Colossians 3:13; Hebrews 12:2; 1 Peter 2:21; 4:1; Revelation 3:21.

[24]See Matthew 5:9; Luke 20:36; Romans 8:14, 19; Galatians 3:26; 4:5-7; Hebrews 12:5-10; 1 Peter 1:3, 23; Titus 3:5.

were juxtaposed in 1 John 2:15-17, and God is the reference in the rest of 1 John 3:1. We cannot limit it too severely, though, because the past tense of "did not know" seems to indicate an historical point in time. John can speak of either Christ's or God's not being known (1 John 3:6; 4:8; John 16:3). However, John 1:10, identical to what we have here, speaks of Christ's saying "the world did not recognize him." In John 8:19, Jesus says, "If you knew me, you would know my Father also." The *him*, then, refers first to God, but unmistakably also to our means of knowing God, Jesus Christ. So just as the world showed it does not know God by rejecting and, indeed, crucifying His Son, the world's rejection of us exhibits that we are truly God's children.

John then contrasts our present condition with what we will be in the future (1 John 3:2). He can assert that we are children of God "now" because he just established that fact in the previous verse. His only reference point for "what we will be" is that other child of God, Jesus Christ. The physical body John saw (cf. 1 John 1:1-4) was just like ours, but His glorified body in the fullness of its splendor is yet to be seen, when Christ re-"appears." As God's children, we will be transformed to be "like him," our brother. The personal pronouns, then, refer here to Christ. The New International Version footnote suggests that "when he appears" could be translated "when it is made known," but this is unlikely since we are still in the context of 1 John 2:28.

The logical consequence of being like Christ at His second coming, according to John, is that we should try to be more and more like Him now in our demeanor. If we put our "hope in him," as we should, then we should purify ourselves, "just as he is pure" (1 John 3:3). That this is in contrast to John's opponents will be elucidated in the next few verses. The pronouns, then, in verse 3 refer to Christ. This is certain because *he* here is actually "that one" already mentioned in 1 John 2:6 as referring only to Jesus in John's letters.

Whom do you resemble most in your family? Many people look more like a cousin or an aunt or uncle than their parents. Perhaps for you, it is your sister or brother, or mother or father. Spiritually, the closest you can get to being like God is being like Christ because He became a real human being. He experienced the emotional traumas and the physical pains that you do. He was ostracized, humiliated, tired, and sick. Yet He did not sin. Make it your goal to become more and more like Him so people can come to know Him through you and God through Him.

We Must Take Sin Seriously (3:4-10)

Occasionally, a basketball player will tip the ball into the other team's goal while going for a rebound. Or a football player may get confused and run toward the opposition's goal. Those are obvious mistakes that benefit the opposing team. Usually, mistakes are more subtle in sports, but any mistake a player makes ultimately benefits the opposition. We don't usually blame them for their mistakes, though, unless it is obvious that they aren't doing their best or because they are angry, not concentrating, or just being lazy. Then we boo them.

Just as no one expects perfection in an athlete, no one expects a Christian to be perfect, either. But God does expect diligent effort to live a life worthy of the perfect salvation Christ has achieved for us. In 1 John 3:4-10, John says that anything short of perfection in our walk works on behalf of the opposition, the devil himself. Despite the fact that we play on Christ's team, our sin enables the devil's team to score points. Therefore, we must take our sin seriously. It betrays our leader, Jesus Christ.

John asserts what he considers a universally recognized truth about sin: "Everyone who sins breaks the law" (1 John 3:4). Probably not even John's opponents will argue with this fact. By saying "everyone who," John narrows this from a general observation to an individual responsibility. When he adds that "sin is lawlessness," he seems to be trying to do something more than define sin as anarchy. Rather, he endeavors to associate sin with "the man of lawlessness" mentioned in 2 Thessalonians 2:3-7. When we sin, we contribute to his unswerving opposition to God. For that instant, we become an antichrist and side with John's opponents.

In contrast to us, John says that "no sin" is in Christ (1 John 3:5). In fact, His purpose in coming to the world was to "take away our sins." Christ's sinless perfection is only alluded to in John 8:46, but it is stressed in 2 Corinthians 5:21; Hebrews 4:15; 7:26; and 1 Peter 2:21, 22; 3:18. His work for our sins, resulting in His death, is a resounding theme of the New Testament, but notice that John 1:29 uses the same words that are used here.

John portrays in the starkest terms how our sin violates our relationship with Christ. Just as a teenager staying out all night may break household rules, our sin breaks the rules of living in Him. Just as Peter denied Christ,[25] we portray ourselves to the world as not

---

[25]Matthew 26:69-75; Mark 14:66-72; Luke 22:54-62; John 18:15-27.

even knowing Him when we sin (1 John 3:6). John wants us to see the utter incongruity of calling ourselves Christians and being unconcerned when we betray Christ. Peter was disgusted with himself for what he did and sought forgiveness. We dare not treat our sin as irrelevant since Christ died for it.

That's probably what the separatists did. For their benefit, John adds, "No one who continues to sin has either seen him or known him" (1 John 3:6). John has already declared that he has seen Christ (1 John 1:1-4). Therefore, he knows firsthand of His sinlessness and His displeasure with sin in those who follow Him. John has stressed over and over in this letter that his opponents do not know God, as they claim. Their lack of concern about sin is further proof of it.

The New International Version's translation, "keeps on sinning" and "continues to sin," is an attempt to keep John out of contradicting what he says about our sin elsewhere (1 John 1:8, 10; 2:1; 5:16). Simply translating the word "sins," as the New American Standard Bible does, is more literal and closer to John's point. He is speaking in ideal terms. One who allies himself with the Sinless One should not sin either. John is well aware that Christians do sin. But he wants to impress upon us that when we do, we betray our allegiance to Christ. John wants his readers to take their sin seriously and not fall for the teaching of his opponents, which denies the need to care about our sin.

This becomes apparent in verses 7-10, where he clarifies and reiterates much of what he has said, not only in verses 4-6, but also 1 John 2:28—3:3. John expresses his worry over the false teachers' impact on the orthodox believers and then repeats his point that we should model Christ's righteousness (1 John 3:7; cf. 2:29). He then explains that sinful behavior, whether from a Christian or a non-Christian, is "of the devil," and that "the Son of God" came to earth "to destroy the devil's work" (1 John 3:8). Glimpses of the second idea are also found in John 12:31 and Luke 10:18.

John's logic for why a Christian should not sin is clear: if a Christian is "born of God" (as John says in 1 John 2:29—3:2), then he literally "does not sin" (NIV: "will [not] continue to sin") and is not even "able to sin" (NIV: "cannot go on sinning") because he has the divine "seed" in him (1 John 3:8). Spiritually speaking, a Christian is as much God's child as I am my father's son. There is something of the Father in him. John may mean the Holy Spirit—as he did when he talked about our "anointing" from Christ (1 John 2:20, 27). Regardless, by *seed,* he indicates that the ability to overcome sin in our lives comes from God rather than from ourselves alone.

Finally, John says that "children of God" and "children of the devil" are divided by how they behave (1 John 3:10). Being oblivious to "doing what is right" and making no attempt to love others identifies a person as being outside God's family.

Because we are God's children, we have within our grasp the resources to be like Him. Even though His Son has paid the price for our sins, our love for God and our commitment to Christ should inspire us to act righteously and with love. We should be distraught that we add one more sin for Christ to bear, and devastated when we contribute to the cause of our enemy, Satan, when we sin. That's what John wants. Our path through Christianity should be one of growth and improvement. With Christ as our model, and as God's children, we need to become more and more like Him each day. It might be worthwhile to ask yourself today whether you have yet moved beyond infancy into adolescence, or from young adult to middle age.

CHAPTER TWENTY-ONE

Living by Love

1 John 3:11—4:12

The thesis statement in 1 John 3:11, that "we should love one another," not only initiates a new section; it begins the second half of 1 John. The word *message* indicates this. The only other time it appears in the New Testament is in 1 John 1:5, where it signals the thesis statement that governs the first half of the epistle.

For the most part, John has finished arguing with his opponents about the place of sin in the life of the Christian. His dominant concern in the last half of the letter is the crucial role of love in the life of the Christian. He speaks to his loyal readers, but his eyes do not stray too far from his enemies. Apparently, not only do they downplay the value of positive behavior toward others; they, in fact, are treating John and those who hold to his message with disdain. Their lack of love for their fellow Christians, John believes, discredits their movement entirely.

We Must Love, Not Hate, One Another (3:11-15)

Few things are more upsetting than hearing or reading news about the innocent's suffering. Refugees created by war in Central America. Victims devastated by earthquakes or floods. Fetuses aborted by their mothers. As bad as these things are, what is worse is learning of the harm hatred does to the innocent. Someone sprays machine-gun fire into a classroom of children. A young girl is abducted and raped. A woman is routinely battered by her husband. Evil hates what is good because purity shows in relief just how ugly the evil is. So unhappy, angry people lash out to break the mirror that magnifies the horror of their soul—just as the wicked queen sought to kill Snow White. Hate destroys. Only love creates.

Having made the connection between being God's child born out of love and loving one's brother (1 John 3:10), John here develops the theme (1 John 3:11-15). First, he issues an assertion about love

(1 John 3:11). Then he provides a negative illustration (1 John 3:12) and makes a number of deductions from this (1 John 3:13-15).

John says we must "love one another" (1 John 3:11). This is the first of five times John will say this in 1 John (3:23; 4:7, 11, 12), and the admonition appears again in 2 John 5. It is unlikely that he means anything different when he says that we should love our brother, something he mentions at least four times (1 John 2:10; 3:10; 4:4, 20, 21). In his Gospel, John records Jesus' saying, "Love one another."

John follows this statement with the startlingly negative command that we "not be like Cain" (1 John 3:12). He briefly recalls the story from Genesis 4:1-16 and then assesses the source and the motive of Cain's despicable action of murdering his brother, Abel. The Genesis account spells out neither of these. John draws these out for his own purposes. He says the source of Cain's actions was "the evil one," meaning the devil or Satan. Very likely, John thinks every murderer has given himself over to Satan. Cain was just the first and, thereby, becomes the archetype of murderers.

When John depicts Cain's action as having "murdered his brother," he does not use the normal verb for murder. It is a word that denotes special brutality, even butchery. In grotesque vernacular, John says Cain carved Abel up. Cain's motive, John says, was jealous resentment. John says nothing of God's rejection of Cain's sacrifice. He delves inside Cain and sees evil, which hates goodness. To Cain, Abel stood for and would constantly remind him of his own inadequacies. Abel prototypes all those who are innocent and good, just as Cain prototypes all those who are evil and bad. Wrongly, Cain thought killing Abel would remove his public humiliation, for God put a mark on his forehead (Genesis 4:15).

In 1 John 3:13, John draws the first of his deductions from Cain. He warns his readers that, just as Cain hated Abel, so "the world hates you." The world hates all that is God's, including us, His children. John feels at one with his readers in this rejection by the world and, for the only time in his letter, he addresses them as "brothers." Almost certainly, John includes the separatists with the world, just as he indicted them for their love of the world earlier (1 John 2:15-17). John, I think, is shocked at the vehemence coming from his opponents' camp toward him and those who have remained in the church. Such satanic attitudes, John will later spell out, show their true colors: black, not white. How can one hate the church without also hating Christ and God himself?

Another deduction John draws is that Cain helps us identify who we are and where we are going. Unlike Cain, who proved himself to be in the death camp, having "love for our brothers" demonstrates that we are in the life camp. He explains, "Anyone who does not love remains in death" (1 John 3:14). This is almost a contradiction in terms: to live in death. Nevertheless, all people live in death unless they put their trust in Jesus Christ and act out their faith in love for others. That's how a person moves from the death camp into the life camp. More to the situation at hand, John may be disclosing that he himself has found the capacity to love the separatists, even though they hate him, and he is encouraging the loyalists to do the same. In this way, they manifest the trueness of their position.

John further explains that hate is murder without opportunity (1 John 3:15), as Jesus himself taught (Matthew 5:21-26). So an attitude of hate toward another person puts us in league with murderers and, by implication, with Cain and "the evil one." Of course, a murderer destroys life. Thus, he is in no way associated with life, much less "eternal life." This is no categorical pronouncement of the eternal fate of all murderers. It is a logical, general deduction John makes to inspire his readers to love and to distance themselves from hate. It also becomes a judgment of damnation on his opponents if they don't change.

The world in which we live constantly exerts pressure on us not to be too good, too fair, too generous, too loving, too forgiving, or too spiritual. Surprisingly, we get this in the church sometimes, too. The crowd gets nervous and even resentful if someone gets too far ahead. John calls on us not to let the world, or even the church, hold us back from loving as we should. Moral mediocrity is no virtue. Moral conscientiousness is a dynamic that drives spiritual maturation. Show that you are worthy of the eternal life Christ attained for you: love one another.

We Must Demonstrate Our Love by What We Do (3:16-18)

Only an hour ago, I was walking through the corridors of our administration building at St. Louis Christian College and came upon a young couple. As I passed, Janine held out her left hand with her ring finger adroitly arched so I couldn't miss it. Of course, she was wearing a diamond. Rick proposed to her last night while atop the Clarion Hotel while the restaurant revolved to reveal scenes of St. Louis. Toward the end of the dinner, he declared his love for her and slipped the engagement ring on her finger. Rick's love for Janine is now expressed in solid gold and cut diamond for all the world to see. It is no longer something for us to wonder about.

John declares that our love as Christians should not be left to doubt, either. Love that demonstrates we are God's children is concrete and observable. John presents a positive example of this in the person of Jesus Christ, and then he presents some deductions for us to heed.

In 1 John 3:16, John offers Jesus as the archetype of love because He "laid down his life for us." The identical words are spoken by Jesus in John 15:13, though John has inserted *Jesus Christ* for *one* and *for us* in place of *for his friends.* Jesus is the opposite of Cain. Cain self-seekingly murdered another and destroyed life; Jesus sacrificially offered himself in place of all mankind in order to give life. He suffered what we deserve for our sins. What He did was not just a feeling nor a display for us to admire. This supreme, historical act of love accomplished something for us that is real and necessary. Jesus did something for us; He didn't just grandstand.

The second half of this verse contains John's first deduction from what Jesus did. He applies it directly to us by replacing *Jesus Christ* with *we,* and *us* with *our brothers,* and by making the verb present tense instead of past. John can say "we ought to" do this, not only because Christ did it first for us, but also because Jesus said that people who are "my friends" will behave this way (John 15:14). John has already stressed imitating Jesus (1 John 2:6, 29; 3:3, 7) and obeying His commands (1 John 2:7).[26]

John expresses his second deduction from Jesus' sacrifice for us in verse 17. He acknowledges the reality that situations that call for us to sacrifice our lives for others may never present themselves. However, real opportunities for sacrificial giving probably pass before us every day. Specifically, he mentions the down-and-outer who needs help. The failure to "have pity" on such a person undermines our claim to be a Christian. We are not imitating "the love of God" so evident in and through Jesus Christ if we cling to our "material possessions" when someone is in need. These are of the world anyway. In fact, *material* is, literally, "of the world." The only lasting value from these things comes from giving them away. The words

---

[26]Many New Testament passages challenge Christians to imitate Christ in their conduct. See 1 Corinthians 11:1; Philippians 2:5-8; 1 Thessalonians 1:6; 1 Timothy 6:13, 14; Hebrews 12:2, 3; 1 Peter 2:21.

has no pity on him literally mean "shuts his bowels against him." For Jews, the bowels were the seat of emotion, whereas we speak of the heart. To prevent our natural human emotions from signaling us to do something to help a person in need is not only un-Christian; it is inhuman.

John's third deduction, issued as an appeal follows from the first and the second. "Dear children," he writes, "let us not love with words or tongue but with actions and in truth" (1 John 3:18). He contrasts verbal pronouncements of love with love that is expressed in "actions and truth" (reminding us of James 2:14-17). Observable deeds demonstrate love to be genuine. Expressions of concern, even when uttered sincerely, trivialize a person's hunger and cold. They hurt, not help. To speak and not do misses an opportunity to imitate Christ's sacrificial love.

Imitating Christ's sacrifice for us is daunting. However, it is basic to our claim to be Christian. John does not allow us to view it as unreachable. He knows we are not God. But he also knows our daily lives teem with situations that require our loving attention in the name of Christ. All he asks is that we be open to the possibilities that come our way. They may seem minor to what Christ did, and they are. But they do parallel His actions, and that is significant. So be ready to imitate Christ today.

We Must Find Security Before God in Jesus (3:19-24)

We can buy insurance for just about anything. Most of us insure our cars for liability, collision, and comprehensive, our bodies for health, life, and old age, and our homes for fire and hail. If we're smart, we insure our vacations with traveler's checks and buy credit card protection. Using our money this way provides protection against the unforeseen.

Insurance isn't the only way we seek protection. We also put locks on our doors, install dead bolts, mount smoke detectors, and buckle our seat belts. Some of us look at religion as a kind of insurance against eternity, and this viewpoint contains a measure of truth. However, unlike normal insurance, only one company writes valid policies for eternity insurance, and it underwrites policies only in the name of Jesus Christ.

John tells his readers here what secures their position with God. It is faith in Jesus, who He is and what He did for us, and obedience to His command to love others. John's rivals brush aside Jesus' significance and any concern for behavior. They probably view these as crutches—even hindrances—to the elitist brand of Christianity they pander. John may also fear that this letter may be making his readers feel skittish about their own relationships to God.

The word *truth* bridges verse 19 to verse 18, although the bridge is somewhat superficial since the term carries different meanings in the two verses. In the former, it means "sincere," and here (verse 19), it means "valid Christianity"; it is something "we belong to." When John says, "This then," he does not just refer back to acting out love for others in our behavior (1 John 3:18). He really encompasses Jesus' demonstration of love for us described in verse 16. He will clarify this a little later (1 John 3:23).

Despite the New International Version's translation of *know* and *set* in the present tense, both words are actually future. John is not speaking generally but has in mind future, individual crises that will dash our confidence in our relationship to God. When we somehow fail God, John foresees a big problem with self-condemnation. As he says it, "Our hearts condemn us" (1 John 3:20). We get down on ourselves and think God must be disgusted with us. He may be, but we must never shortchange God's mercy and His capacity to forgive. Thus, John says, "God is greater than our hearts." We may not be able to love every beggar that comes our way (1 John 3:17), but God can. We must never think His ability to love is so limited as ours. John further suggests that the truth that God "knows everything" should provide comfort, not solicit fear. Perhaps this means that He can assess our good intentions even when we fail. Certainly, it means that He knows our desire to please Him and our remorse when we don't.

A secure relationship with God is also the basis for a productive prayer life (1 John 3:21, 22). John introduces this benefit as further encouragement to keep our hearts from being malevolent. A growing "confidence before God" promotes good communication with Him in prayer. When John says that we "receive from him anything we ask" (1 John 3:22), we must understand that he speaks of the ideal. It is not that God becomes our bellhop. Rather, our requests fall more and more in line with what He wants for us anyway. Other New Testament passages speak of God's granting our prayers; many of them are in John's Gospel.[27] The underlying assumption is always

---

[27]See Matthew 7:7, 8; 18:19; Mark 11:24; Luke 11:9; James 1:5. In John, see 14:4; 15:7; 16:23, 24.

that the requests coincide with God's will. Here, John makes this even more explicit than in some passages by stating the condition that "we obey his commands and do what pleases him" (1 John 3:22). By doing God's commands, we come to know God and His will. Our prayers almost unconsciously fall more and more in line with His plans.

John boils down God's commands to two: believe in Jesus and love one another (1 John 3:23). In doing this, he captures the core of Christianity. A reader might think that his only concern is love, since the word is used forty-seven times (counting both the noun and the verb forms). John has spoken of the command to love as both new and old (1 John 2:8-11). But being a humanitarian alone does not make one a Christian. Sensitivity to others must come out of faith in Christ because this is something both Christ and God "commanded." Thus, John mentions faith first. However, doctrinal belief by itself makes Christianity sterile.

Specifically, John says that we must "believe in the name of his Son, Jesus Christ." A person's name signifies who he or she is. To believe in someone's name is to believe in all that the name stands for, to believe in who they are, what they are like, and what they can do. To believe in the name of Jesus is to believe that He is God's "Son," that He is the "Christ" (or Messiah), that He did die for our sins and rose from the dead, that He is coming again, and that He is the only way to a saving relationship with God. As we have seen, John's opponents don't believe these things. Pointedly, they deny that the man Jesus was God's Son in any real way. John articulates the essential content of our faith and may even have in mind our public confession. Those who have left the church have rescinded their confession.

John can speak of living "in him" with reference to God or Jesus in his letter (cf. 1 John 2:5, 6, 14, 24, 27-28; 3:6; 4:12; 5:20), but here God is uppermost in mind. This is the first appearance in 1 John of the notion of a simultaneous indwelling of God in the Christian and the Christian in God, but the concept will keynote verses 13-16 of the fourth chapter. That same section also expands on "the Spirit he gave us," which also first comes up here (1 John 3:24). Earlier, I said that *anointing* referred to the Spirit given by Jesus (1 John 2:20, 26). Here, and in 1 John 4:13-16, we see that John can conceive of the believer's receiving the Spirit from God. Once again, we notice that John's notion of the Godhead is fluid. He can interchange God and Christ as it is appropriate to the context.

Giving the Spirit, then, is a substantive way in which God marks us as His children. Evidence of the Spirit's indwelling is not entirely subjective, as some think. In John, neither is it manifested by the speaking in tongues or some gift. Rather, it shows itself by the power it provides us to obey God's commandment to love one another and by the conviction it gives us to confess faith in Jesus Christ.

Emotional depression is often remedied by realizing that someone loves you and by doing something kind for someone else. We can treat our occasional spiritual depressions similarly. To get off dead center, we need to look to the Spirit God gave us for just such occasions. He can reconvict us that what God's Son, Jesus, did for our sins on the cross is real. He can also spark us with the needed lift to get our heads out of our hands and do something kind for someone. If we do this, we will soon see our prayer lives picking up again and our confidence about who we are in Christ becoming buoyant again.

We Must Distinguish the Spirit of God
From the Spirit of Falsehood in What We Believe (4:1-6)

In our fifteen years of marriage, my wife and I have changed residences ten times, two of these across the Atlantic. We know something about moving. Packing boxes and loading trucks are dreaded demands. However, one of the most stressful aspects of moving is neither of these. Rather, it is the sorting: wearable from no-longer-wearable, junk from heirloom, useless from maybe-can-be-used-sometime. If clothes, books, papers, toys, and furniture aren't separated in this way, we waste enormous physical energy hauling too much stuff around. Parting from a dated shirt or an old toy can be tough. Separating the wanted from the unwanted is difficult. However, we must do it.

In this section, John provides clear guidelines for sorting out teaching that is truly God's from teaching that is not. The first (1 John 4:1-3) outlines correct doctrine about Jesus. The second (1 John 4:4-6) delves into the origin of true teaching.

John shifts directions here, soliciting his readers' attention with the address, "Dear friends" in 1 John 4:1. That explains the chapter division. But the word *spirit* in this verse recalls 1 John 3:24, where the same word appears. However, the link is weak since the word is specific in the former use and general here.

John summons his readers away from doctrinal gullibility and peraps even charismatic naiveité. Probably, John's readers tended to accept all teaching reputed to be inspired. If a person said he or she inspired or perhaps their teaching was accompanied by some unusual phenomenon, few were inclined to question it. Most of us today are reluctant to attack what our ministers say from the pulpit or what our teachers say in the classroom. We, as well as the early Christians, are wise to keep in mind the danger of declaring false or satanic something the Spirit might have said (Mark 3:22, 29). However, there are limits to what we should accept as His teaching. Thus, John begins: "Do not believe every spirit" (1 John 4:1). John insists that we must distinguish "whether they are from God." In fact, not just a few, but "many false prophets have gone out into the world."

The existence of false prophets is true generally, but John's intentions probably are more narrow here. He used the same verb in 1 John 2:19 to describe the separatists' departure from the church. He has also identified them with the world in (1 John 2:15-17; 3:13). The guidelines for discerning true from false teaching in the verses that follow, then, are aimed specifically at fending off the recruiting efforts of John's opponents.

The purpose of the first guideline (1 John 4:2) is to flush out true from false beliefs about Jesus. Will the teacher publicly confess that "Jesus Christ has come in the flesh"? The confession strikes squarely at the teaching of John's opponents, which denies the genuine humanity of God's Son. Anyone who denies this or any other fundamental belief about Jesus does not warrant a hearing by the church on other matters. The Spirit is not with him. Paul presents a similar guideline in 1 Corinthians 12:3, as does John again in 2 John 7.

John says this denial indicates something worse than just being void of the Spirit. Not only is the teacher who denies Christ's humanity "not from God," but John identifies the person with "the spirit of the antichrist" (1 John 4:3). John's readers have heard this spirit "is coming" in earlier teaching. That he "now is already in the world," John established in the second chapter (1 John 2:18, 19, 22). There, as here, John considers his opponents antichrists. What else can they be, if they not only deny basic truth about Christ but teach against it with the purpose of drawing people out of Christ's church?

John then conveys his second guideline for distinguishing true from false teaching (1 John 4:4-6). He calls his readers to attention again, this time using a word that means "dear children" rather than "dear friends." He uses a linkword connection again. This time it is *the world,* used twice (1 John 4:3, 4) in the same utterly negative sense that we found in 1 John 2:15-17. It represents all that is antagonistic to God.

John proclaims the victory of those who have remained loyal to the truth. They "have overcome them" (1 John 4:4). Against the onslaught of the separatists, John's readers have stood firm and held the church together. Their fortitude confirms that they are truly God's children. They have done this not because they are so strong, but because the one who is in them "is greater than the one who is in the world" (1 John 4:4). The Spirit of God is mightier than the spirit of the antichrist. God's true children overcome "the evil one" (1 John 2:13, 14). Because the loyalists have won, it must be they, not their rivals, who truly possess God's Spirit in their teaching.

The fact that "the world listens to them" (1 John 4:5), while the church has not, further confirms the false teacher's anti-Christian nature. If that is the case, they speak what the world wants to hear and, therefore, must be from the world and not from God. In contrast, John represents those who are from God, as he says in verse 6. Anyone who follows apostolic teaching "knows God," whereas "whoever is not from God does not listen" to it. Receptivity to the message of the apostles versus the message of the world displays trueness. The very fact that the separatists have opposed John and his teaching reveals that the true origin of their teaching is not God. Rather, it comes from the evil one.

John concludes: "This is how we recognize the Spirit of truth and the spirit of falsehood" (1 John 4:6). He refers to the two guidelines addressed above. Denying Christ's true nature amounts to watering down the gospel. In this form, it becomes more palatable to the world but distasteful to the church. It reveals its origin by who accepts it.

A vital task of the church, then, is to distinguish between true and false teaching. This task belongs on the minister's job description. That's why he must be a student of Scripture. But it is not the minister's job alone. More often than not, ministers are the ones who lead their congregations into false teaching and cults. Probably, it was the leaders who initially left John's church. Therefore, the task of discerning teaching belongs to everybody in the church. This means we all must strive to understand the Bible. This is one of the reasons God gives us His Spirit. Are you ready for the challenge that could come in your church today?

Our Love Originates With God (4:7-12)

Children are created by parents who love one another. When babies are born, they may have the capacity to love, but they do much more receiving of love than giving. They do not act out their love for their moms and dads. They sleep and cry, eat and dirty their diapers. Moms and dads, on the other hand, spend almost all their time working out their love for their babies in very practical ways. At some point during adulthood, the child's and the parents' love begins to balance. By the time the parents are retirees and their health recedes, the children are doing most of the loving deeds while the parents are receiving. From where has the children's love come? Doesn't it mirror the love they have seen their parents show them? Like a solar panel, children absorb the love from their parents and then use it to generate love themselves.

At least three times in this section, John exhorts his readers to "love one another" (1 John 4:7, 11, 12). Basic to his reasoning that love is essential among Christians is that love's origin is God. He then details two more related reasons, that God has demonstrated His love by sending Jesus (1 John 4:9, 10) and that His love continues to be demonstrated by the love we exhibit (1 John 4:11, 12). What he says here expands on the second prong of assurance he listed earlier (1 John 3:23), just as the remarks in the first section of the chapter (1 John 4:1-6) expand on the first. It displays the core of his teaching (cf. 1 John 2:9-11; 3:11ff) and contains the most widely known teaching of the New Testament and the foundation of all Biblical truth: God is love.

Again, he attracts his readers' attention by addressing them as "dear friends" (1 John 4:7). Immediately, he grounds his call for mutual love on the nature of God. First, he says that "love comes from God" (1 John 4:7), in the sense that God holds exclusive rights on it. If we see someone doing something loving, then the logical deduction is that God has given him this ability in some way. Second, he says that "God is love" (1 John 4:8), meaning that love describes His character and being, and even that His deeds define for us what love is. In a general sense, all acts of love by people originate in God since He created man in His image (Genesis 1:26, 27). However, in a special sense, a person who "has been born of God and knows God" should generate substantively more of the Father's love than those who are oblivious to Him or who oppose Him outright. Their relationship to God should be obvious by the way they behave.

Some try to take these verses to prove that any humanitarian is a Christian. This is just not possible, however, because it ignores the larger context of what John has said. First, this section is an expansion of 1 John 3:23, which lists the confession of Christ and mutual love as the essence of Christianity. Second, John has just devoted a considerable amount of space to the importance of true doctrine about Christ (1 John 4:1-6).

John's opponents probably agree with John's idea that God is love, just as they agree with his statement that God is light (1 John 1:5). However, they want to keep these in the abstract world of ideas. They consider themselves above the ethical ramifications of both of these concepts of God. John strikes out at their views, which shut God off from man and invite Christians to be irresponsible in how they live.

For this reason, John goes on to spell out the dramatic, loving action God has taken for the benefit of mankind. God "sent his one and only Son into the world," and He did so "as an atoning sacrifice for our sins" so that "we might live through him" (1 John 4:9, 10). John has already mentioned that Jesus' sacrificial death shows us what love is (1 John 3:16). He has also already explained that Jesus' death provided the "atoning sacrifice" that we needed to bridge the gulf of sin separating us from God (1 John 2:2). What is new here and appropriate to this context is God's role in His Son's incarnation in human history and resultant death on the cross. It was His idea. The Son came at God's request. "God so loved the world . . ." says John 3:16. The cross, then, is the ultimate display of God's love for us. To John's mind, it should provide plenty of motivation for Christians to show love to others.

John formulates this very conclusion: "Dear friends, since God so loved us, we also ought to love one another" (1 John 4:11). He then adds a third reason to love one another. He begins by laying down an accepted Jewish principle about God, based on Exodus 33:20-23 (which also appears in John 1:18). Most likely, he assumes that the separatists also hold that "no one has ever seen God" (1 John 4:12). Regardless, if someone wants to see God—and the separatists would be curious—John says he knows a way it is possible. John maintains that God can be seen when "we love one another." His reasoning is persuasive. If all love originates in God and "God lives in us" (as 1 John 3:24 says He does if we obey His commands to believe in Jesus and love one another), then our loving actions are, in a sense, God's. They expose God in us.

But John goes one step further. He says: "His love is made complete in us" (1 John 4:12). God's love does not reach its full potential until it produces children who love as He does. Notice that John does not speak of individuals here. He has in mind God's family, the church, reaching out to the world in love as God did—interacting in love as do the Father, the Son, and the Holy Spirit.

John has provided us with three powerful reasons to love in these verses. Why is it, then, that we are often so unloving in the church? Do we not see that love is foundational in the life of the Christian and of the church? I'm sure our problem has to do with our sinfulness and the worldly values we drag into the church, but we must not give in to them. Is there someone in your church to whom you need to apologize? Have you been mean and divisive toward your minister or someone else in your church? Hear the implications of what John has said! To the extent that your church doesn't show love, it blocks people's ability to see God. Our job as God's children is to illuminate God to the world by our love. We must strive to be worthy of God's presence among us and in us.

CHAPTER TWENTY-TWO

Being Confident of Eternal Life

1 John 4:13—5:21

Reading this last segment of 1 John is like exiting a cave into the sunlight. At first, we are not sure where we are going. Everything looks the same as where we have just been. As we get closer to the mouth of the cave, the cave gets lighter until we finally see it. Much of what John says as we begin this section seems to cover the same ground he has already covered about love, obeying God's commands, and believing in His Son. However, he mentions eternal life (1 John 5:11), and he admits that giving his readers confidence in their eternal life has been his goal (1 John 5:13). His final description of Jesus (1 John 5:20) is as eternal life.

When we look back to the first chapter, we recall that John began his letter by saying he had seen the eternal life (1 John 1:2). So, he rounds out his letter by identifying this eternal life as Jesus. Between the two, we pass by a declaration that Jesus promised eternal life (1 John 2:25) and a deduction that murderers do not have it (1 John 3:15). Clearly, *eternal life* is not mentioned as often as *love* by John. However, it is a theme that is never far from his mind. Finally, it comes to the forefront at the end of his letter.

We Must Believe That Jesus Is the Son of God (4:13-16a)

All of us have certain convictions. Those we hold most strongly have a large influence on how we live our lives. Some of these may be scientific in nature, like believing in the force of gravity or that the earth revolves around the sun. Others may be intuitive, like believing that prices always go up or that anything that can go wrong will go wrong (Murphy's Law). Everyone operates with convictions about God or some kind of worldview, whether he is conscious of it or not. God may be thought to be distant or accessible, angry or forgiving, existent or nonexistent. Accumulation of goods, betterment of mankind, or looking out for number one may drive our lives.

Even within Christianity, certain convictions may vary. One may be a premillennialist or an amillennialist, a Calvinist or an Arminian, a Methodist or a Roman Catholic. One Christian may believe that crew cuts for boys, no makeup for girls, and no movies for anybody are mandatory, while another Christian may not.

In this section of our text, John affirms one conviction that is required of all who bear the name of Christ: "Jesus is the Son of God" (1 John 4:15). This is not the first or the last time he makes this stipulation in his letter. Nevertheless, it should not be overlooked. John is still trying to assure his readers that they are better off in the church than with the separatists. To do this, he wants to mark out guideposts to help his adherents differentiate themselves from his opponents. The surest guideposts are belief in Jesus, love for others, and possession of God's Spirit. These guideposts were introduced in chapter 3 (1 John 3:23, 24), and John has already developed his thoughts on the first two of them (1 John 4:1-12). Here, he points to the central placement of belief in Jesus and reaffirms the importance of the Spirit.

John begins with the announcement that the presence of God's Spirit in us evidences our mutual abiding in God (1 John 4:13). For the most part, he has simply rephrased what he said in 1 John 3:24. Once again, *know* is in the present tense and indicates an assurance that can be tapped at any time. John also repeats what he had said of a reciprocal relationship between God and the Christian, but, this time, he specifically includes his readers with *we* and *us*. The biggest change involves how he speaks of the Spirit. This time, John specifies that God does not give Christians His entire Spirit but rather "of his Spirit." Although the New International Version's capitalization of *Spirit* follows from our Biblical knowledge of the Holy Spirit, it disturbs the image John is trying to project. The idea that God shares His very own inexhaustible being with us by giving us part of it completes John's picture of mutuality.

The *we* in 1 John 4:14 does not include John's readers but, instead, refers to John and the apostles. Central to their role in the church is that they "have seen" and do "testify" of Christ. In 1 John 1:1 and 2, where John speaks of Christ as "the Word of life," he guarantees their expertise and truthfulness with the same language. In contrast to that passage, John here is not so discreet about what the apostolic witness involves. It is "that the Father has sent his Son to be the Savior of the world" (1 John 4:14). This testimonial parallels what John says above about Jesus' being "sent . . . as an atoning sacrifice for our sins" (1 John 4:10). *Father* parallels *God,* and *the Savior of the world* parallels *an atoning sacrifice for our sins.*

God is called Savior in the Old Testament because He delivers and preserves His people.[28] He is also called Savior in the New Testament, almost exclusively in the pastoral epistles,[29] although Jesus bears the title often.[30] Jesus saves the world from our bondage to sin, as John specifies in this epistle (1 John 2:2; 3:10). To call God our Savior is also appropriate because, as our passage says, God "sent" His Son.

Although *Savior* stands in for *atoning sacrifice* here, they are not equivalent in meaning. *Savior* describes the results of Jesus' actions on our behalf. *Atoning sacrifice* describes what Jesus had to do to obtain our release: He had to be killed as a pure sacrifice to atone for our sins to enable us to be in God's presence. John's use of *Father* here (1 John 4:14) enhances God's own sacrifice in sending His "one and only Son" (cf. 1 John 3:9) to a gruesome death.

Here, John's doctrinal dispute with his enemies reemerges. This verse (1 John 4:15) reminds us of verse 2, where John called for a confession of Jesus as both genuinely human and divine. John digests the language here to make it a matter of professing that "Jesus is the Son of God." No doubt, he assumes all that he included in the previous profession. The simplified language intensifies the meaning. Before, the confession described what Jesus did. Here the confession demands that one acknowledge who Jesus is. Jesus did not become the Son of God at some point in time. In His essence, He is and always has been a person of the Godhead, "the Son of God."

According to John, acknowledging this about Jesus shows that a person participates in the mutual abiding with God. His confession demonstrates that "God lives in him and he in God" (1 John 4:15). Again, his confession does not stand alone. It is the center post, supported by the possession of God's Spirit and by loving others.

---

[28]God as "Savior" in the Old Testament: Deuteronomy 32:15; Psalm 25:5; Isaiah 17:10; 45:15.

[29]God as "Savior" in the New Testament: 1 Timothy 1:1; 2:3; 4:10; Titus 1:3; 2:10; 3:4; Jude 25.

[30]Jesus as "Savior": Luke 2:11; John 4:42; Acts 5:31; 13:23; Ephesians 5:23; Philippians 3:20; 2 Timothy 1:10; Titus 1:4; 2:13; 3:6; 2 Peter 1:1, 11; 2:20; 3:2, 18.

"And so," John concludes, "we know and rely on the love God has for us" (1 John 4:16). This traces us back to what he said in verses 9 and 10. Our assurance in Christ is grounded on God's love for us. We "know" God's love because we know what Christ did. We also "know" God's love "for us" because we have a part of Him, His Spirit, in us. Knowing God's love in these ways should provide the confidence we need to "rely on" it.

Whenever you begin to question your assurance of eternal life with God, read these verses over again. Perhaps you're in that position right now. Don't hesitate to review in the Bible what the apostles testify about what Jesus did. Search within to hear the witness of God's Spirit. Don't be afraid to speak with confidence of your reserved place with God. To do less is to insult His Spirit and to denigrate Christ's sacrifice. There is no place for arrogance since we are so dependent upon God, who bought our ticket. But, because He did, there is warrant for assurance.

We Need Not Fear God (4:16b-18)

All of us have fears. Some fear the dark, some heights, or others small rooms. Others fear flying in an airplane, going to the dentist, growing older, or having a baby. Most everyone fears failure, the future, and death. But fears can be overcome. A common remedy for fear is experience. Fear recedes the more a person flies safely. As they grow into it, people can find that aging isn't so bad after all. Experience can lead to confidence and even expertise. An experienced mountain climber does not even think about falling. Crashing is the furthest thing from an airline pilot's mind. Experienced people don't worry about these things any more than you or I worry about stumbling on the sidewalk.

Many people fear God. Most people should! However, John says a Christian should not fear God. What God did for us in Jesus Christ was done to bring down the barrier of fear. How can someone fear God if his relationship is so good that he "lives in God, and God in him"? We don't fear our children, nor do our children fear us. If fear does exist in our house, it reveals a total breakdown in relationships. Similarly, John says fear of God is a telltale sign that a person does not reside in God's house, nor God in his. He is not a Christian.

John repeats many previous remarks in this section, apparently for the purpose of eliminating his readers' fear of God and instilling confidence in their relationship with Him. He begins by saying, "God is love" (1 John 4:16). When he stated this before (1 John 4:8), he related it to a person's lack of loving behavior in contrast to God's evidence of love in sending His Son. Here, the purpose seems related to the mutual indwelling between God and the believer. If we and God are intertwined, the fact that He is love means that we live "in love." This is true not only in the sense that we love God and God loves us, but also in the sense that our love carries over into our relationships with others. Have you ever noticed how two people in love seem happy with the whole world? That's the way our relationship with God should affect us.

When John says, "Love is made complete among us" (1 John 4:17), he is repeating what he said in verse 12. By saying *among us,* rather than *in us,* he makes it clearer that the goal of God's love is reached in His relationship with the church as a whole, not just with individuals. However, this perfection of love is accomplished by the mutual indwelling between God and individuals. John stipulates this by adding the preface, "In this way" (1 John 4:17), referring to the previous sentence.[31]

The purpose of this perfection of love is so that we in the church "will have confidence on the day of judgment." Although John did not use the term *Day of Judgment,* he expressed the same desire for us to be confident when Christ returns in 1 John 2:28. There, our confidence is based on maintaining upright behavior and sound doctrine about Christ. Here (1 John 4:17), our confidence is based first on the completion of God's love in us, as previously stated, and second on our being like Christ.

The *Day of Judgment* is a term used in the New Testament[32] but not in the Old. It emphasizes the condemnation of sinners that will occur in the "last days" or in the "Day of the Lord," to use the more common Old Testament terms. In his Gospel, John speaks of the last day (John 6:40). Earlier in this letter, he warned of the last hour (1 John 2:18; see my comments on that passage for a fuller discussion). Based on the similar concerns of 1 John 2:28 and 4:17, John appears to associate this day with the return of Christ.

---

[31]The earliest editions of the New International Version did not carry this phrase. Happily, it was added in the 1984 revision. You will also find it, or something very similar, in the New American Standard Bible, the King James Version, the Revised Standard Version, and the New English Bible. Including it is more faithful to the Greek text than is excluding it.

[32]See Matthew 10:15; 11:22, 24; 12:36; 2 Peter 2:9; 3:7; Jude 6.

The phrase *we are like him* is really stated more strongly by John than the New International Version indicates. More literally, John says, "We are as he is." This reinforces the idea of our mutual abiding with God (cf. 1 John 4:16). What is especially striking is that *he* does not refer to God here, but rather to Jesus. We know this because the word *he* is actually *that one,* which in 1 John always indicates Jesus (1 John 2:6; 3:3, 5, 7, 16; 5:16). The fact that 1 John 3:2 also speaks of becoming like Jesus when He returns confirms this conclusion. As I have said before, John maintains a very fine line between God and Jesus in this letter, and this is another example.

John does not mean that we are perfect reproductions of Jesus right now, any more than he did in 1 John 3:2. His intention compares with what he said about the world's hating us (1 John 3:13). The world hates God and rejected Christ. Compared to that, our lives run fairly parallel to Christ's—at least, they should. That's the reason the world hates us. John says this here to build our confidence. If we are like Christ, we should not be afraid of God's condemnation any more than Christ is.

John restates this in terms of love, declaring, "There is no fear in love" (1 John 4:18). If we live in God and God's love lives in us, how can we fear Him? As Christians, we know God has already accepted us through the blood of His Son. God's discipline and His power may leave us awestruck and fill us with respect and reverence, but it should not cause us to cower in fear or to run away and hide. If we know Him, we know all His actions toward us are based on His love for us. "Perfect love," meaning God's love made complete among us (cf. 1 John 4:7), eliminates fear of "punishment" on the Day of Judgment. Fear of it only reveals we are not part of God's true church, that we are "not made perfect in love," as John puts it (1 John 4:18).

Many of us carry around two wrong ideas about God from our childhood. The fact that they are in conflict may not seem apparent until we are older. Both impair our Christian maturity. The first idea is that God is angry. We think this because thunderstorms scare us, and He does some frightful things to people in the Old Testament. The second idea is that God's love for us means He gives us whatever we want. This arises because we confuse God with Santa Claus. The truth about God is that He does love us, but He will not hesitate to punish those who reject Him. Those of us who are committed to Him through Jesus may be disciplined just like children, but this happens because of His love for us. His love means He provides what we need to be the best servants for Him we can be. Thus, we should not fear God, but we should respect Him. Our respect should lead to confidence in our relationship with Him.

We Must Love Our Brothers (4:19-21)

Occasionally, our five-year-old twin sons, Gavin and Kyle, get into a fight that results in one of them hitting the other. This happened recently while we were looking at houses with our realtor. She imparted some wisdom from having reared six children. She said to Gavin and Kyle: "When my children would fight, I would tell them to go do it outside where I couldn't see it. I would tell them that I loved them both and when one of them hits the other, he also hurts me."

When John tells us that a Christian should love his brother, his reasoning runs along the lines of our realtor. God loves all of us as He has shown by sending His Son to die for us. When we hurt another person by what we say or do, we injure God, too. This is especially so if that other person is a Christian brother or sister.

John's brief statement about why love should characterize Christian behavior is based on what he said in 1 John 4:9 and 10. In fact, except for the word *first,* the wording ("because he first loved us") is identical to that in verse 10. Thus, *first* refers to God's ultimate act of love in sending His very own Son to atone for our sins on the cross. John purposely supplies no direct object for *we love* so that we cannot limit our love to Christians only. No doubt, that is where John's emphasis is because his opponents have scorned him and the loyalists who have remained in the church. However, Christ died for everyone, not just for a few. Therefore, God's umbrella of love covers the earth, and the Christian should love as He does.

John's affirmation that "anyone [who] says, 'I love God,' yet hates his brother . . . is a liar" (1 John 4:20) recalls a number of previous verses. In 1 John 2:9-11, he says that a person who hates his brother walks in darkness; 1 John 2:22 says that a liar is a person who denies Jesus Christ; 1 John 3:11-15 says that a person who hates his brother is a murderer and that hate characterizes the world's attitude toward Christians; and 1 John 3:18 says that our actions should be consistent with our words. John can brand a Christian "a liar" for hating a fellow Christian because, in doing so, he betrays himself. He blows his cover. He really belongs to the world, which denies Christ and hates His followers. His attitude and behavior negate his confession of love toward God.

John further argues here that our ability to see our brother should make it easier to love him than God, since God cannot be seen. Once again, John uses this Jewish axiom about God's invisibility (cf. 1 John 4:12) to press a point. Support for his reasoning can be seen in romance. People fall in love with and marry people they have met rather than people they have not. In fact, many love relationships disintegrate when the couple becomes geographically separated.

Probably, John visualizes the deprived person he mentioned earlier. "If anyone . . . *sees* his brother . . ." (1 John 3:17). Here is a visible person with visible needs. Here is a ready opportunity to demonstrate love. If the opportunity is acted on, a Christian's actions can be viewed by others to verify his declarations of love for his fellow man. With God, who is invisible, one can so easily confess devotion while doing nothing to show it to others. One displays it, John says, by loving those who can be seen.

As chapter 4 concludes, John adds another reason the Christian should love others, especially others in God's family: God commands it. It is a necessary corollary to loving God. The actual command, "Whoever loves God must also love his brother" (1 John 4:21), does not appear in Scripture. However, Jesus does bring the two Old Testament commandments (Leviticus 19:18; Deuteronomy 6:4, 5) together (Matthew 22:37-40; Mark 12:30, 31; Luke 10:27, 28). Also, John speaks earlier (1 John 2:7, 8) and records in his Gospel (John 13:34; 15:12, 17) that Jesus gave the command to love. Thus, John views God in this verse as giving this command through Jesus, His Son.

For John, then, love for God and love for others are not separate spheres. Love—for God and for others—is one entity. As Christians, we must not attempt to divide our love. To do so creates mere humanism or monotheism out of our Christianity. Christianity is what it is because it weds ethics and worship. Think about that cantankerous person you dislike or that grubby person in need. Now imagine that person is God, who you know loves you. Can you not help but love him now?

We Must Obey God's Commands (5:1-5)

One of my favorite hymns is "Faith is the Victory," by John Yates and Ira Sankey. Images of Christian soldiers at war set to drumbeat rhythm makes my commitment to Christ feel vital and my Christian life so action-packed. The key phrase in that hymn, "Faith is the victory that overcomes the world," paraphrases 1 John 5:4.

The military imagery of this verse typifies the entire section. God is pictured as the commander to whom we submit our loyal obedience (1 John 5:2, 3). Jesus is projected as the righteous cause that drives us forward (1 John 5:1, 5). Our opponent is the world (1 John 5:4, 5). Because of the overwhelming forces against us, God's demands are rigorous (1 John 5:3). However, they don't seem oppressive because we know they derive from His love for us and His desire for us to be victorious. Because of our loyalty to God's leadership and our belief in our cause, John assures us, we will overcome our enemy and claim victory (1 John 5:4, 5).

Here John denotes the third evidence of being "born of God." Previously, he specified that "everyone who does what is right" is born of God (1 John 2:29; 3:7), and "everyone who loves" (1 John 4:7). Now, he cites "everyone who believes that Jesus is the Christ" (1 John 5:1). Normally, the confession to which John requires adherence emphasizes Jesus' sonship (1 John 2:22; 3:23; 4:2, 3, 15). The fact that John substitutes "the Son of God" for "the Christ" when he rounds out this section (1 John 5:5) indicates that the terms are synonymous for him. As noted before, he usually underscores sonship because his opponents denied Jesus' full humanity.

In the clause that follows, John makes a general observation from human experience from which he will draw a spiritual deduction in verse 2. He witnesses that love for someone usually transfers automatically to his or her children. Grandparents are classic illustrations of this. But we can see this in friends, too. For instance, my best friend and my wife's best friend are so loving toward our children that we call them Uncle Mark and Aunt Cathy.

The phenomenon of love-transfer also applies to our Christianity. John deduces that our love for God should transfer to loving "the children of God." Although this makes good sense, John has reversed his usual logic, which reasons that love for God's children demonstrates love for God (1 John 3:14, 15, 17-19; 4:20). To this, John adds a second proof of our love for God's children: "carrying out his commands." He may very well have a thick catalog of commands in mind. However, the only commands of God he has cited in his letter are to love one another (1 John 2:7-11; 3:23; 4:21) and to believe in Jesus (1 John 3:23). John assumes, then, if someone is following God's orders as he is supposed to, he is also loving his fellow Christians.

John then strengthens his case for the need for obedience to God by intertwining it with our love for God. As far as he is concerned, these two relationships to God cannot be separated. Love for God must be nonexistent if we have no regard for what He expects from us. Further, John reflects on the nature of God's commands in order to encourage his readers to follow them. In saying they "are not burdensome" (1 John 5:3), he may be influenced by Deuteronomy 30:11; Matthew 11:30; and Matthew 23:4. Regardless, to non-Christians, new Christians, or struggling Christians, God's expectations for us may appear heavy. However, it is only from the outside looking into Christianity that it seems like this. Once inside, we know it is not true. It's not that God doesn't have high standards. It has more to do with a change in attitude that occurs in us.

That's the reason John's explanation is "for everyone born of God overcomes the world" (1 John 5:4). All who are truly God's children have made a choice. We have chosen decisively to turn our backs on the recruiting efforts of the world. The world's perverted ideas about God and evil attitudes lure us no more. The key to "victory" over the world, John says, is "our faith," which he clarifies as belief "that Jesus is the Son of God" (1 John 5:5). Conviction about our cause—faith in who Jesus is—provides the power to resist the world with its counterfeit causes or no causes at all. Whatever we are asked to do to promote our just cause is what we want to do. We feel no burden about it. One of our primary orders is to love one another. That means we take care of our wounded. We don't begrudge other people's tasks because they are different from ours. We sacrifice ourselves, if necessary, to save others. We keep up our end for the good of the company. We are as loyal to one another as we are to God our commander. Together, victory over the world is assured.

I have purposely used military language above to help you see that conceiving of the Christian life as a military battle has real value.[33] Perhaps you can think of more parallels than I have drawn. It might be of value as you ponder these verses to consider your own role (and the corresponding rank) in the Christian army and the assignment God has given you. Do you seek any advancement in the future? If so, what new responsibilities would you like to have? Perhaps it would be useful to reflect on others in your church in the same way.

---

[33]John is not the only one to use military imagery. Consider Romans 13:12; 2 Corinthians 6:7; Ephesians 6:10-20; Philippians 1:27-30; 1 Timothy 6:12; and Jude 3, 4.

We Must Trust God's Testimony (5:6-12)

Many television game shows require deciding whether or not someone is telling the truth. On the old *To Tell the Truth,* people had to discern which of the three guests actually was the person described to the panel. Even on today's *Hollywood Squares,* people must decide whether or not the celebrity in the square is answering a question truthfully or is bluffing. Whom we should trust is a question that involves us on many levels in real life. Whose advertising gives us the best information on which brand of peanut butter to buy, at which store to shop, or where to go on vacation? Which religion tells us the truth about God and how to live?

The Bible contains a fascinating account of someone who, almost like a game-show guest, had to decide whom to believe about God. Job had lost all he had, including his seven children. He sat on a dung heap, boils all over his body, and three friends, Eliphaz, Bildad, and Zophar, visited him and philosophized about why all this happened. Job fiercely rejected their testimony, which amounted to telling him it was his own fault. A fourth man, Elihu, then came and chastised both Job and his friends for their false views of God. Finally, God himself came and testified to Job about himself, which Job quickly accepted.

Accepting testimony, especially the testimony of God, is the subject of 1 John 5:6-12. Four witnesses are brought forward to testify for Jesus Christ, God's Son. They come to galvanize our faith in Him against the detractors. They also come to challenge the unconvinced to accept their testimony and to be converted. Deuteronomy 19:15 says that conviction of a crime requires a minimum of two witnesses. In John 8:14-18, Jesus says His own testimony about who He is should be sufficient because behind Him stands the testimony of God himself. John marshals more than enough witnesses to support his case.

The first two witnesses, whom John calls "water" and "blood," walk in together (1 John 5:6). John emphasizes that the testimony of his first witness, "water," cannot stand alone. It must be corroborated by the testimony of "blood." The actual testimony John envisages coming from these symbolic words is open to question. The interesting view of both Luther and Calvin that John speaks of the sacraments of baptism and the Lord's Supper has very few supporters today. The main reason is that John says, "He did not come"—which is past tense and must introduce something historical about Jesus and not contemporary worship practice. Besides that, John's own historical situation concerns opponents who deny certain aspects of Jesus' life, not the sacraments.

One of the earliest suggestions, from Augustine, is that John has in mind what he recorded in his Gospel (John 19:34, 35) about the soldier's spear bringing forth blood and water from Jesus' side. This is intriguing because it does argue for the reality of Jesus' death against John's opponents who denied it. However, 1 John reverses the order from "blood and water" to "water and blood," something John would not likely do if he wanted us to make the connection. Also, this suggestion makes pointless John's concern that some believe Jesus came "by water only."

The most common opinion today is that John uses "water" and "blood" to symbolize Jesus' actual baptism and crucifixion. The compelling aspect of this view is that it contends with John's opponents, who very likely believed Jesus was divine only from the time after His baptism to the time before His crucifixion. It explains John's mention of "by water only," too. John may be proclaiming that acknowledging that it was God's Son who was baptized leads to the conclusion that it was also God's Son who was crucified.

This third view also clarifies the role of the Spirit as the third witness. First, the Gospels record that the Spirit accompanied God's testimony that Jesus is God's Son at Jesus' baptism (Matthew 3:16, 17; Mark 1:10, 11; Luke 3:22; John 1:33, 34). Second, John's own Gospel (7:38, 39; 14:16, 17; 15:26—16:16) contains Jesus' promise that the Counselor, whom He described as the "Spirit of truth," would come after His departure (i.e., His death). So the Spirit testifies both that God's Son came to earth as a man and also that He died as a man. This is strong testimony against the views the separatists are spreading in the church.

Most modern translations of 1 John 5:7 and 8, including the New International Version, correctly omit the extraneous words included in the King James Version because of its dependence on the Latin Vulgate text of the New Testament. The over-zealous scribe's clumsy attempt to double the witnesses and then to divide them into Heavenly and earthly witnesses was nearly immortalized.

In this passage, then, John summarizes and orders his three witnesses up to this point. "The Spirit" ranks first because He is a member of the Godhead. Also, not only did He testify historically by appearing as a dove at Jesus' baptism and as fire at Pentecost (Acts 2), He continues to testify to believers personally since He lives in them. "Water" and "blood" remain in the historical order of Jesus' baptism and crucifixion.

Further, John draws our attention to the fact that his three witnesses are "in agreement." If their testimony about who Jesus is and what He accomplished conflicted, they would not be very impressive. As it is, they agree that Jesus is God's Son and that He died on the cross for our sins.

Some suggest that John's switch to the present tense (1 John 3:7, 8) means that he now is thinking of their witness as contemporary and effected in the church's continuous practice of baptism and the Lord's Supper. Such a drastic change in meaning within two verses is unlikely. Besides, as I have explained, the Spirit was already introduced as a present witness in verse 6.

John introduces his fourth witness in 1 John 5:9, God himself. Quite rightly, he points out how much more persuasive "God's testimony" should be to us than "man's testimony." We already accept a person's sworn testimony in court. The question this verse raises is: "In what does God's testimony consist?" Does He simply vouch for the three witnesses already presented, or is His testimony something additional? In my view, the latter is more likely for three reasons.

First, the verb describing God's testimony "about his Son" is present perfect, "has given." If God is intended to replace the Spirit, we would expect the verb to be present tense. If the water and blood testimonies are in mind, we would expect past tense. The present perfect is best understood here as indicating a separate testimony.

Second, John goes on to say that a believer has God's testimony about His Son recorded "in his heart" (1 John 5:10). Perhaps the testimony of the Spirit might qualify here, but not the historical testimony of Jesus' baptism and crucifixion.

Third, John elucidates what this testimony is: "God has given us eternal life, and this life is in his Son" (1 John 5:11). This kind of testimony corresponds nicely to the idea that it is in the believer's heart. Eternal life is more than a promise for a Christian. It also entails a quality of life in the here and now that is akin to our future life with God. Probably, it is equivalent to what he has called, in previous verses, God's living in us and our living in Him.

This testimony from God, then, amounts to the Christian's sensing this shared life with God and recognizing the change in his life since he committed himself to Christ. He is convinced that this "eternal life" has come about only because of his belief in Jesus. Thus, John concludes: "He who has the Son has life; he who does not have the

Son of God does not have life" (1 John 5:12). No life is worth living apart from Christ, whether now or in the future. Life is contingent on the fact that Jesus actually was God's own Son in the flesh from birth to death to resurrection and that what He did for us on the cross was vital and real.

Rejecting God's testimony about His Son is a very serious matter. In John's view, it amounts to calling God a liar (1 John 5:10). This goes against every grain of theology, even that of John's opponents. He urges them, as he does us, to give a fair hearing to the four witnesses he has called: water, blood, the Spirit, and God. Perhaps you know a fellow Christian who is drawn to the counterfeit claims of the Mormons, the Jehovah's Witnesses, the Moonies, or others. Ask your friend to examine these cults in light of John's four witnesses to Jesus Christ. Be mindful, though, that John's witnesses are not so much a matter of rational apologetics as they are a matter of history (water and blood), which leads to experience (the Holy Spirit and eternal life). One must get into Christianity to appreciate fully the witness it bears to itself.

The Author Writes to Assure His Readers of Their Eternal Life (5:13-21)

A positive mental attitude can make a difference in life. Great accomplishments in sports, science, or just about any field are possible if a person believes in himself. In Christianity, a positive spiritual attitude is important, too. I have been involved in a great number of high-school camps and youth revivals over the years. One of the most recurring problems I have seen is that of Christian youth who are unsure about whether or not they are saved. One has to instill in them a positive spiritual attitude. This is achieved not so much by getting them to believe in themselves as in getting them to have confidence in God: that He really loves them and that believing in Jesus Christ really does restore them to Him. Our assurance rests in God through Christ rather than in ourselves.

Without a positive spiritual attitude, a Christian will go through life afraid of God, always wondering whether or not he is saved. As a result, he will be miserable and be a horrible witness to Christianity.

John discloses here that his overall purpose in writing this letter is to assure his readers that if they "believe in the name of the Son of God," they "have eternal life" (1 John 5:13). This is very close to his purpose statement in John 20:31. Here, he is mindful of the hammering that his readers have endured at the hands of the false teachers who have left the church. He knows that these teachers have ridiculed those who have remained in the church for holding on to such old-fashioned ideas about God and Jesus Christ in light of their new ideas. He wants to certify that they have done the right thing, even though they still may feel weak and confused.

Their anchor and ours is that "name." As noted in comments on 1 John 3:23, they must secure their anchor to the fact that Jesus is who He says He is, and is the One to whom the four witnesses here testify: "the Son of God." He has indeed confined himself to the full experience of humanity from birth to death and, though sinless, died a gruesome death to save us from eternal damnation. Because of Him, "eternal life" is both a future hope and a reality in our lives now.

Having stated that his purpose is to give assurance, John enumerates two types of assurance Christians have. The first is prayer (1 John 5:14-17). Of course, it is not very assuring if a person does not pray regularly. We must experience prayer. We cannot receive the assurance that God "hears us" if we do not pray. To a certain extent, John is enlarging what he said about prayer in 1 John 3:21, where he also suggested it as a means of gaining confidence. Here, he specifies what I assumed in my comments on the earlier text, that successful prayer requires asking "anything according to his will." Meaningful prayer flows from the attitude of a submissive child, not a spoiled one. Indeed, prayer involves more than just asking for things. It is how we develop our personal relationships with God. In prayer, we experience that mutual abiding John promises. Through attentive prayer, we can know we know God and know that God knows and accepts us" That is the assurance of prayer.

In concluding his remarks on prayer, John focuses on prayers of intercession for fellow Christians (1 John 5:16, 17). John's concern for a "brother" who has committed "a sin that does not lead to death" is serious. However, he also sees successful intercession that causes God to "give him life" as another confidence-builder in our own relationship with God. A distraction from John's main point arises in these verses because of his distinction between sin that "does not lead to death" and sin that "leads to death." He warns his readers not to intercede for people whose sin is in the second category.

No doubt, John has in mind the separatists and people like them who, once committed to Christ and His church, turn their back on Him and walk out. John's warning is not hateful. Rather, he considers prayer for such people wasteful, useless. It will not build confidence because it will do no good. Such people have known the truth; they have found God in the church. Yet they consciously choose to deny the truth and, in person, if not in words, become liars about Christ and His significance. It parallels what the Gospels describe as the unpardonable sin against the Holy Spirit (Matthew 12:31, 32: Mark 3:28-31).

The second type of assurance that John gives here involves a summary of three facts about the Christian life (1 John 5:18-20). Each fact begins with "We know." These are settled truths that define our status in God.

The first one (1 John 5:18) reprises the essence of 1 John 2:1 and 3:9. John describes a present ideal that presumes an eschatological reality. The Christian certainly should have put away old, sinful behavior, but he also should be pursuing increased holiness that befits one "born of God," who will one day remain eternally in God's presence. Also, because a Christian has declared himself to be on God's side in the spiritual battle, he receives protection from Jesus, "the one who was born of God." Presumably, if he moves away from Jesus as the separatists have done, he is prey for "the evil one." To be sure, John is not so naive as to think Christians don't sin at all. He has just spoken of Christians' needing intercession because of sin (1 John 5:16, 17), and earlier he supported the need of personal confession of sin (1 John 1:8-10).

The second factual assurance (1 John 5:19) synthesizes John's remarks in 1 John 3:8-10 and 4:1-6. It emphasizes the distinction between being "children of God," which we are, and being subjects of "the evil one." It should not be too difficult for a person to know which group he is in. Calling the evil side "the whole world" also presumes that Christians are in the minority. Without help, we face impossible odds.

The third assurance (1 John 5:20) designates the help that God supplies. It is that "the Son of God has come." He has not only come to rally our side but also to supply us with "understanding." We are not automatons to God. We are rational beings with the need to know our purpose. Jesus explains God to us, for He is the Word of life, as John calls Him in the opening verses of this letter (1 John 1:1, 2). Here, John calls God "him who is true," and he reinforces the fact that we are "in him." We are, most assuredly, within God's circle, but only because we have been brought there by "his Son Jesus Christ."

So Jesus not only supplies us vital knowledge about God, He also accomplishes the work vital for our access to God. Without Him, we would be lost, slaves of the evil one. Appropriately, then, John not only completes his letter by saying Jesus is "eternal life," as he intimated at the start (1 John 1:2), but also that He is "the true God." John, more than any other among the New Testament writers, does not flinch about identifying Jesus with divine personhood (cf. John 1:1, 18; 20:28).

Finally, John admonishes: "Dear children, keep yourselves from idols" (1 John 5:20). It's possible that he means actual idols to false gods. However, since this has not been a concern of the letter, it is much more likely that he refers to anything that draws us away from the true God and especially away from a proper understanding of Jesus Christ. Throughout this letter, John has been concerned with people's being led away into false beliefs and practices under the guise of Christianity. The church must continue to be concerned about this, and 1 John stands ready to encourage us.

This last section of 1 John touches on a number of practical matters for us to consider.

First, one practice that we can look to for assurance in our Christian lives is our baptism. Here is a physical manifestation of our uniting with Christ and the church. Here, also, is an act accompanied by our first public confession of His "name."

Next, this assurance in baptism or in the items John mentions in this section should not be taken to mean that we cannot fall away from Christ. False assurance is even worse than honest doubting. John knows very well that people can forsake the name of Christ. That's what causes him to write his letter, and it's especially prominent in 1 John 5:16 and 17.

Third, we ought to take seriously John's concern that we intercede to God for the sins of others. We ought to be very careful about writing off backsliders or even heretics from our prayer lists.

Fourth, we need to be bolder about proclaiming that eternal life with God is only found in Jesus Christ. Heresies, cults, philosophies, and wacky ideas about life abound. People should feel the truth of Christianity breathing down their necks. We should never shrink from keeping Christianity in the forefront of the public arena.

CHAPTER TWENTY-THREE

Thanksgiving and Warning

2 John and 3 John

Both 2 John and 3 John are brief and adopt the standard Greek format of a personal letter, as I mention in the introduction, "Getting Acquainted With John." Only 3 John is actually a personal letter; 2 John addresses a church as if it were a person. Both letters approach their audiences similarly. After the formal openings, the body of each letter begins with a compliment, which is followed by a serious warning. It is warning the readers that supplies the impetus for writing these letters.

The actual content of 2 and 3 John is different. Second John is a boiled-down version of 1 John, probably sent by John to an outlying area of Ephesus to warn a church of the spreading heresy. Third John was probably also sent to an outlying area of Ephesus. Its major concern is to set up a hospitality center for traveling missionaries after a nearby church leader rejected John's request. The unspoken problem may or may not relate to the heresy that occasioned 1 and 2 John.

Some in the Church Remain Loyal to God (2 John 1-6)

Many people make pledges or commitments to various causes. Maybe it's the local PTA, the Rotary Club, a political candidate, the Boy Scouts, the United Way, little league baseball, neighborhood watch, nuclear disarmament, or the United Auto Workers. Perhaps financial contributions are given or volunteer assistance supplied every once in a while for a few years. Usually, our support and involvement eventually wanes. The kids grow up. We become disenchanted with politics. We find other causes more interesting. Few people maintain avid participation in the same organization for their entire adult lives.

Unfortunately, the same is true with people in the church. We have all seen people come and go. Rare is the person who comes, digs in, and continues to use his or her energy in the same local church. As he writes 2 John, John perceives a similar situation. Many have left the church in Ephesus, and they are sending missionaries to more remote congregations under the guise of the orthodox church. John is alarmed at the prospect because of how few in those congregations are deeply rooted in their faith. After his opening remarks, he writes in verses 4-6 to encourage that minority.

John identifies himself as "the elder" (2 John 1). As I explained in the introduction, he may have called himself this to establish his authority in a congregation in which he has had little personal contact. He addresses his letter "to the chosen lady and her children." All attempts to establish that John refers to an actual woman fall flat by the time we get to verse 5. This is not a love letter, but a pastoral letter. John personifies the church as a woman and Christians as her children. Doing so corresponds to 2 Corinthians 11:2 and Ephesians 5:22-32, which picture the church as Christ's "bride," and 1 Peter 5:13, where Peter calls the church in Babylon (i.e., Rome) "she."

The word *truth* occurs twice in verse 1 and once in each of the next three verses. In each case, it stands for Christian truth or the gospel message. It is something we know (2 John 1), live in (2 John 2), and walk in (2 John 4). So, in verse 1, John is saying that his love for his readers is grounded in his commitment to the gospel. It does not fluctuate with his emotions. It is as steady as his loyalty to Christian truth. Further, John expands the circle of those who love his readers to include "all who know the truth," meaning the rest of those steadfast in the church. He attributes this circle of loving support to the fact that "the truth" has been internalized in those concerned and that this truth will remain "with us forever." Based on John 14:15-17, John probably has associated in his mind truth and the Spirit.

Verse 3 is the formal greeting of the letter. It departs from the simple "Greetings," which most Greek letters used. Obviously, John lengthens this, but he also Christianizes it in a number of ways. First, he multiplies the content of the greeting to include "grace, mercy and peace." In this Christian letter, *grace* must refer to God's love for unworthy humanity, *mercy* to His unbounded capacity to forgive man's misdeeds, and *peace* to man's need for salvation. Second, John specifies a dual divine source of these blessings: "God" and "Jesus Christ." Further, he identifies Jesus as "the Father's Son," which we will connect in verses 7-11 to John's warning in the letter. Third, rather than being an appeal to God, John's "blessing" is a statement of fact. Despite the fact that the verb is in the future, "will be," John states the blessings as present realities in the context of "truth and love." Again, truth is objective truth, the gospel message. Love is the love of God expressed in the sacrifice of His Son and made evident in the lives of believers. These two words forecast the subjects of the letter: *love* in verses 4-6 and *truth* in verses 7-11.

John begins his efforts at positive reinforcement by characterizing some of his readers' behavior as "walking in the truth" (2 John 4). Certainly, it means that they are remaining devoted to the original gospel message. However, as we will see in verses 5 and 6, John considers this closely connected to walking "in love." He also speaks of it in terms of obeying what "the Father commanded us." Despite the reference to God, John probably is thinking of commandments of Jesus. (See 1 John 2:3-11; 3:23; 4:21; and Jesus' own identification of His teaching with God's in John 7:16.)

The most striking feature of verse 4 is the word *some.* When we understand that John is trying to be as positive as he can at this point and can only exclaim that "some" of this congregation's members diligently pursue a Christian life, we see that this is a sad situation. How does he know this about them? It is unlikely that he has visited them recently, or there would be no reason to write this letter. Perhaps some of them have visited him recently and reported the information. He also could have learned the news from a letter. Regardless, contact with a member, most likely a loyal member reporting the impact of the heresy, probably prompted John's letter to this church.

John emphasizes that the command he repeats is not "new" (2 John 5), as if others are issuing so-called new commands. His statement that the command is "one we have had from the beginning" reminds us of 1 John 2:7 and draws attention to John's personal contact with the historical Jesus. As he reveals in his Gospel and in 1 John, he knows that love is the foundational command of Christ to His followers. Love for the Father is shown by "obedience to his commands" (2 John 6). Obedience to God's commands means loving one another.

Our mutual commitment to the gospel, then, is supposed to spur my efforts to love you and your efforts to love me, despite how difficult this can be sometimes. Too often, we in the church get this backward. We cite our commitment to doctrinal purity as justification for acting ugly toward someone who expresses a different idea from ours. This is wrong. There is no justification for being unloving to someone, especially a brother or sister in Christ. Our concern for doctrine, first and foremost, should cause us to love others, even when we disagree. The next section will set out just how deep theological differences can go.

Others Come to Deceive (7-13)

Just this week, a major grocery chain here in St. Louis was caught mixing fresh ground beef with ground beef that was past the fresh date and selling it as "fresh." The backs of cereal boxes are notorious for making a flashy item appear to be free until you read in the bottom corner that the item requires purchasing more boxes of cereal than one can eat in a year and sending them more money than the item is worth in the first place. Cigarette ads routinely picture the smoker in a setting of fresh, mountain air when smoking actually blackens the lungs with tar. Beer commercials always film fun social settings and never the loaner guzzling in the corner of a dirty bar. A very fine line separates putting a product in a positive light from the intent to deceive. Certainly, what the grocery chain did was deceptive and illegal. The advertisements noted are simply slick. Nevertheless, as consumers, we must watch out so that we are not deceived by either.

John warns his readers to be on guard against spiritual deception. His immediate concern is not with their own congregation but with traveling emissaries spreading the heresy he wrote against in 1 John. Their numbers must be substantial because he describes them as "many deceivers" (2 John 7). It is very possible that these travelers represent themselves as being from the legitimate church when they actually are from a break-off group. John fears that an unsuspecting church like the one to which he is writing will offer these deceivers hospitality as they have offered to others. If this happens, a dangerous foothold will have been gained.

The impostors are the same as the false teachers in 1 John. We know this because John uses the same language to describe them and their false doctrine. Three expressions in 2 John 7 call to mind his warnings in 1 John. He says they "have gone out into the world," just as he spoke of the false prophets in 1 John 4:2 (see also 2:19). He associates such a person with "the antichrist," as he did the separatists in 1 John 2:18-23 and 4:3. Finally, John characterizes the deceivers as denying "Jesus Christ as coming in the flesh," which is virtually identical with what he says in 1 John 4:2 and 3. Like the separatists in 1 John, then, they do not reject the fact of Christ's incarnation. Rather, they reject the full humanity of Christ. They reject that Jesus was God's Son from conception through the crucifixion and resurrection.

John prepares his readers to resist the heresy by drawing attention to the fact that they could lose their salvation (2 John 8). The New American Standard, New English, and Jerusalem Bibles, as well as many commentators, take exception to the New International Version's *you* in "what you have worked for," preferring "what we have worked for." I agree. The work for their salvation is not theirs alone, but John's too. It will have been in vain, if, in the end, John's readers are not "rewarded fully."

John stipulates that teaching that leads to God can only be found in Jesus Christ (2 John 9). A Christian teacher cannot sidestep the issue of who Jesus is and His declaration to be God's Son and still call what he is talking about Christianity. Such a person "runs ahead." He may think what he teaches is advanced because it goes beyond the rudiments. However, if it cuts itself off from the rudiments, it is adrift, and whoever jumps aboard is doomed. On the other hand, those who remain on the main ship piloted by the apostles and purchased by Christ's blood will reach God safely.

In verses 10 and 11, John comes to the practical solution that will alleviate his worry. He tells the congregation to turn away these emissaries of heresy. He means this both in an official sense, no "welcome," and in the sense of hospitality, no "house." Because most inns were dirty, immoral, and expensive, traveling missionaries relied on Christian people along the way to put them up. That's the reason hospitality normally is considered a virtue in the New Testament.[34] Here, the virtue comes from not supplying hospitality. If each family does what John requests, the heretical teachers will be forced to move on without gaining even a hearing in the church. To aid even one of these rascals, John says in verse 11, amounts to supporting "his wicked work," which purposes to denude the church and denigrate Christ.

John closes his remarks on the subject by apologizing for their brevity (2 John 12). He plans to make up for this by visiting them personally very soon. Very likely, John has run out of room on his

---

[34]See Acts 16:15; Romans 12:13; 1 Timothy 3:2; 5:9, 10; Titus 1:8; Hebrews 13:2; 1 Peter 4:8, 9.

sheet of papyrus. For the moment, this brief letter of warning from an apostle should be enough. He is well aware that the church deserves a fuller explanation. Thus, he promises to visit. Perhaps he plans a tour to match that of his opponents.

Verse 13 reveals that John is writing not as an apostle alone. His letter carries with it "greetings" from a "sister" congregation. The word *chosen* may very well indicate that this is the mother congregation that planted this more remote church by sending out its own missionaries, perhaps under the direction of John. If our earlier speculation is correct, this mother congregation would be in Ephesus.

We today still need to apply John's tactic against heresy. We should prevent teachers of cults and their literature from being allowed in the church. This is not to say that we should bar hospitality to everyone with whom we disagree. Rather, the central issue is Christ. We can brook no movement away from who the Bible says He is and what the Bible says He did to gain our salvation. Is there value in inviting a Mormon or Jehovah's Witness into your home when they knock on the door Saturday morning? Perhaps—if you know your Christianity well enough to persuade them of the truth. However, if you are not so certain, politely saying, "I'm already a committed Christian, so no thanks" is the best thing to do. Certainly, no value can come from inviting them to speak at your Bible study or at church.

Gaius's Faithfulness and Hospitality Are Praised (3 John 1-8)

The outreach of the church depends on hospitality today almost as much as it did in the first century. Church families house touring choirs. The revival speaker needs a place to stay, as does the visiting missionary and the summer intern. The youth group requests hosts for their monthly after-church gatherings. In my second youth ministry, I stayed with a wonderful family every weekend for nearly two years and daily one entire summer. In the home in which I grew up, we welcomed such opportunities. Not only were we able to share in important ministries, we met some wonderful people.

Gaius, the Christian gentleman to whom John writes in his third letter, has regularly opened his home to traveling Christian workers. He has done this so warmly that emissaries of John have commended him personally to John. After the opening remarks, John uses the first part of his letter, verses 5-8, to praise Gaius's exemplary conduct and to request officially that Gaius continue his gracious practice toward people John sends out.

As in 2 John, the apostle John again refers to his official capacity by calling himself "the elder" (3 John 1). Also, just as he probably had not visited the congregation addressed in 2 John, it is unlikely that John has met Gaius personally. His high opinion of Gaius is due to the reports of others. Most likely, then, he calls Gaius "my dear friend" out of convention. He goes on to explain his friendly manner to a nonacquaintance as being based on their common devotion to "the truth," meaning the Christian message (the same meaning it has in 2 John).

In verse 2, John offers a blessing on Gaius's behalf. The blessing is twofold and is based upon John's certainty of Gaius's spiritual advancement. He prays that Gaius's "health" and general physical welfare might balance his acknowledged spiritual maturity. This is not a health-and-wealth gospel John enjoins. Rather, it is a practical relationship. In order for Gaius to continue to entertain traveling missionaries—as John will soon request—Gaius must continue to have financial resources and physical well-being. John could ask for no more than for these to match Gaius's spiritual capacity. It may very well be that both Gaius's health and finances are being threatened in some way.

After this greeting and blessing, John commends Gaius for his loyalty to the apostolic message of Christianity. Probably, Gaius has proven this by entertaining more than one party of traveling "brothers." By his emphasis on "the truth" (3 John 3, 4), John may be indicating that a problem of false teaching underlies this letter, as in 2 John. We have no way of knowing whether it is the same heresy as in 1 and 2 John, but it could be. Anyway, Gaius's steadfastness to the truth pleases John immensely.

Notice, Gaius's faithfulness includes not only subscription to doctrine but also compliance in behavior. Gaius is "walking in the truth" (3 John 4). John's reference to Gaius as one of "my children" tells us that Gaius's conversion to Christianity must have been the result of John's evangelistic efforts, either personally or through an assistant.

John's praise moves from the general to the specific in verse 5. Gaius is steadfast in the faith, but he also is consistent in offering hospitality to traveling Christian workers. Even "brothers" who are "strangers" have been welcomed. Upon return to John's church, a certain band must have mentioned Gaius individually for his "love." When this trait is added to Gaius's other trait of commitment to the truth (3 John 3, 4), Gaius becomes of model of Christian character, as John summarizes it in 2 John 3. With "you will do well" (3 John

6), John makes a polite request for Gaius to continue offering hospitality. He especially has in mind those who go out from him.

The appeal to "send them on their way" probably refers to providing missionaries the food and supplies needed for journeying to their next destination.[35] The Didache, a practice guide used by the second-century church, maintains that, although traveling Christian workers should not request it, money and provisions should be provided to get them on their way. To do this "in a manner worthy of God," as John advocates, is to recognize that these travelers between the Christian congregations are God's representatives. Therefore, one should not be chintzy in supplying them with provisions.

John's reference to "the Name" (3 John 7) as the motivation behind the travels of these Christians indicates "Christ," as it does in Acts 5:41; Romans 1:5; and 1 John 2:12. Twice (1 John 3:23 and 5:13), John fills out the reference to make this unmistakable. John reveals that conventional church practice did not allow for Christian travelers to rely on non-Christians for assistance. To do so would disgrace Christ by putting the spread of the gospel message on the level of false religions.

It was common practice for pagan philosophers and cult missionaries to travel from city to city and to ask for money to support themselves. This is one reason Paul took the extreme measure of refusing support money even from Christians (1 Corinthians 9:11-18). The standard, though, was to accept help from fellow Christians but, for the sake of retaining rich soil for the planting of the gospel, help from nonbelievers was rejected. For Christians, as John says, it was—and still is—a way that Christians "may work together for the truth" (3 John 8). We can't all journey beyond our local church to spread the cause of Christ, but we can share in the efforts of others to do so by providing financial support and by offering a place to stay when it is needed.

This passage always reminds me of something an elder I know would always say when he had the opportunity to present the offering meditation in Sunday-morning worship. What he said may have made the financial secretary nervous, but it always calmed the visitors present. He simply said: "If you are a visitor here today, we don't expect you to give anything; don't feel you have to pay for

---

[35]See Acts 15; Romans 15:24; 1 Corinthians 16:6, 11; 2 Corinthians 1:16; Titus 3:13.

your seat." Warren is right. Church bazaars and raffles are also inconsistent with Biblical teaching because they seek funds from non-Christians. It's not that we are to rely on ourselves alone, either. Rather, we should be able to trust God to supply the resources from within His church for the efforts He endorses.

Diotrephes' Rebuff of the Author Will Be Disciplined
(3 John 9-14)

Parents dole out discipline in varying measures. A child who forgets to turn out a light will likely be dealt with mildly. However, a child who looks straight into his parent's eye and defiantly says, "No!" will be handled more severely. Dr. James Dobson recommends spanking as an appropriate measure for such an open challenge to parental authority.

Before John closes this letter, he censures Diotrephes for defying his apostolic authority. As in the home, the lines of authority in the church occasionally need to be enforced. Apparently, Diotrephes has taken it upon himself to block any attempts by others in his local church to cooperate with the apostle. He has openly rejected John's letter requesting hospitality for traveling missionaries. Not only that, he also demeans the apostle personally in whispers to others. Such defiance must receive the personal discipline of John himself, so he plans to come. Gaius is to pass this warning along.

One of the major points of discussion regarding this text is whether or not Diotrephes and Gaius are members of the same congregation. When John says "the church," both in verse 9 and in verse 10, it would seem so. If so, why does John need to inform Gaius of what Diotrephes was doing? Perhaps Diotrephes had rejected John's letter by disposing of it secretly before word of it surfaced. But how could Gaius not have known that Diotrephes was refusing to supply hospitality to traveling brothers and was booting out of the church anyone who did so? Very possibly, the closed homes under Diotrephes' authority may have been the very cause of the brothers' coming to Gaius for hospitality. For whatever reasons, Gaius is not under Diotrephes' authority. The simplest explanation for this is that Gaius is a leader of a congregation within the general vicinity of Diotrephes' church. He has enough local church support and the resources to defy Diotrephes.

Another major point of discussion in these verses concerns the nature of the rift between John and Diotrephes. Is it theological, organizational, or personal? We know it has become personal because

John believes dealing with Diotrephes will require public exposure of Diotrephes' "gossiping maliciously about us" (3 John 10). Perhaps Diotrephes is an ambitious, charismatic leader who ridicules John's age. Maybe the church is so far from Ephesus and has been out of contact with John for so long that Diotrephes has become used to doing things his own way and simply resents the intrusion. Possibly, Diotrephes has grown so weary of the controversy between John and the false teachers in Ephesus that he has decided it would be best to reject all traveling missionaries from either camp.

Despite the fact that John does not mention it specifically, I tend to think Diotrephes has sided with emissaries of John's opponents referred to in 1 and 2 John. Personal attacks on John seem to be an underlying feature of the heresy (1 John 3:13-15). Diotrephes' motivation for putting people "out of the church" could include the fact that they are a minority who support the orthodox message of John.

In verses 11 and 12, John uses the character of the letter-bearer as a teaching point. The eleventh verse opens with a command that is proverbial in nature. It is a general truth to say that we should "not imitate what is evil but what is good" (3 John 11). However, the implication is more specific: Diotrephes is a bad model of Christian behavior. In fact, John's statements suggest that Diotrephes' behavior reveals such evil that he is not a Christian at all. The phrase "has not seen God" (3 John 11) can mean nothing else (1 John 3:6; 4:20). Diotrephes, then, seems to be in Christianity because he enjoys wielding the power of his position. The church seems to be a haven for people like that, and I guess it always will be.

Anyway, Gaius is not to imitate Diotrephes, and we already know he doesn't. A better model of Christian character is Demetrius, who carries this letter to Gaius. Demetrius bears the commendation of "everyone" (3 John 12). He stands up to the objective standards of "the truth itself," again meaning the gospel message but particularly its behavioral expectations. Importantly, John also certifies Demetrius with his apostolic stamp of approval. The need for John to endorse Demetrius may be twofold. First, Demetrius probably is a stranger to Gaius. Second, he may have been among the missionary workers sent packing by Diotrephes. Third, so many heretical missionaries may be traveling around, in light of 2 John 7-11, that Gaius may want to be sure he is not hosting one of them.

The closing verses of this letter (3 John 13, 14) parallel verses 12 and 13 of 2 John. John decides to contain his letter to one sheet of papyrus. He will be able to communicate more in depth when he sees Gaius personally. So he will save that for his planned visit. He extends the "peace" of Christ to Gaius. (This abbreviates his greeting in 2 John 3.)

"Peace" was and still is the customary greeting among Jews. For them, it encompasses the harmony that belief in God brings into the world. Jesus extends this greeting in John 20:19, 21, 26, but He also gives His followers peace in John 14:26 and 16:23. Elsewhere in the New Testament, the gospel is called peace (Acts 10:36; Ephesians 2:17; 6:15) as is Christ himself (Ephesians 2:14, 15). So, for Christians, a greeting of peace brings together the message of Christ and all its spiritual, social, and eternal ramifications.

John closes his letter to Gaius by conveying warm wishes from friends. He asks Gaius to reciprocate by conveying greetings to his acquaintances in Gaius's church. Saying "hello" by name would be a fitting end to a letter that Gaius probably would have read aloud to the church. It demonstrates John's pastoral nature.

No one likes to be disciplined, to witness someone else's being disciplined, or to hand out discipline. It is not fun, as all parents and teachers know. But it is essential sometimes, especially in the church. Autocratic elder rule in a democratic society probably is not the best style of leadership, generally speaking. At times, however, elders need to take official positions on behalf of the local church and uphold them for the good of everyone. Christ invests in this leadership body surrogate authority. Elders must seek to act for Him in sticky situations and not out of their own enjoyment of power. If they do this, where discipline is called for, elders should enact it. Their decision should be obeyed by the party concerned and supported by the church. To do less is to make a sham out of the church. By prudent pruning, Christ's church can grow into its full potential and the peace of Christ can reach the world.